Pat (Patricia) Kirkwood was born on 24 February 1921, in Pendleton, Manchester, and made her stage début at 14 at the Royal Hippodrome Theatre, Salford, as a solo performer, billed as 'The Schoolgirl Song-stress'. She went on to star in eighteen musical productions, including *Black Velvet, Top of the World* at the London Palladium, Cole Porter's *Let's Face It, Starlight Roof* (with the 12-year-old Julie Andrews), Noël Coward's *Ace of Clubs*, Leonard Bernstein's *Wonderful Town*, and most memorably, the title role in *Chrysanthemum*. Described by the critic, Sir Harold Hobson, as 'the greatest principal boy of the century', she starred in fourteen pantomimes, five of them in the West End. She has appeared in three Royal Variety Perfomances. She made her first film, *Save a Little Sunshine*, at 16. Others include *Come On George*, opposite George Formby, *Band Waggon*, with Arthur Askey, *No leave, No Love*, opposite Van Johnson in Hollywood, Lewis Gilbert's drama, *Once a Sinner*, and *After the Ball*, opposite Laurence Harvey. On television, she had her own series, *The Pat Kirkwood Show*, and played Marie Lloyd in *Our Marie*, Vesta Tilley in *The Great Little Tilley*, and Eliza Doolittle in *Pygmalion*. She played the title role in *Peter Pan* in 1953, and in recent years has played the lead in ten straight plays, including Somerset Maugham's *Lady Frederick* and *The Constant Wife*, and Pinero's *The Cabinet Minister*. Her last stage appearance, in *Noël/Cole — Let's Do It*, was at Chichester Festival Theatre in 1994, the year in which Michael Aspel presented her with the red book in *This Is Your Life*. She lives in Bingley, West Yorkshire, with her husband, Peter Knight, formerly President of the Bradford and Bingley Building Society, and their West Highland terrier, Jamie McGregor.

THE TIME OF MY LIFE

Pat Kirkwood was the undisputed queen of West End musicals. Beautiful and dynamic, she was the only British star to rival Broadway's Ethel Merman for vocal power. She conquered Las Vegas in a record-breaking cabaret season and became the first woman in Britain to have her own television series. But her life was an irrational blend of triumph and tragedy. At the peak of her fame, she was trapped in a loveless marriage. A romance with Baron, the Court photographer, led to her meeting with Prince Philip, and to decades of speculation by royal biographers. Here, in this candid account of her glittering career, she tells the truth about that celebrated encounter.

PAT KIRKWOOD

THE TIME OF MY LIFE

Complete and Unabridged

CHARNWOOD
Leicester

First published in Great Britain in 1999 by
Robert Hale Limited
London

First Charnwood Edition
published 2000
by arrangement with
Robert Hale Limited
London

British Library CIP Data

Kirkwood, Pat
  The time of my life.—Large print ed.—
Charnwood library series
  1. Kirkwood, Pat
  2. Singers—Great Britain—Biography
  3. Women singers—Great Britain—Biography
  4. Actors—Great Britain—Biography
  5 Large type books
  I. Title
  792.6′028′092

  ISBN 0–7089–9209–9

Published by
F. A. Thorpe (Publishing)
Anstey, Leicestershire

Set by Words & Graphics Ltd.
Anstey, Leicestershire
Printed and bound in Great Britain by
T. J. International Ltd., Padstow, Cornwall

This book is printed on acid-free paper

for Peter

Acknowledgements

Thank you to the many who have encouraged me to write this book, especially my husband Peter, for his endless patience, understanding and sensible advice, Juliet Burton, my literary agent for the sustenance of her cheerful optimism and, not least, that fine actress, Patricia Hodge. Without their inspiration this book could never have been published.

Foreword

Following a preview performance of Sondheim's *A Little Night Music* at the Royal National Theatre a few years ago, Sir David Hare and I were discussing its qualities and the word 'glamorous' came into the conversation. 'Yes, but what exactly is glamour?' he challenged. I had never thought to question it. Glamour is Pat Kirkwood.

For many, many years glamour was what the theatre offered best, a shining, more polished, more exciting version of man or womankind. Pat Kirkwood was the ultimate example. Before the War, stars produced in Britain were of the Gertrude Lawrence, Binnie Hale variety, glamorous, of course, but more girl-next-door with a lightness of voice and manner. America had Ethel Merman, Dolores Gray and Mary Martin — zonking big stars who would strut their stuff in musicals but whose voices and dynamism could also front a big band with ease. Then along came Pat. She was the first home-grown version of a big American musical star, yet owed nothing to emulation and everything to being simply herself — a hugely talented and outstandingly beautiful woman. For many years during and after the War she dominated the West End like a Colossus. Her presence in any restaurant would create a hush; in any night-club would guarantee an entrance round of applause: her

1

every professional and social activity was newspaper worthy. She was a legend that my generation inherited at least by name, if we were not fortunate enough to witness her in performance.

Then I got lucky. In 1976 I was asked to play the juvenile role in *Pal Joey*. Pat Kirkwood was to play Vera. My mother was hysterical with delight. It really is true what Jerry Herman says in *Mack and Mabel* 'Somehow the ceiling seems a little lighter . . . it feels like someone lit a roaring fire . . . ' the very moment Miss Kirkwood walks in the room — in this case a predictably drab church hall somewhere in Maida Vale. I was captivated from day one — the rich velvety voice which seems to flow from the depths of her soul; the radiant face with the permanently moistened eyes she ingenuously claims are due to blocked tear ducts, but which in performance can break your heart; the figure and legs of a 20-year-old that made her the patron saint of principal boys. Unexpected though, was her sheer down-to-earth Northern-ness that immediately joined us at the hip. On the opening night I stood in the wings of the Royal Lyceum Theatre in Edinburgh to watch her deliver 'Bewitched, Bothered and Bewildered'. I had never seen anything like it. Thereafter I watched every night. At the end of the song, as she elevated ' . . . am I!' to its conclusion, she would run her fingers through her hair, a simple gesture which in one stroke fused the song to the singer, bothered and bewildered but both bewitched and bewitching.

2

I have ever since counted it as one of the most privileged experiences of my professional life, so I am thankful for all our sakes that Pat has written this book. In the year of Noël Coward's centenary, we should remember that of all the ladies for whom he actually created shows, only she and Elaine Stritch remain alive. Every page, as he would say, 'pins a memory down'. She writes as she speaks, as if we were still in that Maida Vale rehearsal room in enthralling conversation. Kirkwood devotees can share the details of a fascinating life. Readers who perhaps have never even heard of her can take more than a glimpse into a world which was formative in the entertainment business this century, but which we shall probably never see again.

Bewitching and yes, David, most definingly glamorous.

Patricia Hodge
February 1999

1

Early Days

I was in the wrong place, although I was not aware of it at the time; certainly if I had known my mother better I would have realized that this was par for the course. So my first appearance was in Manchester instead of Liverpool — Pendleton in fact, which, Mother constantly reminded me, was a leafy suburb in those days, chock-a-block with 'des res'. One of these was the Seedly Terrace Nursing Home, where I emerged into the light on Thursday, 24 February 1921 at 12.45 p.m., wisely, just in time for lunch.

The reason for this disorderly change of plan was because Mother, along with three younger sisters, had left Liverpool and my father for a visit to Eccles, Manchester, where her family home was. They were a lively family: Grandma Carr played the piano, Grandpa Carr sang, and 'musical evenings' were frequent. The visit was such a success that Mother decided to stay on a bit. This was disastrous for my father, who had made all the arrangements for my 'first entrance' in Liverpool. These he had to undo and start again with Manchester.

Mother had insisted on a nursing home rather than an 'at home' although, at that time, my father was hard-pressed to meet this command. I can understand my mother's wish to be with the family. Grandpa was the nicest one ever, possessed of great charm, six feet two in height, handsome, with a fine head and a glorious deep baritone voice; he always seemed to be enjoying life and everyone who met him became enchanted with his warm, larger-than-life personality. Grandma, too, was striking, tall with a slim waist and upright carriage. All four daughters were tall; in fact the family were giants, gregarious and fond of entertaining. Although Grandpa was a strict and at times fearsome father, his daughters had inherited his gifts of self-assurance and love of life, which supported them well through their difficult times.

After Mother recovered from my appearance I was whisked off to my parents' house in Rusholme, a suburb of Manchester six miles from the city. The first recollection I have is of learning to walk when I was eighteen months old, and it is quite vivid in my memory. When I was three things started to happen. First, I fell through a cucumber frame whilst trying to reach some children playing in a garden nearby. My mother, after I had been patched up, decided I was lonely — I wasn't — and that it was time to have another child. My father had not wanted children at all; they had been married for four years and didn't need them, he said; but Mother had always longed to have a boy and was so bitterly disappointed when I arrived that she refused to look at me for some time. Father had made it worse by creeping into the room soon after I was born, going straight over to the cot, ignoring Mother completely, leaning over me and saying, 'Isn't she beautiful!'

'What about me?' demanded Mother.

'Oh you look as if you have just been on holiday,' he chirped.

It was some time before the waves settled after this, especially as Mother had had nineteen hours' labour with me — I was labelled a 'lazy baby'. In fact she never forgot 'Father's bloomer', which had a long-reaching effect on Mother's attitude towards me. As a result, she brought me up to believe I was hopelessly plain.

My brother was born three years and three months after. This was the good thing that happened that year. I adored my new brother, Brian, a chubby rosy smiling doll who made a lot of noise. Of course, Mother was completely devoted to him and I lost the companionship we had shared when I was her small confidante. Strangely I never resented this nor felt abandoned in any way; my baby brother added such novelty and excitement to our lives, especially mine. He was barely two days old when misfortune struck again. This time Mother had had a home birth and Granny Kirkwood (Daddy's mother) had come to stay, to help. She took me to the park after lunch. There were some swings there and I immediately ran to them and perched myself on one. Of course I could not swing as my legs would not touch the ground but Granny K. gave me a push once or twice. She then sat down on a park bench some distance away. I could not swing myself, but

Granny never moved from the bench. I called to her in vain and then decided to go and get her. Mine was the first swing in a line of others and in order to reach Granny I had to walk across in front of them. I walked past two and then looked up to see, outlined high against the sky, an enormously tall girl with black bushy hair, standing on the swing and about to descend. She wore a look of horror. There was a loud bang followed by a black space. Then I was being carried along by people and I could see the leaves of trees passing above me. Then blackness once more. The swing had crashed into my forehead on the left side and cut open my eyebrow. Consequently I arrived home looking like a pirate, with a large bandage over my left eye and round my head and sporting six stitches. Mother was in bed nursing Brian, so I climbed in as well and felt much better. I carried the scar across my eyebrow all my life but found a solution to the problem when I was twelve by plucking out both my eyebrows and using a soft B pencil to make two thin arches instead, for which I was sent home from school. The eyebrows never grew properly again, not surprisingly. I read somewhere that Lana Turner had done exactly the same thing, which comforted me somewhat.

I was nearly four when the following occurred: Mother had a woman friend called Auntie Minnie — real aunts were called just that, but Mother's friends were also 'aunties'. One day, as she left, she gave me a shilling, which was a handsome present then. I went out to play, clutching my shilling tightly. Not far from our house there was a large square with a green where we used to play with the other children from the area. On this occasion there was much excitement as a man with a donkey had appeared on the green and was walking it up and down and calling, 'Donkey Rides — twopence for a donkey ride'.

I felt my shilling in my hand burning to get away. 'I would like a donkey ride, please,' I said, feeling very brave.

The nice man made sure that he ran beside me and kept one hand on the saddle. What joy it was and how important I felt, free and happy, what with the warm smell of the donkey and the saddle in the sun.

I gave my shilling to the donkey man, but when he put tenpence carefully into my hand I refused it, saying in quite a loud voice, much to his surprise and amusement, 'No, thank you. We would *all* like a ride'.

So, we had one. I felt quite drunk with power! After this I realized it was time to go home, so off I went. When I came in I was just about to tell Mother of the great adventure I had experienced when I saw she was looking at me sternly.

'Where is the shilling?' she said.

'Oh, I spent it,' I replied happily.

Suddenly Mother's right arm was raised high — I was standing close, facing her. Then there was a loud bang and I knew no more until I awoke in my parents' bedroom, which was darkened and still. I had been unconscious for twenty-four hours, so Mother told me. Apparently the doctor had said I had had a 'brain-storm'. That was her explanation, but when I grew up a little I realized that she would never have admitted the truth to the doctor, that she had hit me on the side of the head with all her strength. This contravened my grandmother's instruction: 'You must never hit Pat, she is a very unusual child'.

The next day the mother of one of my friends came to visit and mentioned the story of the 'donkey party' to my mother and what a wonderful time we had all had because of my shilling. Mother was full of remorse, and consequently I was thoroughly pampered and fussed over for the rest of the day, which I spent surrounded with an aura of angelic smugness and satisfaction.

Having managed to reach the age of five, I heard on the gramophone a song called 'Ukulele Lady', which I learned by heart. I used to go to the tall trees at the end of the garden and rehearse over and over. Brian needed constant attention, so I was more or less left alone to do as I wished. However, I was quite content to discover for the first time the joys of solitude and song. There was always something to explore or 'pretend games' to invent for my friends who I called in to experiment on with my various dramas. Many years later one of these friends told me she was once petrified when she came into our garden 'by request' to find a large circle of small girls sitting cross-legged on the grass with myself standing in the centre, all in complete silence. When she began to speak no one stirred. Then, apparently, I held up my hand: 'Hush,' I hissed, 'we are waiting for the fairies to appear!' She left rather quickly.

Father was a shipping clerk with Manchester Liners when he met Mother. She was eighteen, Daddy eight years older. Mother's father was the son of a director, P.J. Carr, whose company had been responsible for building one of the first railways in England, the Wirral railway in Cheshire. Grandpa succeeded him but devoted too much of his time to 'the good life' and not enough to the firm. He was asked to resign, but because his father had filled the position so admirably, and because he had to support a wife and two young daughters he was given a job loading trains. This was a grim time indeed. My mother, then aged eight, was accustomed to great comfort, nannies and servants in abundance and all the benefits of a well-to-do family. Suddenly it all disappeared, the family home was sold and they were forced to move to a small, modest house. No more parties were held, nor musical evenings with, sometimes, the whole of the D'Oyly Carte opera company as guests; the glorious voice of Grandpa was stilled.

At this time my grandmother was expecting another child, a daughter, Eileen. Grandpa made a brave effort but it was difficult for him to adjust to life as a train loader after having been a director. He worked hard but sometimes he drank and when he did, all his frustrations and anger were vented on his wife and daughters. His weak point was his uncontrollable temper and

11

when he arrived home the worse for drink, his daughters used to tremble with fear. My grandmother, though, was a strong and courageous woman, as indeed were all her daughters, and she always stood firm against these onslaughts. She was the only person who could handle Grandpa at these times. Eventually another daughter was born, making four altogether: my mother, Aunt Freda, Aunt Eileen and Aunt Kathleen — called 'Poppy'.

My mother and her sisters were forced to go out to work. Mother was the first to go — she was sixteen. She went first to a velvet factory, then managed to get work with a shipping company — Manchester Liners — and it was here she met Father. Aunt Freda went into nursing and became the youngest matron in England, a state lecturer, a major in Queen Alexandra's Nursing Service and she was also to the fore in the F.A.N.Y.S. She was known in the family as the 'sergeant-major'.

Aunt Eileen was gentle, sentimental and kind, easily hurt and, as Granny said, the beauty of the family, with chestnut hair, green eyes, a peachy complexion. She became a buyer for a very exclusive and wickedly expensive gown shop in Manchester, until she married a cotton tycoon, who whisked her off to Karachi, India (now in Pakistan), where his business was. She had a wonderful time there, in those days of the British Raj. I was her favourite niece and she used to send Mother the most glorious shantung silk material for dresses for me. She taught me the Charleston when I was six. Later she and her husband retired to the Isle of Man. Aunt Eileen was killed in a plane crash flying home from Speke aerodrome. She was only thirty-six. Grandma, who went to the airport to see her off, saw the whole incident: the plane crashed into a hangar in the fog and the whole thing, including two more aircraft, went up in flames. My grandmother was traumatized.

Aunt Kathleen — 'Poppy' — was youngest and the prettiest of the girls, dark-haired with enormous brown eyes, and considerable charm. She was of a happier disposition than her three sisters having been born when times were easier for the family. She decided to be a nurse, too, like Aunt Freda, but this did not work out — probably she was a disruptive influence amongst the doctors and surgeons — and after a year she left and stayed home with Grandma. Later she married an exceptionally good, kind and patient man, who adored her all his life and spoiled her dreadfully. After he died, many years later, she married his elder brother, Richard Metcalfe, the chief orthopaedic consultant at St James' Hospital, Balham. Her two children by her first marriage, Michael and Tilly, both loved her as their father had done. She died peacefully at seventy-three, was much missed and still is. Grandpa, having fathered four daughters, constantly declared to whoever would listen, 'Ah! Any fool can make a boy — it takes a man to make a girl.'

Father was not approved of by my grandparents. Granny considered him to be 'beneath' her eldest daughter, mainly because he came from a large family of modest means — eight in all, of which he was the eldest. There were four sons and four daughters, one of whom had eloped and disappeared. Two of them, Aunt Gladys and Aunt Muriel, were stunning beauties. Granny Carr resented this as she always considered her own daughters to be the most beautiful of all — though she did have the grace to say, 'I thought my daughters were beautiful until I saw the Kirkwood girls'.

There were many confrontations about my father which ended when Mother announced, dramatically, 'I would go through fire and water for him,' capping this with 'And if I don't marry him, I will never marry anyone!' Thus, they were married, Mother in lavender of all colours, in 1916, during the First World War, while Daddy was on leave.

Mother made it crystal-clear to Brian and me that my Father was to be 'Daddy' to us, but that she must always be called Mother and nothing else — no 'Mummy', 'Ma' nor, heaven forbid, 'Mum' — and so it was, until my brother, with great temerity, after being scolded one day when he was eight, drawled, 'All right, Norah!'

Mother was so stunned by this that she actually laughed and from then on Brian called her Norah, but only at home. I resented this, as I was still stuck with 'Mother', but I was quite philosophical about it, realizing Brian could get away with anything as far as 'Norah' was concerned.

When they married, Mother was nineteen and Daddy twenty-seven. They were both virgins.

This was the custom in those days, and I know it to be true because, many years later, when I was married myself, Mother told me what a terrible time they had had on their wedding night. The day after was worse for my father, as he insisted on wearing his kilt. Daddy had been in the Liverpool Scottish Regiment — known to the enemy as 'the Ladies from Hell'!

Mother and Father were absorbed totally in each other and remained so in spite of the cruel separations that were to come. Theirs was a life-long love affair, tempestuous, peaceful, joyful, miserable, funny. I do not know if Daddy's family was at their wedding but I doubt it. Sadly Mother's family were set against the marriage and remained so even after Brian and I were born, the first grandchildren. We never saw the Kirkwood family except on rare occasions. My Aunts Muriel and Gladys, my father's sisters, I only saw once, until many years later, when I was playing at Liverpool's Royal Court Theatre, in a musical called *Chrysanthemum*. They came to see me perform and we had a wonderful talk and much laughter late into the night. I always felt immediately at home with Daddy's family, who were gentle and relaxed with a wonderful sense of humour; there was none of the aggression nor tension of the Carrs about them, and I felt the loss of not having been able to know them through all the years.

The climax to the animosity felt by the Carrs for the Kirkwoods came to a head when I was nine and Brian six. Grandpa and Grandma Carr came to see us for tea and were still there when

Brian and I went to bed. I was asleep and was awakened by dreadful shouting — my Grandpa in full voice, which was quite terrifying. Then my Father's voice came through, measured and firm and calm, followed by a movement in the sitting-room downstairs, like a chair being thrown over, then Grandpa's voice again. He stormed out of the house along with Grandma, but before he went he shouted, 'Keep that man away from me.' So that was that. Daddy forbade Mother, Brian and I ever to see the Carrs again. How we missed Granny Carr.

When I was seven and Brian four we removed to Withington, a quiet suburb of Manchester, and into a Victorian terraced house. How I loved it. There were attics to play in, and cellars where there were always puddings and custards cooling on a raised concrete table slab. It was peaceful down there and dim, not dark, as the cellars were only just below ground and had windows that let in the light; there was no damp. I often go back to that house in my dreams: it was such a happy place and time.

By this time Brian had developed into his own man, a loner, who frequently disappeared for hours at a time but always turned up for lunch! These absences were longer when we went on holiday; so much so that it was a regular occurrence for Daddy to ring the police to try and find him. He never had to explain to them what happened, for as soon as he gave his name the police replied, 'Oh yes, Mr Kirkwood, Brian is lost again, eh!'

We stayed often in a friend's house in

16

Blackpool during the summer. We also visited Hoylake and St Anne's for some holidays, but were always happier with our good friends in Blackpool South. There was an only daughter called Stella, who I began to think of as a saint. She used to allow me to wear her high-heeled shoes for the 'concerts' I would give in the garden for all the neighbouring children. I used to charge a halfpenny each, but if anyone did not have that or forgot it I let them in anyway. Anything for an audience! A wide archway framed the front door that looked out on to the garden, so I used to sing, tell stories in my high-heeled shoes — once in a silver brocade pair I had found in Stella's cupboard. She was a bit put out as they were brand new, but she, being a saint, let me continue to wear them.

A school friend of mine was also on holiday at Blackpool during one visit and we used to haunt the Pleasure Beach, which in those days was not overcrowded. I even went on the Big Dipper — responsible for quite a few deaths and serious accidents — by myself, as my chum would not dare. It was a frightening experience and not at all fun alone. In fact I came off with shaking knees. Because I was so frightened, I decided to go on it again immediately and this time not to be scared at all. I eventually tottered home, broke, and a nervous wreck. My friend thought it hilarious and laughed cruelly and continually. I did not see her next day.

When we were low in funds we used to stand at the doughnut stall and sniff at the wonderful aroma of the frying doughnuts. 'Let's ask him for one, he's got plenty,' said my friend; she was rather a forward girl with some good ideas sometimes. Of course she expected me to ask, because, as she said, she had had the idea and now it was my turn.

'Could we have a doughnut?' I said with my best toothy smile.

'Got yer money?' the man said.

'Oh no, we haven't any money,' I said cheerfully, whereupon my friend dug her elbow into my ribs, rather unreasonably I thought.

'Then go away,' the man said.

How mean, we agreed, and how rude. We decided not to give up and made a pact that we would go to the stall every morning and after asking for a doughnut would stand and stare at him until he gave in, ashamed. We did this for a week. It did not work, though towards the end of the week he burnt a couple of the doughnuts, much to our delight; also, we decided, he did not look too well and would not last long.

Once, on holiday at St Anne's, there was a regular open-air concert party on the beach and I was hardly ever away from it. The artists, especially the girls, wore full stage make-up, which looked extraordinary in the sunshine. I loved the deep blue eye-shadow and black lines round the eyes and the bright red lips; one girl even wore a large black beauty spot on her cheek. The men had brick-pink tanned faces and a lot of wrinkles, it seemed to me. They were people from another planet and I longed to speak to them.

One afternoon a large placard was put up by

18

the side of the stage announcing that a singing competition would be held. All competitors would be expected to learn by heart the song 'Springtime in the Rockies' — a sheet inscribed with the lyrics was posted up at the side of the stage — and the best interpretation would win the prize. The competition would be held in two weeks' time. I feverishly copied down the words from the sheet and stayed up late in my bedroom trying to memorize them. To my surprise I found this easy and after two days I had the words firmly in my head. To make sure, I was at the concert party every day staring at the song sheet. The audience sat on deck chairs, for there was no theatre as such: it was all open-air, except for the actual stage and proscenium with dressing rooms behind. Two older girls were standing beside me one day, very tall and sneery, watching me studying the song sheet. 'What do you think you are doing?' one of them drawled.

'I'm learning the words,' I said importantly.

'What! You?' said the taller nastier girl. 'You can't sing. You'll never do it.'

'Oh yes I will,' I answered haughtily. 'I know the words and I'm going to win the competition.'

They both hooted at me. I'll show them, I thought. On the day of the competition I was there early, and waited impatiently for the show to begin. At last all the competitors were called and we went up on stage one by one. I had arrived first, so, of course, I was the first to go up on the stage. I was full of confidence: that is to say, I was full of confidence when I stepped forward. The pianist played the opening chord. I suddenly saw the audience before me, all staring at me in expectation. The pianist played the chord once more. I still stood dumb and rigid. All those people in front of me waiting for me to sing! Once more, the pianist played the chord, this time quite loudly. I didn't hear it, for I was frozen, without a word of 'Springtime in the Rockies' in my head, simply a blank. The audience were smiling benignly, some chuckling kindly. They began to sing the song, with me mute and rigid. And so it was until the very end. Then they clapped, laughing good-humouredly — they were applauding themselves! When the last note died away I burst into tears, ran across the stage, down the steps and, oh misery, past the two horrible tall girls, who were hysterically relishing my utter downfall.

2

Schooldays

My education I would call 'serviceable' — that is, two private schools, one elementary school and a grammar school. Mother had insisted that I go to a private school in spite of Daddy's protests that he could ill afford it. I was utterly miserable there, being the youngest in the school: all the girls seemed enormous to me. There were two mistresses besides Miss Knight, the principal, who was rarely seen. She wore a pince-nez and closely resembled a large raven. One mistress, Miss Long, always wore brown and had a long, gentle, mournful face. The other mistress, a Miss Webb, always wore black and terrified me — it was obvious she had taken a violent dislike to me at first sight. She used to hold my work up to the whole class and sneer, 'Look at this for a morning's work.' There were many reasons for this. First, the other girls were much older than I and therefore well advanced in their studies. I was completely green, though I could already read as Mother had taught me. Miss Webb, though, was one of nature's bullies and I was a gift from heaven to her, being just five and small for my age. So it turned out that I was to be her 'whipping boy'. I was never out of the corner, with my face to the wall. She was a short stout woman with jet-black hair, narrow

21

black eyes that glinted, a large nose and a greyish sallow complexion. All this, with her black dress, reminded me of an enormous spider about to pounce. I found I could not do anything right; I was so frozen with fear and humiliation that I became unable to absorb any subject I was taught.

One day after this I was given an opportunity to elevate my position at school. Miss Knight had made one of her rare appearances one morning for a nature lesson. She instructed the class to collect, during their lunch-time, some samples of leaves and branches for further nature study. This was my chance, so on my way back to school I started collecting. I decided I would have the biggest and best collection of leaves in the school, in order to show Miss Webb that I was not a dunce after all. I began with enthusiasm. It was one-and-a-half miles to school from home. Some time later I staggered up the stairs to the classroom. I could neither open nor even see the door as I was loaded down with my collection of privet, so I pushed with all my might. Lo and behold the door crashed open and I and my bundle fell on to the floor to an amazed silence. I looked up to see desk legs and human legs facing me. I was covered in dust and dirt, and my face was black; the class was in the middle of a history lesson! No one laughed; I suppose it must have been quite a shock to them as it was impossible to see me under my collection — as if a walking hedge had suddenly burst through the door. Miss Long took me upstairs to wash my face and hands and dust me down. Miss Knight remained speechless. I received no punishment, everyone was much nicer to me and, best of all, Miss Webb treated me not only with respect but a modicum of fear as well.

I was sent to a new school, another private establishment called Beechwood, which was a large sprawling Victorian building run by the Misses Harvey, whose home it had been all their lives. I assume that when finances had been low the three sisters, with great fortitude, decided to do something about it and turn it into a school. The sisters could have stepped straight out of a nineteenth-century novel. Miss Laura, the eldest and the headmistress, was always immaculately coiffured and dressed. Her hair was arranged in the Edwardian style, with four kiss curls on her forehead that never stirred. She always wore a pince-nez and a high lace collar. Her appearance was deceptively gentle and feminine and her head always held high. Miss Laura was very definitely in charge. Miss Millie, the second sister, was extremely tall and straight, with a similar hairstyle but minus the kiss curls, which would have looked absurd above her rather long, lugubrious and flushed face, in the centre of which rested a surprisingly red nose. Also a faint but strange odour clung to her. One of the older girls gathered us together one day and whispered that 'Miss Millie drank gin!' She knew it was gin, she said, because her parents drank it in the evening and she recognized the smell. We began to like Miss Millie more after this intriguing discovery! Miss Ellen, the eldest, was my favourite. Her white, rather wispy hair was constantly escaping from its bun; she was tiny and very frail with a parchment yellow face which lit up with a most beautiful smile, and her large eyes were childlike and soft. On handing round the hot milk, at 11 a.m. each morning, she used to make little jokes which she enjoyed more than anyone. This was the only time we saw Miss Ellen as she did not teach.

Once more I was one of the youngest and smallest pupils, but I improved somewhat in this gentle atmosphere. However, a large girl with a horsy face and teeth took a firm dislike to me. She used to stand in my way as we were leaving to go home and thump me and jeer at me. I tried to hit her back but I could not reach her for she was so tall; in any case, my punches were not strong enough. One thing rescued me most times, though, and that was my fleetness: she could not outrun me. This period seemed to be bully-dominated for me.

After I had escaped old 'horse-face' I had one other hazard to face. Our house was over a mile away from the school — of course, we all walked there and back in those days — and just before I turned into the main road near our house, a schoolboy with five of his 'helpers' stood in my path barring my way. I had seen the ring-leader before as he lived near us and I had thought then what a nasty face he had. He wore a permanent grin, his schoolcap was always askew and his eyes were slanted and malicious. His face was red and shiny. He started to push me around and the others tried to thump me, but I got away and ran. This occurred two or three times on my way home and I began to dread the walk; but they were routed one day when I was carrying a heavy book-filled satchel and decided enough was enough. I lifted the satchel high in the air and brought it down with all my strength on the top of the bully's head. His eyes went most peculiar and his permanent grin departed. So did I, at a brisk trot. The bullies never stopped me again — bullies always run away if one fights back — and the ringleader was not seen about for some days.

Of course, life was not all thumps. I made some very good friends, who were more my size. One of these was a thoughtful girl who announced one day, after a quiet think, whilst I was leap-frogging over a hitching post, 'You know you would be very popular, Pat, if it wasn't for your awful voice!' This gave me pause to wonder what I could do about it and what on earth was wrong with it. I decided to ignore the whole thing and leapt over another hitching post to show I did not care.

I liked Beechwood School: we had French, drawing, and embroidery lessons — dancing, too, taught by a Miss Veeci, an Italian lady. Music and drama were taught by Miss Laura, who one day announced the school was to give a play at the local hall. The play selected was called *The French Doll* and we were to read it through. Miss Laura called on me to read the leading role. I was stunned, but did as best I could. To my utter amazement I was chosen to play the French doll. How anyone could have chosen me is still a mystery: my hair was scraped back into two skimpy pigtails at each side of my head, with bows on the ends which never stayed on, and there was a gap where one of my front teeth should have been! The weeks passed with frantic rehearsals, and I was too busy to feel frightened to death — this came later.

The first scene demanded I be hidden in a large closed hamper in the centre of the stage, armed with an enormous rolling-pin. I had to bang on the floor with this and shout loudly the words 'Let me out, let me out' several times, whereupon a clown doll would come and open the hamper and I would climb out. I banged the rolling-pin with gusto and shouted with my eyes shut and all my strength. From then on it was plain sailing, and we took our bows at the end of the play to as riotous applause as was possible in Withington. Mother came round with tears streaming, Daddy wore a large grin and Brian nodded approval and gave me a hug. Even Miss Laura beamed on me and said, 'Well done, gel.'

What a wonderful evening. There were repercussions, however. I became rather smug about my 'triumph' and was taught a severe lesson. Some weeks later I was chosen to play Gretel in *Hansel and Gretel*, which we were performing in the hall again, Miss Laura having discovered her latent talent as an impresario. During a musical rehearsal Miss Laura played the piano accompaniment, as always, but on this occasion I was standing squarely behind her. As my fellow pupils and I had decided that Miss Laura wore a wig, because her hair was always so immaculate, I decided to make the girls laugh by copying her hand movements on the piano with my own hands round her hair, but lightly so that she would not know. The girls sniggered and one laughed out loud. But what I had not counted on was the reflection in the piano case facing Miss Laura. She had seen my hands darting about on her head! Miss Laura wheeled round, genteely, furiously and, with startling menace, told me to go upstairs to her study and wait for her there. She entered, closed the door and said, 'Now, Patricia!' There followed a bone-crunching lecture on my disgraceful behaviour. Worse was to come: Miss Laura was taking me out of *Hansel and Gretel*. I was devastated, broken-hearted, hopeless and squashed. But I had learned my first lesson, one I did not forget, on the vagaries of the theatrical profession and the ephemerality of fame. Whatever success I did have, years later, Miss Laura seemed always to be standing behind me to remind me to take it all with a large spoonful of salt.

There was to be a change in my life before long. My father had been advised not to continue with my private education as it was a waste of time and money. I was 'only a girl' and did not need such an expensive outlay, as 'I would marry as soon as I left school'. Also, there was the boy to consider. It was more important that he should be properly educated than the daughter if there were not enough resources to educate both children to a high standard. When Daddy informed me of his decision in one of his terrifyingly serious moods, I was not too upset.

Beechwood had become too static for my liking, as there were no physical activities. All my considerable energies were devoted to climbing trees and running, instead of walking, as a good Beechwoodian should. I had enjoyed my three years there but liked the thought of a change and a new adventure. So I said farewell to the Misses Harvey, not without a tinge of regret but with a certain sense of relief. On my last day the 'thumper' with the horse face suddenly burst into tears, and said, 'I'm so sorry I have been so horrible to you. Please forgive me.' I was amazed but, as I was leaving anyway, forgave her readily, thinking to myself how funny people were sometimes and how I wished I had known her better — and she me! Then I ran home.

Cavendish Road School was waiting for me, but not with bated breath, and I soon discovered it was quite different from Beechwood. The elementary school, as they were then called, was a sizeable municipal building with many windows and was set in, what seemed to me, miles of concrete playground. The headmaster was Mr Clarke, a man to be reckoned with but a great principal, and the school was run wisely and excellently under his authority. The school was mixed: the boys were taught by male teachers and the girls female teachers; the genders were kept rigidly separate, even at morning prayers in the hall. At recreation breaks the boys played in one half of the playground and the girls in the other, not even visible to each other.

The teacher of my reception class was a Miss

Cope. She was tiny, about five feet one inch, I should think. Tiny she may have been but what a spirit she had, coupled with a glorious sense of humour that, however, could disappear in a flash when her authority was breached by a disobedient pupil. She was the most brilliant, dedicated teacher possible and the whole class — thirty-two pupils — adored her without exception.

Nevertheless I received many canings from Miss Cope, on my palms with a ruler. They did not hurt much and I always thoroughly deserved them, usually for talking during lessons. We regarded them as simply part of the curriculum. However, I was to discover other punishments in store — the ruler slaps were merely the first course. Miss Cope sent me out of class again one day, not to my comfortable 'leaning wall' but to Mr Clarke himself. So I stood before the great man's desk in the hall entirely without misgivings, as I had convinced myself that I was a favourite of his; he had often smiled at me and patted me on the head. My hated pigtails had given way to long ringlets, which Mother curled up for me each night, so I was rather taken with my new-found glamour. I was in for a rude shock. Mr Clarke left his desk and approached me slowly. He asked me why I had been sent out. 'For talking,' I told him, smiling smugly. He looked at me grimly. There was a sudden movement, both his arms shot out and I was soundly clouted on both ears, my ringlets offering me no protection. I was mortified, dashed, humiliated and aggrieved. Mr Clarke had boxed my ears, *my* ears, I, his favourite. I slunk back to my classroom and Miss Cope regarded me with her arms folded and a satisfied grin on her face.

My next encounter came some time after this lamentable experience. I had settled down somewhat and had not been 'sent out' for at least a week. This time I was caught reading *The Schoolgirl's Own Magazine* during a lesson and, much worse, reading out the funny bits to one of my friends in a whisper. She, the idiot, laughed out loud, and when Miss Cope reprimanded her sharply whined that it was 'all my fault' and so on.

'Come out, Pat Kirkwood' rang through the classroom, as it had so many times before. Miss Cope, who stood tapping her foot with arms folded, eyes flashing, face scarlet and the ruler waving back and forth like a metronome, announced that I was to pack up my desk and leave the classroom. Worse, I was to walk across the hall to Miss Butler's class and stay there for a week. I had a horrible feeling I was not going to enjoy the coming week. I was right. Miss Butler separated my desk from the rest of the class and they were not allowed to speak to me nor I to them. I was not given any work to do nor could I take part in any lessons. In the middle of the morning Miss B. launched herself on a lecture addressed to me. 'It's time you settled down, Madam,' she hissed. 'Last week a girl pupil at Carr Road was asked by a friend of mine which school she went to and the girl replied, 'Pat Kirkwood's school'.' She glared at me through her mascara.

One day, towards the end of this dreadful week, I asked a pupil what the time was, longing for the end of the morning. Miss B. heard me and immediately called me out. 'I'll settle you once and for all,' she intoned. There was something in the corner which she took in her hand and she approached me, her eyes gleaming. It was a long willow wand. She grabbed my hand, turned it palm upwards, stretched it out, then whipped the inside of my forearm about six times or more. I was determined not to cry out, but the pain was so intense that the tears spurted out of my eyes almost of their own volition. But I did not really cry: it was just the tears that let me down in spite of my gritted teeth. The class was completely silent. Miss B. threw the wand on the floor, then, seeing the reaction of 'her dear girls' as well as the large red weals coming up rapidly on my arm, she put her arms round me in a cloud of powder and californian poppy scent from Woolworth's and hugged me, patting my back meanwhile. I preferred the willow wand to this disgusting performance, but I made myself stand stiff and straight like a statue and gave no reaction whatever. When I went home to lunch Mother was horrified, then angry and swore my father would go and see Mr Clarke and complain. But Daddy always abhorred confrontations of any kind so nothing happened. My arm was something to behold, but thankfully it was the end of the week and I was restored to Miss Cope.

A new and different challenge appeared on the horizon. Miss Cope had chosen the play to be performed by her class in the hall on Christmas Eve. Her choice was *King Lear* by Shakespeare, in its entirety, and she announced that I was to play the king. 'Oh thank you, Miss Cope,' I cooed; not having read the play I did not know what I was in for. Indeed, I had never read any Shakespeare until then. So after many weeks of study and rehearsal the play was shown on the afternoon of Christmas Eve. Parents were invited. We were at the beginning of the first scene in Act I when Mr Clarke barked out from his desk-throne, 'Speak up! Speak up!' I glowered at him through my beard and beneath my crown, in a kingly manner I hoped. Fortunately it was the very thing I needed to forget my nerves, but not my lines. I'll show him, I thought. I may not be the best King Lear in the country but I will be the loudest. I found my voice was ready and stronger than I had realized and the first act had no further interruptions from Mr Clarke. Not even a cough was heard. Throughout the last act there was complete silence. Then after the final tragic speech a long pause ensued. Nothing stirred. Suddenly the silence was broken by what sounded like an enormous wave breaking on a stony beach. Through our beards and robes we all looked at each other in fright — what was this? As we exited this sound continued, even when we reached our classroom. Miss Cope's face was a mixture of tears, joy and pride. We found out later that this sound was called applause. The play had been performed in its entirety, unabridged, and I was exhausted. But also, for the first time, I experienced the euphoria of acting as well as I possibly could, with the full approval of an audience. After we had removed our wigs and costumes we dressed and, rather flushed, went out into the hall where our parents were standing with Mr Clarke, who was in a benign mood, almost smiling. He came over to my mother, patted me on the head and pronounced, 'Nothing but the stage for this one!'

I was now eleven-and-a-half years old and my eleven-plus examination seemed extremely unimportant to all the family save me, but I passed with a Grade A and, much to my amazement, obtained a scholarship to Levenshulme High School for girls, an imposing modern school set in sizeable green grounds and approached by a long, straight drive bounded by an abundance of shrubs and bushes. There were tennis and lacrosse courts and a cricket pitch, the whole enclosed in tall slim railings and two enormous wrought-iron double gates. Seen through the gates, the drive seemed a mile long, but the whole effect was quite beautiful.

On my first day I arrived in my new uniform: a green gymslip, cream blouse, green-and-red narrow striped tie, green blazer with the school motto on the top lefthand pocket — 'Temperat Omnia Veritas' — and a black velour hat with a green-and-cream headband. I had arrived on my new bicycle and felt a mixture of excitement, nerves and bravado, the latter disappearing and replaced with awe when I beheld LHS in all its glory and size. A chilly thought entered my head, that this was not going to be easy, this was the crunch, this was earnest. Would I sink or swim? There were a number of new girls; we eyed each other cautiously and walked our bicycles up the drive, where riding was forbidden. We stood about in rather forlorn groups, eyed with curiosity and amusement by the rest of the school. How awful, I thought, to be a new girl.

Then we all marched into prayers to the strains of a Sousa march. With unease I noted the mistresses floating about in their black gowns and mortar boards looking like sinister crows ready to pounce. No one smiled. The headmistress was a Scot, a Miss Robson. She was of medium height and spoke quietly and, indeed, had a most attractive voice, dulcet even. She seemed quite young for the position she held and far from the dragon I had envisaged. She was certainly a change from Mr Clarke and his 'bark' and it occurred to me that my boxed-ears, thankfully, were due for a long rest. In any case, in my opinion, I was far above such chastisements now that I was twelve, with a long plait down my back which reached my waist and my hair swept back straight from my forehead, giving the impression, I fondly hoped, of a serious and studious pupil.

The week started well. After two or three days I was voted captain of the class by my fellow pupils and given a badge to prove it. This euphoria was not to last. By the end of the week I was demoted for talking during lessons and another girl was given the precious badge. I consoled myself with the thought that I did not want the responsibility at my age. I decided I would enjoy my Levenshulme days considerably more being 'free of office' and that, in any case, the class vote told me I was already popular.

At this time Granny and Grandpa Carr had retired to the Isle of Man and bought a most beautiful cottage, 'Briac', in a place called Dreamskerry, just outside Ramsey, close to Aunt Eileen and her husband, who had also retired. In the summer we went for our first holiday to this magical island, staying at the cottage. The feud was over at last and we all rejoiced. We fell in love with the glens so green and mysterious; its fairy bridges, where, as tradition demands, before crossing, you must bow and say good day to the resident fairy; the wild fuchsia buds in the hedges that we used to pop open with a squeeze of our fingers for the sheer joy of hearing the sound; the charming old town of Ramsey and the harbour; the sandy beaches with easy swimming and miles of fragrant golden gorse in bloom which, I always thought, smelled of coconut. We all had a perfect holiday and Brian did not go astray, having now become a responsible young man of nine years.

In Ramsey, by the harbour, there was a large circular café and swimming pool — the Ramsey Café and Ballroom. It was rather swish and run by a man called Mr Hughes. In the afternoon the social hierarchy of Ramsey hostesses, mostly husbandless, assembled for tea. There was a circular floor and a quartet of musicians who played dance music and the popular tunes of the day. There was also a gigolo in attendance called Jimmy Keegan. He seemed terribly old to

Brian and me. He was not really a gigolo; he was a music-hall comedian all winter, but came every summer to Ramsey as an 'escort' for the season.

One afternoon I was at the ballroom having tea with Mother and Aunt Eileen, who, unknown to me, had asked Jimmy Keegan to dance with me. I had never danced before, but he was very kind and tried not to notice his crushed toes. Of course I was thrilled to bits, dancing on a real dance floor with a real professional. To make me feel more at ease, he asked what I wanted to do when I left school.

'Go on the stage,' I replied.

'But what can you do?' he asked.

'I can sing a bit,' I replied, nettled.

'Would you like to sing now?' he asked.

'Yes,' I gulped.

So he led me to the pianist. 'Why not' he said. 'What would you like to sing?'

I sang 'The Girl with the Dreamy eyes' followed by 'It's Easy to Remember' as an encore. It was a great success and I sat down thinking that perhaps I might be asked to stay for the season. What a wonderful dream, I thought. Mother was appalled by the whole episode.

Brian and I were at the Ramsey Café and Ballroom one morning having a swim when Mr Hughes, the manager, came over to us. 'You were very good last week, when you sang in the ballroom,' he said. 'Is your Mother here today? I would like to talk to her.'

'Oh yes,' I replied, 'she is having coffee in the ballroom.'

'What have you done?' said Brian, grinning hugely.

I hurried inside. It turned out that there was to be a gala night and Mr Hughes would like me to sing there, not with the musicians but on the dance floor, in the centre, on my own. In other words, do a cabaret. Mother was not amused, but Mr Hughes persisted charmingly. Eventually she agreed to think it over — talk to Granny and Grandpa, she meant — and let him know the next day. During all this I thought my heart would burst with excitement and longed to interrupt with 'Oh please, please, Mother,' but knew that this might not help my case so stayed silent, though I was jogging from foot to foot with frustration. Mother eventually gave in. I was not sure whether to be delighted or fearful — or both!

I selected three songs and, cheekily, an encore. This was — of all things — 'St Louis Blues'. I had always wanted to sing this as I thought it was very dramatic; I had not considered the taste of the Ramsey Baths clientele, of course. There was just enough time for a rehearsal with the musicians, who were very kind and helpful, as I had no music for them. Luckily they already played the songs as part of their repertoire, with the exception of 'St Louis Blues', which was not well known in Ramsey. It all went well — 'St Louis Blues' especially — although the audience chuckled quite a bit at my nerve. Also many were in shock!

Then something happened that was to change my life, in fact all our lives, Mother, Father and

Brian. Two men had been sitting at a table close to the floor. They looked to me like London businessmen. After Mother had rushed me away to change I heard a tap on the door and there stood the smaller man. 'I am sorry to disturb you,' he said. 'My name is Julie Hyman. Here is my card.'

Mother took it looking bewildered.

'Mrs Kirkwood, I think your daughter is talented, but she needs experience. I am an old friend of 'Aunt Muriel' [Muriel Levy] of 'Children's Hour' on Northern BBC in Manchester. I think you and your daughter should go and see her. She may be able to do something for her. Please take my card when you go.'

It turned out that Mr Hyman was a Blackpool jeweller, from an old established family firm. His companion at the table that evening was a well-known comedian called Len Young. I found out later that when Julie Hyman had declared his enthusiasm for my performance to Young, he laughed and said, 'You are mad, Julie. She is only a band singer and will never amount to anything!' I remembered this incident and the name Len Young for some time and had my satisfaction many years later when I was appearing — top of the bill — at the Opera House, Belfast. In small print at the bottom was the name Len Young!

There was much excitement at 'Briac' that night. Granny had two pink spots on her cheek, having had an unaccustomed glass of wine, Aunt Eileen cried, as she often did, Mother was dazed and Grandpa was beaming with joy, his great voice swirling through the cottage. Brian had not been allowed to go, as he had been considered too young, so I told him all about it, with considerable embroidery, of course, and he listened in amusement. After all, it was Brian who had started it all.

It was now time to return to earth and face Levenshulme High School again. Four weeks went by; all thoughts of Julie Hyman, 'Auntie Muriel' and the BBC had vanished from our lives. Four weeks later Aunt Pop — Kathleen — suddenly arrived. 'Have you done anything about taking Pat to the BBC?' she asked. Mother replied that she had not, that it was all a lot of nonsense and that I must attend to my studies; besides, when would we have the time to go? Aunt Pop asserted herself — I had marvellously positive aunts — ordered us to take the afternoon off, forget school and go at once to the BBC, taking Mr Hyman's card, to see 'Auntie Muriel'. Mother was bullied into doing just this. So off we went to the BBC in Manchester, where we asked to see Miss Muriel Levy and sent in Mr Hyman's card.

Miraculously she emerged from the studio with the card in her hand, seeming rather bemused. 'Well, what exactly do you want?' she asked me reasonably.

Something took over in my head and I was surprised to hear myself say, 'I want fifteen minutes to myself with a pianist, please, the BBC providing the pianist.'

I trembled inwardly at my nerve but, I

thought, She did ask me.

'I see,' she said, rather coolly. 'I'm not sure that can be arranged, but I will do what I can.'

She was really a very nice woman. Some time later I heard that she had remarked to someone 'That girl Pat Kirkwood thinks a lot of herself.' I thought this hilarious, as I had always suffered from a crippling shyness. Indeed I continued to do so until, some years later, following a friend's advice I began to protect myself with a flippant, joky shell.

Not long after this the BBC offered me an appearance on 'Children's Hour'. I was not entirely thrilled at this, but it was better than nothing, I thought, even though the BBC had chosen 'The Good Ship Lollipop' as my song and no argument. It was necessary for me to ask Miss Robson if I could leave early in the afternoon to be at the BBC by three o'clock. Miss Robson was quite amused at the idea and being in a good mood she agreed to my leaving early. So off I went on the fateful day, down the long drive of LHS. It felt rather lonely, but as my classmates, who were in a fever, had said they would wave to me through the windows, I turned round to see them all crushed together, waving like mad, cheering, jumping up and down and completely oblivious to the lesson that was going on. It made me feel better to see them all and I left ready for anything — even 'The Good Ship Lollipop'. Of the envious eyes that watched me down the drive, one pair only followed me onto the stage — those of Beryl Reid.

Although I was nervous I was also 'ready to go'. Violet Carson played the piano; this was before her memorable performances as Ena Sharples in *Coronation Street*. And 'Auntie Muriel' was quiet and considerate. I was very happy and sang 'The Good Ship Lollipop' as if it were George Gershwin! I thought I had done as well as I could and must have been right, because soon after I had another offer to sing on 'Children's Hour'. The same routine was gone through at school, although this time Miss Robson was considerably less amused, and it was with reluctance, after an impassioned plea on my part, that I was given permission the second time. No more was heard of my 'fifteen minutes with a pianist', so I had to make the best of songs like 'Jack-in-the-Box' and other infantile compositions. It was a long way from 'St Louis Blues'! I did a third 'Children's Hour' after another battle with Miss Robson. All this fuss had a disruptive effect on the girls in my class. They nearly all decided they wanted to go on the stage; lessons were chaos on the days when I walked down the drive with my music case, containing one song. Also there were repercussions at home. A boy at Brian's school who had heard the 'Children's Hour' broadcasts — and I had my photograph in the *Radio Times*, in a gymslip — gave his opinion that 'Your sister sounds more like forty than fourteen,' whereupon Brian punched him on the nose and returned home with a black eye, of which we were all proud, except for Mother who was devastated.

Then something happened. My father received a letter from a Mr T.D. Clarke of the Argyle Theatre, Birkenhead. He wrote saying that he had heard my broadcast on 'Children's Hour'. Would I come to Birkenhead and give him an audition, as he was putting together a touring show called 'Let's Make a Record'? There was a tremendous upheaval. Daddy refused point blank to let me go. Mother was decidedly for the project, however. There was a closed-door conference between them that lasted for some time. I was in the garden biting my nails, pacing up and down and trying to hear what was going on by flattening my face against the window. Finally Daddy was worn down into agreeing that Mother and I should go to Birkenhead, returning the same day. This time there was no confrontation with Miss Robson, we simply went. On arrival Tom Clarke and his secretary greeted us; he was a tall thin, smiling man, gently-spoken and wearing thick glasses. I had no music, of course, but I knew by heart all the popular ballads, comedy songs, everything. So, at last, I had my 'fifteen minutes with a pianist' but, oh joy, upon a real stage.

The Argyle Theatre was tiny. One could step easily from the boxes on to the stage, which was also minuscule. In fact it was like a Victorian doll's theatre, and it seemed incredible to me that it had acquired such a tremendous reputation and that such great music-hall stars had ever played there, not just once but time and again. Mr Clarke, his secretary and Mother sat in the stalls. This was it. I sang two or three songs, then at the request of Mr Clarke, two more. Would I please show them how I took a bow? This flummoxed me for a moment, but I suddenly remembered a magician's assistant in the one pantomime Mother and Daddy had taken us to at the Manchester Palace some years ago. She had put her right knee against her left leg and bowed from the waist, spreading her arms out at the sides with her head forward and her face smiling at the audience. I had been very impressed by this and now it popped into my head in the nick of time. So I bowed my magician's assistant's bow. A hoot of laughter came from the secretary in the stalls. I thought this was because my plait, which was by now below waist-length, had fallen over my shoulder during the bow. Anyway I was mortified. But Mr Clarke's voice floated over the small orchestra pit: 'Not bad at all young lady, not bad at all.'

I felt better. Then they all came up on stage. Mr Clarke said he was very pleased with me. I had done well and he would be writing to us in a few days; then he escorted us to the front of the theatre.

By now I was feeling thoroughly depressed. I had expected Mr Clarke to book me on the spot. And there had been no applause at all. And my bow had been laughed at. I was a complete flop. We arrived home. I was sent to bed with a glass of hot milk, feeling that my life was at an end and that there was nothing to look forward to, now nor ever.

'How did it go, Pat?' Brian asked cheerfully.

'Dreadful,' I replied and buried my head in the pillow.

Next morning Miss Robson sent for me. She was furious, her voice quiet but terrifying and her face grave. At the end of a nerve-grinding speech, she said, 'Do you intend to go on with this nonsense or are you now ready to attend to your education?'

Trembling in my shoes, I replied, 'I want to go on with this nonsense, Miss Robson.'

'We shall see. You may go,' she said and terminated the interview.

I wobbled to the door wondering what was in store for me now. Miss Robson sent for Mother two days later and was closeted with her for a considerable time. The same evening at home, there was a conference between Mother, Daddy and me. My father was in his grimmest mood, which was pretty grim; Mother was a nervous wreck; and I decided I did not care what happened to me any more. I knew that next year I was supposed to take my matriculation exams. I had seen some of the older girls going through this ordeal, with hollow eyes, white faces and a general air of complete despair and exhaustion. I had watched them all growing thinner and thinner and dreaded the time when I would have to face the exams myself.

My father ordered me to sit down. 'Now, we are going to have no more of this,' he growled. 'Next year you are going in for your matriculation, and after that you are going to art school' — this because I was rather good at art at Levenshulme. 'No more 'Children's Hour' appearances,' he continued. 'You are to work hard, pass your examinations and forget all this stupid nonsense about the stage.' There was a lot more in this vein; Father was a speaker of some talent, known throughout the shipping business as 'the silver-tongued orator of the west', because he always got his way as to what would be carried on the ships of his company, Furness Withy, of which he was freight manager.

The days passed slowly, the more so because I had been given two detentions that week and Miss Robson told me that if I got one more I would be expelled. I did get one more! When I received my ultimate detention before the threatened expulsion the whole class gasped with horror, including me. This, again, was one of the occasions when I had been blameless. In fear and trembling I decided to see Miss Robson off my own bat. She heard me out and gave her verdict that the detention would be overlooked and also gave me a pat on the head, metaphorically, for the recent improvement in my work. Miss Robson asked my mother to come and see her for a talk yet again! When she returned she burst out with, 'Do you know what she said? She said that something must be done to kill this girl's spirit.' Daddy was shocked and angry. I was not at all, as I knew that Miss Robson would never ever express such a cruel and unreasonable thought, being a just creature. The word she had used, which I guessed was unfamiliar to Mother, was 'curb'. In this, of course, she was absolutely right: I did have too much spirit, one of the faults that would cause me much trouble throughout my life. I was a riderless horse.

Still no word came from Mr Clarke and life was a dreary road when, suddenly, through the letter-box dropped the beginning of a new life. The letter had arrived from my angel saying that he intended to put me into the touring show 'Let's Make a Record'. He would give me a single spot of twelve minutes and expected me to be at the Salford Hippodrome for rehearsals in two weeks' time! Panic ensued. My father was white-faced, Mother delighted and Brian intrigued. I was, for once, speechless. Then the battle began. Daddy was grave and stern and issued his war plan, that I would not, *would not*, accept this 'ridiculous offer' and that after my matriculation next year I was to go to art school in Manchester. Meanwhile, I would attend to my studies and there was to be no further discussion of the subject. The next day, feeling that my life was over and that nothing was ever going to happen, I was passing the locker room and cloakroom, which was always kept locked after prayers. Someone had left the key in the lock. An idea suddenly popped up: Unlock the cloakroom, put your hat and coat on, get on your bicycle and run away, it said; Where to? I asked myself. There was no reply. Something simmered at the back of my head, but I did not open the cloakroom door nor run away. Instead I summoned up all my courage. When my father arrived home in the evening I waited until he had finished his meal and then announced that I would like to speak to him.

Typically straight-faced, he replied, 'Oh,' which conveyed a world of menace, disbelief and more than a trace of warning. 'Yes,' I said firmly and, without waiting to draw breath, off I went. 'If you will not let me accept Mr Clarke's offer I will run away and join Mr Clarke's show 'Let's Make a Record' at Salford Hippodrome.' After this nerve-racking effort I flew up to my room, collapsing on the bed in floods of exhausted tears.

There was a silence and I heard Daddy and Mother talking very quietly, then Daddy's voice, 'Come down here, Patricia.'

This was a bad sign as he always called me 'Paddy' or 'Putty Nose'. I crept downstairs.

'Your Mother and I have decided that since you seem to determined on this foolish escapade, you should accept Mr Clarke's offer.'

I whooped with joy and was about to give him a hug, when he held up his hand like a traffic policeman. 'Your Mother will go with you. After this I will give you one year to find out how very foolish you have been and then you must return home and go to art school as I intended you should.'

If only he had said 'drama school'. But so it was.

Tremendous upheavals followed the drama: Brian was sent to Macclesfield Grammar School; Grandma Carr came to look after Daddy; and on the next Friday I left Levenshulme High School. How I ran down the concrete corridors and stairs with not a glance backwards! I was finished with school, with caps and gowns, with detentions, with gym-slips that were always too big for me. As I cycled down the drive — which was forbidden — I remembered many of the things that had happened to me whilst I had been at school there. Like the day I had cycled home for lunch, which I usually had at school, because my gym-slip had frayed at the back with wear to reveal a large portion of my regulation blue bloomers. This I had discovered after prayers in the big hall, realizing that I had marched into hall with my knickers in full view. I had arrived home in quite a state and refused to go back to school that afternoon. Mother calmed me down and sewed together the offending split, saying as she did so, 'Never mind, darling, we'll be laughing at this some day.'

3

Variety

Mother and I prepared for our great adventure. There was much to do. I had been given one year to prove myself or face 'retirement' and the matriculation! What should I wear? I had been allotted twelve minutes to sing on my own. What should I sing or, rather, which songs did I know? Once more one of my aunts came to the fore — Aunt Pop, who kitted me out with a dress of her own. It was a bottle-green fine wool day dress, perfectly simple, with long sleeves and a white collar and cuffs as the only contrast. Although the dress was beautifully cut and obviously expensive it was not what I had dreamed of wearing. But Aunt Pop had a sixth sense about the suitability of clothes for any given situation and the calf-length dress, with medium-heeled court shoes to match was exactly right, being suitable for my age, fourteen, and subtly suggesting the schoolgirl which I then was. With my hair drawn back into a long plait which reached my waist the whole effect was quite striking. I did not appreciate this then, of course, having in my mind something in gold lamé with a train! Mother and I chose three songs which I knew from the Henry Hall programme I listened to every day, but I had no music of my own, not even piano copies: it was all in my head.

We arrived at the Salford Hippodrome and met the other people in the show: Harry Lester and His Hayseeds — a comedy musical act topping the bill; an Irish tenor; Bobby Farrell; and a young soubrette called Edna Green. The Lesters, who were American, were the kindest of people, a large family who toured together all over the country. In fact the performers were wonderful folk: I was a complete amateur and, to my utter amazement, had been given a prominent spot — what they called in the music halls 'full bottom' of the bill, which was the equivalent of second to 'full top' billing. This was because of my radio broadcasts and the fact that I was a local girl. One would have thought this would antagonize the rest of the cast, considering I was as green as my dress, but not a bit of it. They were all splendid to me. Mrs Harry Lester, who was the most beautiful woman I had ever seen, a top-notch soprano with a brood of young children to care for, took me into her dressing-room and made me up, as I had not the least idea what to do about my face apart from opening my mouth to sing. Her own stage make-up was flawless and she looked gorgeous, so I hoped to emulate her as she dabbed and patted and powdered me gently and spoke in her soft voice to encourage me. Alas, when I looked in the mirror I saw a pink-cheeked china doll with heavily shadowed eyes and a bright red mouth with cupid bow lips, not at all recognizable as myself. This was because Mrs Lester had put her own type of make-up on my face, a style befitting a more mature woman. Somehow it did not fit, it was too heavy for me. I thanked her but I obviously could not go onstage with this make-up, especially as it hardly suited the demure green dress and the plait down the back. So I took it all off, borrowed Mother's powder and lipstick and went onstage as my ordinary self; good or bad, this was it.

Mother was rigid with nerves and white as a sheet but, strangely, I was not a bit nervous. It seemed somehow natural to walk on stage and sing my few songs. I simply felt at home. I sang 'Dancing with my Shadow', a hit by Elsie Carlisle on bandleader Henry Hall's radio show, and two other songs from the same source. My reception was not world-shaking, but at least the audience was quiet and listened. I think they were more curious than anything, as it was not often that they had seen a fourteen-year-old girl in an elongated green gym-slip with a plait down her back walk on and deliver songs they must have heard many times before. The applause was polite but uncertain. Anyway Mother was relieved and for myself I was glad this first professional appearance had passed without any crisis.

There was a crisis of sorts, however. Aunt Eileen was in front with Aunt Pop. They both came back-stage afterwards and in the dressing-room that I shared with Edna Green and her mother, Aunt Eileen, to my horror, collapsed in hysteria. We took her outside, where she cried even louder. Just as we got to the stage door she clasped me in her arms and sobbed, 'Poor little

Pat, in this horrible place, and with these awful people' — right in front of Bobby Farrell and one of the Lester brothers. I felt so mortified and angry at this insult to my new friends that I couldn't speak.

Mother said loudly, 'She's not very well.' Aunt Eileen was taken home, still sobbing, by a cross Aunt Pop. And so ended my first night.

The following week we played the Metropole, Openshaw. This week was rather better and the audience more receptive, perhaps because I felt more sure of what I was doing. Mr Clarke then offered me an appearance at the Argyle Theatre, Birkenhead, as a solo artist. This was thrilling news as the theatre was the 'Palladium of the North', with a unique reputation. Despite being a tiny Victorian theatre all the great music-hall stars had played there, many times in fact; several successful careers had been launched there. Sir Harry Lauder, Marie Lloyd, Vesta Tilley, George Formby senior and all the great names of that wonderful era had played there again and again and it was a great honour for me to be asked to appear there with only two weeks' stage experience. There was also to be a broadcast that week from the theatre; Mother and I reacted with joy at this tremendous news. Even Daddy smiled, but said, 'It's early days yet,' sounding a warning note with his typical Scottish caution.

I could not possibly wear the green dress for such an important occasion and after two weeks of twice-nightly performances it was looking rather battered and droopy. I was sad at the thought of deserting what had been such a good friend, but Mother was adamant and the green dress was retired with honour. Enter Aunt Pop to the rescue once more, for another most beautiful dress arrived via her: ankle-length, of a pale-pink gauzy material, with elbow-length puffed sleeves, a fitted bodice and waist, a round high neck and a wide flared skirt with one row of the tiniest lace frills at intervals. The sleeves were finished at the elbow with a band of similar frills. It looked demure and the kind of dress every young girl dreamed about. That is it looked demure at first sight, but as the material was transparent, underneath the gauzy dress could be seen a fitted, beautifully cut heavy satin underdress, which, even on its own would have been most glamorous and sophisticated. The whole effect was beautiful without being at all suggestive or erotic, simply rather dream-like. There was no cleavage nor any other kind of display, but oh! it was the most beautiful dress I had ever imagined. That I was actually going to wear it made me speechless — I did not know whether to cry or not, so I just grinned.

It was with great joy and anticipation that Mother and I set off for Birkenhead and the famous old Argyle Theatre. We arrived at our first digs and were greeted by Mrs Bell, a rosy-cheeked, black-haired, plump woman with dark sparkling eyes and a nice smile. The digs were warm and comfortable; we had a small bedroom and were 'all-in', that is, we had all our meals there. Anyway Mother and I were so ecstatic that we would have settled for a barn. We did not stop to unpack but took the dress to the theatre — how small it was, but what a lovely fusty atmosphere it had and how friendly everyone seemed and how busy. There was a smell I could not place, but which later I came to know well. It was the smell of greasepaint embedded in the old walls and curtains — in the red plush of the gilt painted seats, in the floorboards of the minuscule stage and the even tinier dressing rooms beneath. Everyone was working hard, whistling away, banging, knocking, hammering; what a row, but how exciting! LIFE, in capital letters, oozed out of this dear little theatre, where from the stage one could almost touch the orchestra, whose musicians were squeezed into the pit. They were rehearsing and I discovered them tuning up and handing out band parts. These important sheets of paper I did not have; nor the envelopes for them, the names of each artist, usually in gilt lettering, written across them on tough cardboard or, if one was the top of the bill, on leather! I had only small sheets from music publishers, which used to give them to artists for nothing. However, after greeting the band with 'Good morning, gentlemen,' as I had been taught to say by Mr Clarke's secretary, the rehearsal began. Top of the bill that week was Ted Ray, who was just beginning to come into his own and had only recently taken this as his stage name. Before that he was billed as 'Niblo the Gypsy Fiddler'. Then there was an Anglo-American husband-and-wife comedy duo called Bobby Wright and Marion and a Mexican troubadour called 'Don Galvan',

54

who played the guitar and sang and shared equal billing with Ted Ray.

I found the Merseyside audience warm and responsive; I suppose the dress had much to do with it and the fact that I was completely unaware that the Argyle audience could be ruthless if they did not like the artist. Many an artist — and some great stars — had been 'given the bird' quite firmly and loudly if the gallery and the rest of the audience agreed they were not up to scratch. I was lucky I did not know this before I went on. The Argyle audience was very kind, but I did not 'tear up any trees', you might say. Mother insisted, on the Saturday night, that I must go and say Good-night to everyone on the bill, but everyone was packing up, so I must have been a nuisance. In one dressing-room, a man and wife act were having a tremendous row and as I knocked on the door something crashed against it, but the wife sang out, 'Come in,' and a brief armistice occurred. They were very kind to me, wishing me luck and 'a full book' — music-hall parlance for every week booked and no empty seats. I bid farewell to the two tops of the bill — Ted Ray first, who was encouraging and sympathetic, his wife stopping to smile at us as she was packing up for him. 'Good luck, kid,' he said and then burst into a song called 'Stay as Sweet as you Are'. I almost cried, so very nice and sincere were they, as indeed, I found all variety performers to be. They are my favourite people, an opinion I have never revised. I loved them from the start.

We now had to go home as we had no more

weeks booked. The time dragged, three weeks crawled by and I began to think my retirement was to become an unprecedentedly early one but — O bliss — I had an offer from the Theatre Royal, St Helens, near Liverpool for a weeks' variety, as the music halls' programmes were called. Music halls developed in the Victorian era, and theatres in those days had bars in the stalls. Drunkenness was frequent. Variety was completely different in my time — sober and strictly well behaved — a night out for respectable families.

The Theatre Royal, St Helens, was an enormous variety theatre owned by a rather eccentric lady who ran it for her pleasure. This was obvious from the first show, when I could see the silhouette of a single figure in the circle outlined against the bar lights behind and five more scattered over the stalls. That was the total audience. Oh well, I thought, never mind: it is only a matinée. The owner insisted on a Monday matinée, which was unheard of in the theatre — but I soon discovered that small audiences were typical. The stage doorman said the theatre was never full, nor had it ever been to his knowledge, so we finished the week having played to about twenty-five lonely souls. I would love to have met this strange lady who indulged in such a fantastic hobby. What fun she must have had, running her very own theatre.

After Birkenhead we were gaining more experience of theatrical digs, and also of landladies. Mrs Ball had been a good start, but we were to find this was not always the case. The

St Helens digs were clean but the landlady was a hardened professional whose meals were sparse and not something to be relished. But it was only for a week and we made some good friends. The Six Harmonists, a musical act on the bill, were a jolly crowd. The singer was Gladys Hay, the daughter of Will Hay, and she was married to one of the musicians. After the empty matinée on the Monday a Mr Grundy came round backstage. He was a theatre-lover, quite dotty about it, and saw all the shows in St Helens, Liverpool and Manchester. He was chairman of the district council or the mayor — anyway, a prominent citizen. He invited the whole company out to his house for supper after the show. It was a beautiful place with extensive grounds, a large swimming pool and enormous kitchen gardens. He was a most generous host and everyone had a marvellous time, including me, although I did not drink or smoke. Lime juice and soda was my drink, and I often wonder how many gallons I must have drunk over the years.

We had a 'week out' in music-hall parlance, meaning seven days of idleness. My father was amazed to hear that I was earning five pounds a week; in fact, he was rather horrified: 'That is more than double what I was earning when I started in shipping.'

'Yes, Daddy,' I replied, 'but you were earning it every week!'

The next assignment turned out to be the Theatre Royal, Hanley. I still did not have an agent; whoever wanted to engage me rang up the

Argyle Theatre, Birkenhead, and spoke to Mr Clarke. Topping the bill again at Hanley was Don Galvan, the Mexican troubadour, and Mother and I were delighted to see him again. He was most concerned that I had no agent and said he would ring his own, who was also Ted Ray's agent, in London and ask him to come down and see my act. He said he thought I could go a long way with the right guidance and said I reminded him of a young girl he had introduced onstage in New York as a rising star: Ginger Rogers.

I was flattered but thought this was all very improbable even if it was exciting at the time. But true to his word, his agent arrived in Hanley, Stoke-on-Trent, in the middle of the week, saw my act, such as it was, and immediately signed me up on his books. Mother and I were ecstatic. The agent was called Don Ross, a Scot. He was married to a great music-hall star called Gertie Gitana, who had topped the bill for many years in all the big theatres, including the tiny Argyle, but was now approaching her retirement. Don Ross was a charming, intelligent man and a first-class agent; we both liked him immediately and trusted him implicitly. We were not wrong.

Mother had evolved a routine for me, with strict rules. The first was that I was not to speak to anyone in the theatre except to say Good morning, if they said it first. The second was that the moment I came offstage after my act, I must go straight up to my dressing-room. This latter rule was impossible to disobey as my Mother would stand in the wings with my dressing-gown

58

and when I came offstage she wrapped it round me without a word and bundled me away. After the show it was straight home to the digs, supper and then to bed. This routine went on for the entire three years I was in music hall, but the rule was relaxed for pantomimes because I was working with a company who were resident for some weeks and we came to know them well. A pantomime company was more like a family and, in any case, it was not possible for Mother to put my dressing-gown on every time I came offstage, as I was on and off all through the show. But it was some while before I was allowed to talk to anyone in the company, and even then I did not know what to say.

It was a strange life, I suppose, for a young girl. Our routine began on Monday morning with a 10 a.m. band call at whichever theatre we were playing. I still had no band parts as such, only the publisher's small printed music sheets, which I used to hand to the musical director, who then distributed them to the musicians. When I think now of how tolerant they all were towards my unprepared and inexperienced self, I am deeply grateful to these hard-pressed men, most of whom worked hard during the day at various jobs and played in the theatre at night. They were bakers, plumbers, house-painters and builders, I discovered, and not one of them complained about my small and practically unusable pieces of paper. In fact at St Helens for the old Sophie Tucker song 'Some of These Days' I had no music at all, so I said to the band: 'Well, you know 'Some of These Days' don't you? It goes like this,' and sang a bit of it for them. How on earth I expected eight middle-aged worthy citizens to know this rumbustious American number I do not know.

After band call on the Monday we would return to the digs for lunch and in the afternoon go out to the 'pictures', as they were then called. Mother never knew how very nervous I was on these weekly Monday afternoons, hardly knowing what was happening on the screen, with my stomach whirling and my head full of thoughts about the dreaded first house that night, wondering if the audience would like me or, horror of horrors, boo me offstage. Each hour that passed brought me closer to that inevitable moment when I had to step on stage. I felt I knew how a condemned prisoner feels when he walks to the gallows. Mother never noticed anything wrong or, if she did, had the wisdom to ignore it.

I have always felt the same reaction throughout the years before a first night. Once onstage I was quite all right, the concentration being intense and after the first night most of the nerves and anxiety disappeared. But I would carry around a vague sense of foreboding a few hours before arriving at the theatre and a restlessness to be there early and safe in the dressing-room. The variety theatres were a valuable training ground for young and aspiring artists, as one played a different town each week and to vastly different audiences. In the second, third and even fourth grade music-halls — the latter I just escaped — the key thing was to register with the audience within a few seconds, to show no fear nor over-confidence and convey that you would stand no nonsense from them. It was important to surprise them into complete attention at first and then hypnotize them into submission, ending in a mutual sense of enjoyment and affection, sometimes even love. All this does not always happen, sometimes only in part and sometimes not at all. One always strove to achieve the first essential element, 'registering', without which one was in danger of 'getting the bird', which means being booed and shouted off. These imperative and difficult lessons I learned little by little through watching other artists and observing the audience reaction. This was the only training I ever had or have had since.

I concentrated on the stars — top-of-the-bills — mainly because I thought I could learn more from artists who were better than I and also had something special to give an audience. Mother was against all this, as she did not want me to 'hang about the stage' when I was not actually on it. But I managed to persuade her that I was learning my business, so I was allowed to watch certain acts and then come straight up to the dressing-room — always 'up', usually under the roof and reached by what seemed like thousands of concrete steps. I must have been the stage managers' curse as every Monday, after I had done my act, I squeezed into the prompt corner in everyone's way, but never taking my eyes off the stage. The long-suffering stage managers never shooed me away nor lost their temper,

61

though I must have been a dreadful nuisance.

Don Ross, my new agent, certainly did not waste any time with the bookings. When the Hanley week finished I received an offer of four weeks' work on 'the bread and butter tour' — a name given in fun to the circuit of the Palace Theatre, Preston; the Palace Theatre, Halifax; and the Metropole, Openshaw. By now I had finally acquired the much-needed band part covers, which contained each musician's part and, of course, one for the musical director as well. These new covers were my pride and joy, being made of burgundy-coloured pressed cardboard with my name written across in gilt paint. On my first band rehearsal at the Palace, Preston, during my first week on the 'B & B tour', I was at the theatre early and sat clutching my band books at the back of the stage waiting to rehearse. I thought that as I was the first I would automatically rehearse first. Not a bit of it. One act after the other came forward, picking up their band parts from the floor of the stage directly in front of the musical director's stand. How very careless, I thought, putting their band parts on the floor in all the dust. I would certainly never treat my own beautiful burgundy and gilt covers in such a way. Time passed. I had arrived at 7.30 a.m. All the acts in the bill came and rehearsed and went away. The musical director and the band were waiting for something or someone, I supposed. Then from the wings a portly, bearded figure emerged. He came up to me, the only person still sitting at the back of the stage with my band books.

'Good-morning, young lady,' he said with a gentle smile. 'I have seen you sitting here for a long time. What is it you are waiting for?'

'I'm waiting to be asked to rehearse,' I answered.

At this the old gentleman's smile became broader. 'My dear, no one is going to ask you to rehearse,' he chortled. 'My name is Percy Broadhead and I would like to instruct you as to the custom in variety theatres for a band rehearsal.'

'Oh! Mr Broadhead, good morning,' I stammered, feeling a fool.

'The first thing you should do,' he said, 'is to place your band books on the stage facing the musical director and the band, making sure that you arrive as early as you can, before any other act has the chance to put their music down.' He went on to explain that there were marks painted on the stage in compartments for the band books. This is to ensure that if you are a singing act you have 'booked' your songs and that no one else on the bill will be free to sing the same ones. This 'first-come-first-served' rule was rigidly adhered to.

That night I 'stopped the show' for the first time and it was a wonderful feeling. This expression means that the applause for an artist is so great that the next act cannot go onstage or, if they do, are turned away by the clamour of the audience for the previous artist to come back. That was the original meaning of the phrase. Nowadays if an artist takes even one extra bow, say three instead of two, it is called stopping the show, which is completely false. To stop the show means just that. It was a heady experience. As I reached the end of my last medley, consisting of 'Dinah', 'Some of These Days' and 'Nobody's Sweetheart Now', all songs with terrific speed and enormous energy, it seemed as if an avalanche had hit me. I bowed and ran off. I was halfway up the stairs to my dressing-room when one of the stage hands rushed up to me and shouted, 'You'll have to go back, they want you back!' So back I went and stood there surrounded by this wave of sound, warm, loud and joyful, which enveloped me like a blanket. I did not know what to do, as I had no more songs to sing, not having much of a repertoire at that time, so I sang the last chorus of 'Some of These Days' and the audience sang it with me. Then they let me go.

Mother was standing in the wings as usual with my dressing-gown at the ready and a straight face. 'O Mother!' I began breathlessly.

Mother said 'Sssh,' wrapped the gown round me and we were off. When we reached the dressing-room she gave me a hug and said, 'Now remember, never say anything at the side of the stage, no matter how well or badly you go. Only when you reach the dressing-room should you say anything.'

I did not understand why Mother made this rule until some years later; it was because 'going well' created enmity in some artists who, perhaps, were not so well received. It is extraordinary how my mother had such an instinct for so many aspects of this theatre, and yet neither she nor any member of the family had been involved in the profession in any way. That night we floated home to our digs on a rosy cloud, which stayed with us all through the week, as the 'show stopping' happened each night. This was to be the first of many similar experiences, leading to completely unexpected results.

Our landladies were great characters. They were always interested to hear anything about the theatre — what the other artists were like and all the successes, disasters, problems and hilarious jokes that are part of theatre-land. One landlady in Bradford had an inexhaustible fund of stories about all the show people who had stayed with her. This fascinated Mother and me, green as we were, so she used to stay chatting away to us until it was time for supper, when she would say 'Well, it's late so I don't suppose you'll want any supper — awfully bad to eat late at night. What about a nice glass of hot milk?'

'O yes,' we used to nod, being quite hypnotized by her persuasive voice and having forgotten our appetites completely until we realized we had been talked out of our supper.

An offer for me from Don Ross to play the Miss Leddington circuit, which meant the Empress, Brixton; the Palace, Walthamstow; the Chelsea Palace; and the Metropolitan, Edgware Road. London at last! The circuit, run by the formidable Miss Florence Leddington, was a much coveted tour by the variety artists as it was a wonderful showcase and, in those days, all the

London managements would come talent-spotting. Also as most of the artists lived in London they had a chance to be at home, saving on train fares and digs.

Our first Leddington date was the Chelsea Palace, a joy to play. The theatre was beautifully maintained. The manager, Mr Chigwidden, was like a father to the artists, although he was a strict disciplinarian when it came to running the theatre. This is why it was such a shining example, the very best of its kind. That week I was sharing a dressing-room, which did not often happen and which I always dreaded, as, being ridiculously shy and over-modest, I never undressed without wrapping my dressing-gown round me like a tent and retreating to a corner or a wall. This used to give some artists I shared with quite a shock, not to say a reason for subdued mirth. Another hazard was that Mother and I could not give vent to our feelings regarding how the act had gone or how the audience was, as we were accustomed to do. As the act had gone very well that week, though the audience was much more restrained than at the Pavilion, Glasgow, we could not do our usual 'triumph dance' round the dressing-room, and I had to make do with an approving wink from Mother. The other artists sharing the room were a female dancing act called the Keneally Sisters, who opened the show. They were blonde and cheerful but considered me to be rather odd when they saw my acrobatic struggles with the dressing-gown. The other occupant was a pretty girl, who was part of an American comedy act;

she was English and rather snooty at the beginning of the week. Mother, who was extremely gregarious, soon established friendly relations with our companions, as she did with everyone she came in contact with, particularly in trains. This was not my idea of fun, as I liked to be quiet and read on journeys, or think about what I was singing next week, or why a certain song had not gone well the week before and what I was going to put in its place. I dreaded being hauled into a conversation with someone I did not know, not having Mother's insatiable appetite for chats. No doubt it was a great gift, but one which I did not possess. So I kept my head in a book the entire journey. In a way Mother's aptitude for instant friendship was a protection for me, as it prevented any of our fellow travellers from attempting to unload their burden of chatter on me, as, when Mother began, there was not the slightest chance of anyone else having the nerve or energy to stop her.

After Chelsea Palace we played the Empress Theatre, Brixton, and again had a tremendous reception. After that we arrived at the Mecca of the Leddington tour, the Metropolitan, Edgware Road. This was a tough and highly critical audience, we had been warned, and if they did not approve of an artist's offering were liable to let them know sooner than straight away, with catcalls, raspberries, thrown pennies and, some-times, squashy tomatoes. In the 'good old days' bottles were thrown as well, but the management had stopped this, for obvious reasons — broken heads and a glass-strewn stage — with a strong steel-wire barrier in front of the gallery.

I was scared, but as always when this happened, a kind of defiant aggression helped me to overcome my fears and strengthen my voice. Attack first was my budding philosophy and I went onstage like a tornado, plaits, arms and legs flying. I belted out my first number as fast and as loud as I could, which in those days was quite something, as I had all the energy and drive of a fifteen-year-old. After a stunned silence, mainly shock I should think, the audience was mine. When I finished the house went mad and I took bow after bow until the stage manager, in desperation, dropped the backcloth for the next act. How Mother and I hugged and danced upstairs in the little dressing-room. Don Ross came round beaming, but retained his Scottish calm, though his eyes were dancing. He warned me not to let up, saying that every performance must be like the first, as the Metropolitan was a great showcase and that important people would be coming to see me after that night and this was the last week of the tour.

Topping the bill at the Metropolitan was a musical father-and-daughter act from France. They had been extremely successful for many years but were now not quite as big as they had been, having become rather old-fashioned. They were still great performers, which was why they were playing the Metropolitan, where the performers were either on the way up or the opposite. Their act followed mine on the bill, which meant that they were standing in the wings when I came off and so I had to pass them. On the first night, after my overwhelming reception, these two artists gave me looks which would have frozen an active volcano and stood solidly together, so that I had almost to squeeze my way offstage. This shook me, as I had never before experienced the hostility and jealousy from other artists that I had heard about. It was quite frightening, and I used to dread my exit after the act, as their behaviour was repeated after each show. I even tried a 'good evening' but this received no reply and seemed to make things worse. However, I managed not to let it disturb me too much: the important thing was that the audience reaction remained warm and wonderful and Mother and I were relieved.

On Wednesday I careered onstage as usual, with plaits and arms and legs waving about, came up to the microphone — which all singers used in music-halls at that time — and, to my surprise, it was not working. Thinking fast, I put the dead instrument to one side and made an announcement: 'Ladies and gentlemen, the microphone does not seem to be working so I will try to do my best without it,' which I then proceeded to do. But as I had been used to the 'mike', mainly because Mother insisted on it ('to save her voice, as she's so young — it must not be strained,' she had announced firmly to various theatre managers), I finished the act but I was aware that the applause was not as strong as it had been all week. I had not yet learned to project my voice to the back of the theatre, I thought to myself, and was upset to think that I had let the audience down. Mother was not upset in the least but downright angry, although neither of us thought to find out from the stage manager what had happened. Worse was yet to come. Mother told me that Don Ross had informed her that he had brought a most important management to see me that very evening and was sitting out front with him. I was inconsolable and burst into tears, thinking I would never get another week's work and would have to go back to Manchester to art school. Suddenly, there was a loud knocking at the door. It was Don Ross, smiling all over.

The 'management' he had brought to see me was no less than the illustrious Prince Littler. 'Ooooooh!' I moaned and Don hushed me quickly. 'The microphone breaking down was the best thing that could have happened,' he chortled. 'Prince Littler was looking for a principal girl for his pantomime at the New Theatre, Cardiff, and before he came to see you was doubtful if you could sing without a microphone in a large theatre. He saw that you could and has booked you for the pantomime. He also wants to book you for a further three years for other pantomimes of his!'

Joy was unconfined, and Mother and Don Ross floated off to have a celebratory drink. Then there was another knock on the door. It was the stage manager. 'Could you come down for a minute, Miss Pat,' he said, rather mysteriously and quietly. We went down to the side of the stage and he led me to the microphone, standing forlorn and disgraced in the wings. 'Look at this,' he said, reaching for the cable that led to the mike. It had been cut clean through.

During our four weeks in London we had been staying in the most wonderful digs at 13 Albany Street in NW1, a tall, four-storey terrace house owned and run by Mickey Cohen and his wife Bea. Mickey Cohen had been a boxer but was now retired. He was a short stocky man with a round merry face and a humorous kind nature. His wife, Bea, looked uncannily like the film actress Billie Burke, slightly faded with soft blonde hair and a gentle voice. She was extremely feminine and appeared quite fragile, but this was deceptive as she ran the large house, the clients and her husband with a velvet-covered rod of iron, never raising her voice or losing her gentleness. She was wise and, I fully believed, a saint. Neither of these two people was young by any standard, but they managed between them to make 13 Albany Street a truly happy and comfortable home, a haven to variety artists tired and worn out after touring the provinces for months on end. So whenever we came to London Mother and I stayed at Number 13, and Mickey and Bea became our guardian angels.

Then came my first pantomime for Prince Littler: *Jack and the Beanstalk* at the New Theatre, Cardiff, in which I was to play Princess Dorothy. As I had never spoken a line onstage except for my announcement at the Metropolitan that the microphone had broken down and to introduce the songs in my acts, I was scared stiff of actually playing a part, if one can call 'principal girl' a part. I didn't have a clue and rehearsals were agony, especially as the chorus ladies thought I was a great joke and laughed at my pathetic inexperience. Many a night I cried myself into a puddle of humiliation and frustration. The director was no help, being a sophisticated West End type, who seemed to take great pleasure in making me say the same lines over and over again. My first entrance was a disaster as I was supposed to trip daintily on to centre stage and deliver these dreadful lines:

> I've slipped away from father's suite
> To be alone is such a treat
> The youth who'd die to win my smile
> I'd like to see again awhile

All this caused great hilarity among the chorus ladies, especially as I did not trip on daintily being used to striding onstage for my act. Also, through nerves, I was quite inaudible and rushed my lines, the quicker to get off. I was nearly sixteen but still kept my two long plaits and was certainly not a beauty. The principal boy was a straight actress from London and extremely dramatic. She frightened me to bits by leaning towards me during our duet 'Lovely Lady' and whispering, 'You must be really in love with me, really feel it!' She had nostrils which used to dilate during the romantic scenes but she was only feeling the part, of course, and soon fell madly in love with the director and was devastated when he left her for the Fairy Queen!

I improved a bit in a week or so and began to enjoy the marvellous atmosphere of pantomime. No other form of entertainment is so joyous, although the hours are long, involving a twice-daily three-hour show with a short break in-between. The cast was wonderful and I became the 'baby' of the shows receiving the legendary kindness and help from the experienced old troupers, mostly variety artists. I was so happy and even got a good review in a local paper, though the critic said I should never play principal girl again.

One night the Fairy Queen was off with 'flu and so the understudy, who happened to be one of the chorus ladies, took over. This understudy had been one of the chief laughers at my expense during rehearsals. Her performance was not, to put it gently, up to standard and almost wrecked the show. After the curtain fell she came to my dressing-room in tears. 'Oh! I am sorry for the way I made fun of you at rehearsals,' she moaned. 'I had no idea how difficult it was to go onstage in front of an audience but I know now. Please forgive me.' I thought this was pretty nice of her, brave too, and forgave her, even though the miserable nights I had endured during rehearsals did flash through my mind at the time.

Prince Littler and his wife came to see the show. We were all nervous and on our mettle as we peeped through the curtains to see him entering his box. He was the least frightening of men, being of a benign countenance and always, it seemed, in good humour, so there was no need to be nervous. We were, just the same! He seemed to enjoy the show and along with his wife came backstage to meet us all. However, when it was my turn for him to have a few words I noticed a slight lessening of his smile. This worried me a bit, but Mother reassured me by saying that by the time he had got to me he must have been tired. When the pantomime had finished its run I received notice that Prince Littler had dropped his option for the two more pantomimes he had contracted with me. This was a mighty blow and dashed any confidence I had acquired so far. I experienced my first real set-back and my first lesson on how precarious life was in the theatre.

Then I was offered a summer show in Scotland, which was to run for four months, June until October, at Largs in Ayrshire, so we packed up again. I was booked to do my single act; the show ran twice nightly, with two matinées a week and a 'free' cabaret on Friday nights, held on the floor of the theatre with the seats cleared away — they were wooden moveable ones — and the audience sitting at tables instead. The cabaret was after the two shows, so it was quite a late night. 'Free', I learned, meant that all the artists did a single act without payment! There were two completely different shows each week. So I was busy gathering songs from all the music publishers. I was still singing in the published keys, which often were too high for me; but it was that or nothing, so I managed to climb up there

74

willy-nilly. I was now earning twelve pounds ten shillings per week — quite a sum for a 'schoolgirl songstress', as I was billed in very small print on the posters.

The first night arrived. I was not too nervous, as I was only doing my own single act and therefore had no new songs to worry about for two or three days; a wonderfully warm atmosphere came up from the audience and the show was going well. I did not come onstage until the second half. I went on in my regulation white pleated skirt with braces, red shirt and white beret with the red pom-pom feeling quite relaxed and did my stint. After the last song there was sudden pandemonium. What had happened, I wondered, was I getting the bird, would I have to make my emergency speech prepared for such a calamity — 'Ladies and Gentlemen, this is my bread and butter,' which Mother had laughed at. People were standing up and clapping, there were cheers and 'bravos'. The noise was indescribable, and I realized with relief that I was not getting the bird at all — quite the contrary, I was stopping the show. I just stood there bemused. They were calling for an encore, but I had no more songs to sing, only the ones in the act. So I walked off and the music struck up for the next act, which was a sketch; the artists walked onstage and began their routine, but not a word was heard so they marched off again. I walked on thinking perhaps the noise would calm down a bit. But no. Down the centre aisle the producer in his dinner jacket came running and in a panic, his face red. 'Sing something,' he cried.

'What?' I replied.

'Anything,' he shouted. It was chaos, but what a beautiful chaos it seemed to me, the whole audience now on their feet. So I sang the chorus of the last song I had sung. When I came off the whole cast, except the two who had finally been able to get onstage, was in the wings, clapping, some in tears. Mother was white as a sheet. I learned later that, as our show at Largs was the first to open the season, many of the artists who were rehearsing for the other shows had come to see ours. I was thrilled by this, as it meant that I had been approved by my fellow artists, the greatest honour of all. The show-stopping continued for the rest of the season, no matter what I sang. I had been adopted by Largs.

As the shows were changed midweek, meaning two completely new productions per week, I had many songs to rehearse, some of which I put in that night after a brief morning rehearsal. I was now taking part in sketches as well; once I even played a very old lady, reddening my nose with lipstick just for fun. I looked like a gigantic clown and when I went onstage the comedian, who was the star of the show, collapsed with laughter and could not go on for some time. 'You'll be a comic yet,' he gurgled. I was soon to learn a hard lesson. I became over-sure of my songs, thinking how clever I was to learn them in the morning and toss them onstage that night. So, of course, one memorable show I was brought down, smack, to earth. There was a song called 'Wake Up and Live', which was one of those that had a word to every syllable and two choruses and a verse. I blithely went onstage that evening knowing it backwards, or so I thought.

It was my opening song. I swept on during the introduction, opened my mouth to sing and nothing happened. Except for the title I had forgotten the words completely, so I invented some words of my own, keeping a grim smile on my face. These words were quite extraordinary; one line, I still remember it, was 'Wake up and live although the clouds are stormy, wake up and live, you must do this for me.' It was a nightmare. I had two choruses and a verse to invent and as it was my first song I could not get offstage but had to continue my act. Somehow I reached the end of this dreadful song: the musicians' faces were a study of confusion and the conductor looked as if he had been struck by lightning. My knees were shaking for the rest of the act but at last I finished. I vaguely remembered someone shouting at the side of the stage rather loudly but I was too intent on my invented poetry to pay any heed. When I came off I bumped into one of my fellow artists, Hilda Meacham, a dear person, a comedienne of considerable talent. Tears were streaming down her face and she was clutching a copy of my song. Mother told me she had seen what was happening, grabbed the music and dashed to the wings shouting the words to me and crying, 'She's making it up! She's making it up! What an artist.' Of course I was beyond such help. The poor woman was in a bad way and had to be given brandy and put to rest on a sofa.

Worse followed, however. Weak with relief, I sought out our conductor and thanked him but asked if he would take out 'Wake Up and Live' for the second show and put in a song I had sung many times instead. I gave him the music of the old song and he said I must not worry, it was all over and he would hand out the band parts to the musicians for the second show. I stood in the wings waiting for the introduction. To my horror the band struck up the opening chords of 'Wake Up and Live'! 'No, no,' I cried to the conductor, but it was too late and I had to go on. This time I not only had to go through making up the words for the two choruses, I had forgotten the words *and* the tune of the verse. So I made up the tune of the verse as well as the words, such as they were. The band had given up by now but the dear pianist stuck with me. However, as he had even less idea what I was singing than I did, he sensibly struck a few chords and let me get on with it. The trouble was, I did not know how to finish the verse, which seemed to be going on for ever, and get back to the dratted chorus. I finally came to the end of it by singing 'So' very loudly and went into the final chorus, the band joining me, now that they knew where they were. It turned out that the conductor had forgotten to hand out the music for the old song. He was abject. So was I. Some friends who had seen the show came round backstage afterwards, and seeing my stricken face asked me what was the trouble. 'The words,' I stammered. 'What did you think of the words of the first song 'Wake Up and Live'?'

'Oh, all right. In fact I thought they were a great deal better than most of the popular songs,' one of them said.

They had noticed nothing and when I came to think of it nor had the rest of the audience, because the act had gone well, though I was not noticing the applause much that night. But I learned that preparation is all and never again tempted the gods by cutting it short.

I was learning all the time, sometimes unconsciously, often through my own mistakes, and although my mother had a natural sense of theatre she did not have the experience to help me much. When something went wrong with a song, or my interpretation of it, which I could sense from the reaction of the audience, I could not put my finger on exactly what it was. As Mother was sitting in front I used to ask her what I was doing wrong. She also knew that something was not working but could not explain to me what it was. I was always desperate to find out and questioned her mercilessly. She used to think a bit and then say, for example, 'I think it's because you put your hand forward at the end' — of the particular song, that is. So I would stop putting my hand forward. Still it was not right. Eventually I came to know that Mother could not really help me much, except to say that I did not give a good performance or did, as the case might be. Instead I discovered a remarkable solution. I went by the audience; that is, when I made a gesture, sang a note, made a movement that was not as it should have been, if I concentrated hard on the audience's reaction at the time it happened, I could feel them draw away from me. As a result I came to know where the fault lay and during the next performance tried another tack until I sensed that the reaction was right.

This instinct served me better than any training could have done or any 'teacher' at a theatrical song, dance or drama school. I learned from working onstage in front of an audience, not through theory. It was the people sitting in front who taught me, chided me, put me on the right track again, punished me, rewarded me and, sometimes, loved me. I always arrived early to hear the audience's reaction to the previous acts and somehow knew from this, when waiting in the wings to go onstage, whether they were going to like me or not. At first, if an audience was cold towards me, I used to work harder to make them like me. I could feel myself going over the top and over-working, but I could not help it, so anxious was I for their approval. This was a mistake which it took me some time to realize and, when I did, a great light came on in my mind, with the solution. If the audience does not immediately take to you, do not fight them; on the contrary, act as if they are not there and perform for yourself. This worked tremendously well and it was a great feeling when I felt them come towards me instead of me going towards them and finally heard the warmth of their surrender when I had finished. It took all my courage, though, to try this out for the first time, and in the back of my mind I could hear, fearfully, my 'bread and butter speech'.

4

Early Films and Pantomime

After the summer season in Largs, everything seemed to happen at once. I made a film test for ABC, and made three films. The first was *Save a Little Sunshine*. The star was Dave Willis, a Scottish comedian of great renown in Scotland, and I was the leading lady, although I had only one song. It was a comedy with music and very few close-ups of me. I was then sixteen and considerably younger than Dave Willis, who had already been established for many years. The director was noted for his penchant for bullying, once he had found a vulnerable target. This time it was my fate to endure his tirades. As I was completely inexperienced and nervous to boot, he really indulged himself to my cost, always when the full cast was assembled for a scene. It was not a happy experience but it soon passed, leaving me, however, with a dread of filming which lasted for many years. Whenever I entered a film studio, especially the set, I felt claustrophobic and could not accustom myself to the silence and the faces clustered around the camera, especially after the space and light of the theatre, with the faces some distance away, which laughed and smiled. There was no applause, no inkling of whether the scene I had played was good or bad. Then came the screams of the demon director: the feeling that I could do nothing right damaged my confidence and I stiffened up like a robot whenever he called 'action'.

The second film *Me and My Pal*, was better. It featured a new director, Thomas Bentley, who did not yell at me as his predecessor had done. The cast of *Save a Little Sunshine* had included the young Max Wall and Tommy Trinder, both beginning to shine. Tommy, in those days, was rather preoccupied, but Max Wall was relaxed and as amusing and eccentric as he always had been. He was an attractive young man, with shiny blond hair and a lovely smile, plus considerable charm. He was blessed with great self-assurance and, of course, a tremendous wit. He entirely dominated the film set even at seven-thirty in the morning. I thought him absolutely terrific, but as I was dreadfully shy I never spoke a word to him, nor anyone else come to that. In any case I could not imagine that he would even notice me, especially in the awful clothes I had to wear and with my plaits done up in a bun. The last day of shooting arrived, then we all went to our dressing-rooms to pack up. Mother went to get the car. There was a knock on the door, it was Max Wall. He entered, closed the door and then smiled that wonderful smile as he walked slowly towards me. I was transfixed. Fear and delight struggled within me. I said nothing. I couldn't. Neither did he. His arms went round me gently and he kissed me on the lips, a most beautiful, soft, tender kiss which lasted forever, it seemed to me. It was the most perfect first kiss any girl ever had. He released me slowly then stood back. 'Where do you go next week?' he asked.

'Coventry,' I whispered.

'I am at Leeds. I shall come to see you on Tuesday morning and we'll have lunch. What is your address?' he asked, without taking his brilliant eyes off mine. Where is Mother? was my first thought, but I said 'O . . . yes,' and gave him the address.

The following Tuesday Max arrived. Mother had talked to me quite a bit and given various warnings and time limits. She greeted Max unsmilingly, but his charm was unassailable and we left with her grudging good will. The first thing he had to do, Max revealed, was buy some new shoes, so we went to a shoe shop, where we spent nearly two hours looking for something that would suit. Nothing did. So we went to another shoe shop, where we spent slightly less time but with a similar result. By now I was beginning to feel restive. One more shoe shop was on the agenda. 'Can't you get some shoes in Leeds?' I asked shortly.

'You must learn to be patient and unselfish' came the reply. I began to wonder when and where we would be having lunch. It was pouring with rain when we left the third shop, which mercifully had supplied a suitable pair. Max then drove out of the town some distance when he stopped the car. It was still pouring with rain. He attempted to kiss me, but by now I was firmly unkissable. He tried again to embrace me but I was so furious — and hungry — that his effort was wasted. 'What's the matter?' he enquired plaintively.

'I'm sorry, I should have told you — I'm engaged,' I was suddenly inspired to announce. Encouraged by his shocked reaction, I continued, 'So I think it is better if we do not see each other again.' And we never did.

I was playing a Sunday concert some time later at the Leeds Empire. My call came and I ran down the three flights of steps afraid of being late, when my heel caught on the edge of the concrete and my shoe bounced down two flights at the exact moment when the doors to the stage opened to reveal George Formby in dinner jacket and black tie. My shoe landed at his feet. I descended the rest of the steps and he gallantly knelt down and put my shoe on. Not a word was spoken as I had to run onstage, almost missing my entrance, gasping a hurried thank-you as I ran. He smiled. There was not a soul about and it was quite a romantic moment, especially as George looked rather handsome in his evening get-up. I had not even known that he was on the bill.

I forgot all about the incident until a few weeks later, when my agent rang to say I had been offered the feminine lead opposite George Formby in his next film *Come on George*. What a surprise and how thrilled Mother and I were. Oh dear, another film, I thought to myself, but, perhaps, being a more important one, with a big star like George Formby, things would be different. The first step was a silent test I had to make for the studio, Ealing Films, for make-up and hair to see how I photographed. This went off quite well. Before we started shooting, however, I was called into make-up and was told that my hair would have to be cut — it was below my shoulder-blades now, the plaits having been finally executed at Largs. Cut it certainly was, up to my ears. I was a shorn lamb and it looked, I thought, awful. Then my make-up was adjusted, hardly any lipstick or eye make-up and a flat white face. So different from my stage make-up, which I had finally learned to do. I was playing a policeman's daughter, but I looked more like a drudge. I asked the make-up man why I had to have all these changes. 'Oh, Mrs Formby wants it,' he said nervously. 'She said your hair was too sexy for a policeman's daughter and your make-up was too theatrical.'

Worse was to come. The clothes I was given could have been bought at any country jumble sale and the hat I had to wear, a navy felt halo, was similar. My agent had asked for a song for me, but this was refused; he then asked if I could, at least, sing a duet with George. This also was refused. I felt handcuffed and frustrated. Things were not improved by the fact that George Formby never addressed a remark to me during the entire film nor ever came near me. It was as if he were frightened and, looking the way I did, I was not surprised! But the film plodded on and when it was fairly well underway the nice make-up man, who was Italian, slowly began to alter my make-up to what it should have been in the first place; the hairdresser, too, set my shorn locks in a quite attractive shiny hairstyle, and I was given a rather chic little linen suit and hat to wear — in the last scenes that is! Still there was no communication from G.F. — not even a cup of tea or a Good-morning. Our director, a great fellow called Anthony Kimmins, and his assistant Basil Dearden, later a notable director himself, assured me that G.F. had probably been warned off me by his wife Beryl, who was apparently, very jealous of George and still madly in love with him. I felt rather sorry for her in spite of her making me look like a scarecrow, because she must have suffered a lot of pain.

The final close-up of the film was to be a kiss between George and me, but in order to achieve this we had to see that Beryl was off the set. I could not understand what all the fuss was about, until I heard about the film George had made some time before with Googie Withers as leading lady. Apparently there was also a kiss in that script, and when the time came to shoot it everyone was so occupied with their work that no one noticed Beryl had just arrived and was sitting behind the camera. 'Action!' cried the director and action he got, but more of it than he expected. George and Googie kissed, but during this rare happening George, when the two pairs of lips were firmly joined, rolled his eyes! Now this was definitely not in the script and before George or anyone else could draw breath there was pandemonium. Beryl gave a loud cry, collapsed into a sea of tears and left the set sobbing heavily. Panic! Everyone stopped except George, who flew after Beryl. Both Beryl and George were in the dressing-room for what, I was informed by the crew, seemed hours and there was no more shooting that day! It seems the fatal kiss was eventually shot, but without the eye-roll.

This was the reason for such caution now. Tony Kimmins, our smashing director, solved the problem. Someone would have to go out of the studio and telephone Beryl. Someone did. 'Telephone call for you, Mrs Formby,' floated through the set. All was ready to go and I was instructed by Tony to 'Grab him and let him have it and don't break till I say 'cut'.' As I was so utterly fed up with all these capers, together with losing my locks, looks and entire persona I decided to do just that. It all worked and that was one more film I could forget, except for Tony Kimmins, Basil Dearden and the helpful cheery crew who hauled me through and kept my spirits up.

A few days later, we had wonderful news. Prince Littler had not dropped my option after all; he had been dissuaded by his wife, formerly Nora Delany, a famous and well-loved principal boy until she married Prince Littler and retired. She told him, I later learned, that the reason I had been such a rotten principal girl was because I was really a principal boy. 'I could tell by the way she sang and looked in the finale line, when she was just being herself — also her walk,' Mrs Littler explained. So I got the part of Dandini in *Cinderella* at the Prince's Theatre, Shaftesbury Avenue, London, with the great star Stanley Lupino as Buttons. I was sixteen. He was a star comedian of the London theatre and British films. Mother's introduction to Stanley Lupino was more dramatic than my own — she tripped down a flight of steps right into his arms!

Stanley Lupino was a joy to work with, considerate and helpful to everyone, and especially to me as I was so young and inexperienced. We began rehearsals. I was given only one song to sing as Dandini, but it was well placed and in front of a backcloth, which was good as a large elaborate set might take the audience's attention away from me! I was well aware that this one song could either make or break me. At least that is what I believed, and so I was anxious to find the right song — but which one? I had already combed the publishers before we started rehearsals and had found nothing suitable. One morning Mrs Littler was sitting in the stalls watching rehearsals. She called me over. 'You are doing very well, young lady, but what have you chosen to sing for your spot?' she wished to know.

I admitted that I had not been able to find a song as yet and there was no time during rehearsals to look further.

'We will see about that,' she smiled mysteriously. Mrs Littler then proceeded to explain to me the various tricks and pitfalls of playing onstage with other performers. This conversation opened my mind considerably to the competitive element that I had not considered was such a large part of our profession. I learned from her that morning how to cope with being upstaged by a fellow performer, that is, being manoeuvred into a position whereby one finds oneself having to speak one's lines with one's back to the audience. There were many more lessons I learned that morning from dear Nora Delany — another angel who helped me enormously — and I stored them all away in my head, never to be forgotten. I was sad in a way. I had never dreamed that these wonderful magical people would ever stoop to such tricks. But I supposed it was better to know than to lose face.

One morning I arrived at the theatre to find Mrs Littler awaiting me. 'No rehearsals for you this morning, my dear,' she informed me. 'We are going to find a song for you.'

Whereupon off we went to Feldman's Music Publishers. We were shown into a large oak-panelled room. Behind an enormous desk sat a white-haired gentleman with a kind face and direct gaze. When he saw Mrs Littler, his face broke with a smile. 'Good morning, Nora. It is a pleasure to see you, my dear. So this is the young lady in search of a song?' He sounded surprised. I supposed it was because I looked nothing like an actress with my hair in a bun, no make-up and dowdy clothes. In fact I looked, in those days, rather old-maidish and more mature than my sixteen years; all this and my painful shyness added up to an unlikely figure for the theatre to adopt. The white-haired man was Frank Rubens, head of Feldman's and an important personality in the music publishing business.

'What type of song were you looking for young lady?' he asked me quizzically, thinking, no doubt, that I would answer 'Ave Maria'. But I had given much thought to the choice of song. I explained to him that as I only had one song to sing it had to be something startling and effective and up-tempo, the faster the better, with a touch of humour. This time it was Frank Ruben's turn to be surprised. His eyes widened and twinkled. 'I think I have the very thing, just come in, no one has worked it yet,' he enthused. 'It's American called 'You Can't Stop Me from Dreaming' — could be a show-stopper.' It had better be, I thought grimly, for if I didn't stop the show I would have been the worst failure ever, to myself — retired, with a broken heart, at the age of sixteen. I could see the headlines, though how this tragic event would be headlined, considering that no one had ever heard of me, was something I did not consider.

Mrs Littler brought me back to earth with a brisk, 'Come along, Pat, try it out and let's see what happens.' So a pianist was found and I rehearsed 'You Can't Stop Me from Dreaming' for the first time. It was the perfect song.

On 24 December 1937 *Cinderella* opened at the Prince's Theatre and the world was far away beyond the magic lights, the red plush, the swishing curtains, the scent, the warmth, the joy and terror of a London first night — my first ever. I must do well, I must stop the show or I shall die, I whispered to myself. 'Sixteen-year-old Actress Dies on First Night after Being Booed Off-stage' went the headlines in front of my feverish eyes. Not even a mention of my name, how rotten — of course no one has ever heard of me, perhaps they never will after tonight. My thoughts tumbled out, round and round in my aching head. Curtain up and I was on for my first entrance, a scene with Madge Elliot, who was playing Prince Charming. It all went well in front of a wonderful audience and a packed house.

The show was running on oiled wheels; it was a beautiful production, with magnificent clothes and scenery, and it seemed no time until the interval. Suddenly I was onstage on my own before a front-cloth and starting to sing 'You Can't Stop Me from Dreaming'. During the last few bars I swept my hat off and raised it aloft, as I exited with a hop and skip and a sideways run — a fast one. The house went mad — that is the only possible way to describe it. I was numb with relief. The Ugly Sisters, Freddie Foss and Ken Douglas, who had been in pantomime at Cardiff the previous year and were like benevolent uncles to me — both experienced and dedicated performers — stood blocking my exit and pushed me back onstage as the applause and bravos went on. The noise was deafening, with people standing up and shouting and clapping. They did not stop, so the stage hands took away the front-cloth, behind which was set the gates of the palace — an enormous set. Two major-domos in white powdered wigs stepped forward to begin their lines. They could not be heard. Three times they tried to speak through the noise. Freddie Foss had me in an iron grip in the wings and would not let me go. Eventually the frontcloth was lowered again and the major-domos and the gates of the palace disappeared. I went on and sang the song once more. The strange thing is that my reaction to this extraordinary, unreal and completely unexpected ovation was simply surprise; no delight, pleasure, satisfaction — simply surprised disbelief.

What I was not aware of at that moment was what had been happening in the dark centre of the stalls, where Mother and Aunt Freda were sitting. Apparently when I made my finale entrance, an elderly dowager-type sitting in front of Mother stood up, banged her stick on the floor and in a loud 'shires' voice declared, 'That little Dandini is splendid — she'll be the Prince next year!'

This caused Mother to lean forward and, with tears pouring down her face, cry, 'Oh thank you, she's my daughter.' Aunt Freda was thoroughly disgusted at this and didn't speak to her again the rest of the evening. I was greeted with great warmth in the dressing-room and old Emmy, our dresser, handed me a large tumbler of fresh orange juice. I loathed the drink but she plied me with it whenever I came offstage, saying I 'must keep up my strength as I was only a little 'un.' She was such a darling that I always drank it. In the midst of all this jollification there was a loud bang on the door and Mother, who was near, opened it, loudly announced 'wrong room', then closed the door firmly. There was a slight pause, then another determined bang, and this time it was opened to reveal Ralph Lynn, our most famous comedy star. We all stood at attention as he burbled in his unmistakable voice, 'I s-s-say, I'm so s-s-sorry to b-b-barge in like this. I was looking for Miss Kir-Kir-Kirkwood.' As there was a long flight of steps down from the door it was difficult to see where anyone was.

'Here I am, Mr Lynn.' I gasped, thrilled to bits.

He came down the steps, then right up to me, took my hand in his and stammered, 'I j-just wanted to say how m-m-much I enjoyed your performance, my dear. You were absolutely splendid and I wish you all the luck in the world.' To think that this great star had climbed all those horrible steps up to the roof to say this to a complete unknown. Now, no longer young, he touched me and all of us in the dressing-room with his kindness. I could not speak; I was so thrilled, so excited, so emotional, I just stood there. He understood, of course, being considerate, so he simply smiled round at us all, bewitched and silent, and took his leave. A fitting finish to an unforgettable evening.

The reaction to the opening night throughout the West End was amazing. A few days later as Mother and I were walking to the theatre a famous figure approached us. It was Sydney Howard, a great comedy star. He took my hand, saying, 'Miss Kirkwood?'

'Yes,' I gulped.

'So you're the little lady everybody is talking about,' he said, smiling, then wished me luck and walked on. 'You Can't Stop Me from Dreaming' had been a golden choice and the reaction from every audience was the same as the first night, but the frontcloth was not taken away so soon.

Mother confessed to me that she had had a conversation with Stanley Lupino that went as follows. Mother: 'What am I to do with her — shall I put her into a drama school?'

Stanley: 'No, no, on no account, just keep her working — she's intelligent and she will learn better and faster that way. No schools!' he insisted.

Well! I thought to myself, this might sound all right, but I might make some awful mistakes. I would probably benefit from someone else's knowledge, an experienced artist like Stanley Lupino must be right: I had better get on with it. I recall that *Tatler* magazine reviewed the show and at the very end said, 'Pat Kirkwood was an adequate Dandini . . . '

In spite of the great fuss, nothing happened after the run of *Cinderella*, as I had already been booked for more variety shows and another summer season at Barrfields Pavilion, Largs. Still, it all seemed rather tame after London. So, we were off on tour again and soon settled back into our old routine. By now I had become accustomed to stopping the show wherever we played, although my billing was still in small print. In fact, if my act did not go better than the top of the bill I was really upset, not in any spoiled, cross way but because I was anxious about my voice or my repertoire. I was not in the least cocky or smug; I simply wanted to give my very best all the time and never fall below standard.

5

More Variety

If Mother, sitting in the audience, ever heard any adverse comments on my performance or appearance she never failed to tell me. These criticisms hurt and upset me at first, but after a while I became angry instead. 'I'll show them,' I growled and went onstage like a virago, which was always appreciated by the audience, who responded with wild enthusiasm. When Mother saw this turn of events she decided I worked at my best when rattled, and evidently made a plan, of which I was not aware until some years later. She proceeded to relay to me any criticism or comment that would achieve this effect, even sometimes, when they were nonexistent, making up her own. Although Mother meant well, it occurred to me when a friend informed me of her machinations that it would have been kinder if she had occasionally passed on some good comments too, but she never did. Perhaps she did not want me to become spoiled, not being aware that this would be the last thing I would ever become, being far too aware of how quickly things change. Every artist needs encouragement and praise from time to time, especially from someone who's close. This I never ever had from my mother, not even after an enormously successful first night nor, even more necessary, after a disastrous one. Not once did she ever say 'You gave a good show tonight,' or 'Well done, dear, I'm proud of you,' or even 'Never mind, you were fine,' if the show happened to be a flop.

I still had no sign of a booking from Moss Empires, which owned almost all of the big variety theatres in Britain, such as the London Palladium and Hippodrome, and the enormous variety theatres in the provinces — all the 'number ones' as we used to call them. The theatres were not only very large but beautifully managed, with proper dressing-rooms backstage and sumptuous auditoria. It was the dream of every up-and-coming variety artist like me that they would, one day, be booked to play these first-class venues — and a nostalgic memory for those who had played them in their heyday but were now, because of changing fashion or, simply, their age, playing second-, third-, or fourth-rate theatres.

These splendid artists still performed with consummate professionalism onstage, but after they had walked off or in the daylight their eyes were tired and sad. There was another lesson for me to learn, though I was still too young to absorb it. This particular lesson can be learned only after several falls and stumbles on the way; indeed few of us ever learn it or even wish to: the lesson that we should never be seduced by success nor vanquished by failure if we wish to have more than an ephemeral career.

Don Ross told me he had spoken to the great George Black, chief impresario of Moss Empires and a formidable figure indeed. He was called

'GB' when he wasn't around; otherwise it was 'the Guvnor' or 'Mr Black'. I called him 'Mr Black'. He had seen my act and 'they are keeping an eye on you but waiting till you settle down a bit, as you're far too busy onstage at the moment.' So, no luck! But what did they mean by 'busy'? I thought perhaps I moved about too much and/or worked too hard, but that was the only way I knew how to make the act work. I did not change anything as it would make me self-conscious, unable to be myself. Still, I was disappointed.

Suddenly, one day, we had a telephone call from the office of Jack Hylton, the leader of his own well-known orchestra and then one of London's leading impresarios. The caller was Frank Barnard, his manager, saying their touring show *Secrets of the BBC*, starring Phyllis Robins, Bryan Michie and Robb Wilton, was in trouble as Phyllis Robins was ill and they needed a replacement right away. Could I get along to their office in Wardour Street that morning? Luckily Mother and I were in London, as I had a week out, so off we went. Here we were met by Frank Barnard and Bryan Michie. There was another man standing behind Frank Barnard's desk, a shadowy figure I did not notice much. Mr Barnard explained what had happened and asked if I thought I could go on in Phyllis Robins's place that same night at Hackney Empire.

I was just about to say 'Yes please,' thinking I would only be required to do my normal act. Then Bryan Michie explained further. I would have an opening number to learn, and I would have to sing it solo with the entire company onstage. Also, I had to learn a duet with Dennis Lawes and, more, I was expected to learn to ride a trick bicycle round the stage, with a saddle that went up and down, dressed in nineteenth-century clothes. Then I was to do my act. I sat silent for a bit. Bryan Michie, Jack Hylton's long-time right-hand man, beamed his large and benevolent grin at me. He was an enormous man, not only impressively plump but tall as well. 'Come on, Pat, you can do it. I'll pull you through,' he roared and suddenly I thought, Yes, I can. So all afternoon in the concrete backyard of the Hackney Empire I rode this bicycle with the up-and-down saddle; thank heaven for my cycling years, I thought.

The opening night went well. I managed to remember everything and not fall off the bike. All the 'pros' were wonderful to me: Izzy Bonn, Rosie Lloyd — the sister of Marie Lloyd whom I was to play years later on television — Bryan Michie, Dennis Lawes, Robb Wilton — they all came to congratulate me, especially for stepping in at such short notice. As Phyllis Robins had decided not to continue with the *Secrets of the BBC* tour I was asked to stay. So I did. It was a comfortable experience being part of a show on tour, instead of having to look after all travel and accommodation details oneself.

At last I was playing the Moss Empires theatres, although only as a 'fill-in', not booked by them. The tour was a long one, for which we were thankful. Every Friday evening in between shows — we were playing twice nightly with a Wednesday matinée — we were paid our wages by a man from Jack Hylton's office. He always paid mine to Mother and I never really noticed him — he was just someone from the office to me. I learned much later that he had been in the office when I went to meet Frank Barnard and Bryan Michie about *Secrets of the BBC*. He had been the shadowy man behind Frank Barnard, but I'd never really noticed him. One evening, after being paid my salary and 'the man' — I did not even know his name, nor want to — left, Mother said, 'That fellow is keen on you.' I was even more amazed than Mother that any male, a grown-up one especially, would cast an eye in my direction. I was firmly convinced that I was as plain as a boot and would die an old maid. I laughed, rather prematurely, not knowing what was in store for me. I was also flattered and intrigued, even though I still could not remember what he looked like. How could I know that those few words of my mother would completely change my life. If only she had never uttered them.

Next Friday afternoon we went to the pictures — we were playing Coventry that week. As we were coming out of the cinema Mother nudged me furiously. 'Look, there he is — he's been sitting behind us.' Sure enough, there was 'the man', whom I recognized for the first time as the person who paid our salaries. Mother hurried me out and to the theatre as it was time we were there. That evening the 'fellow who was keen on me' did not leave as soon as he'd paid, but started to chat. It seemed that he had seen my act at the Palace Theatre, Blackpool, when he was the assistant manager and had been very impressed. Not long afterwards he had met Jack Hylton, who was appearing at the Opera House and became friendly with him, playing golf with him many times. Apparently JH took a liking to him and suggested that he give up his job there and come and work in his office as an assistant to Frank Barnard, his then manager. It seems 'the man' made JH laugh a lot and he wanted him around. It was 'the man' who had suggested me as the replacement in *Secrets of the BBC*.

So, the saga began. He (John William Atkinson Lister was his name) was fifteen years older than I and extremely experienced. He asked me out and Mother, surprisingly, after a while, agreed but checked on where we were going and put a curfew on our return. We went to a matinée at the Empire Cinema, Leicester Square, and then to a Chinese restaurant in Soho. Strangely, although I was still extremely shy and this was my first date with a man, I found him easy to talk to. Maybe it was because he came from the north of England, as I did, but he was from Yorkshire, which should have warned me from the start. John was of medium height, slim, with abundant hair and light green eyes, was not exactly handsome but rather nice-looking and he had a sense of humour. He made me laugh, which is always fatal to a woman although I was still only seventeen. My plait I now wore in a large chignon on my neck when I was not onstage. The Chinese restaurant was a wonderful adventure for me and I loved the delicious new flavours of the food and the exotic atmosphere. I did not drink, nor did he — another danger signal — so we had jasmine tea. He took me home right on Mother's deadline and made a date for the next Sunday. I went to bed feeling a mixture of elation, surprise and wonder. The next Sunday we did exactly the same thing, though this time I found myself talking to him as if I had known him for years and he listened, actually listened to me — what a joy. Again we had a marvellous time, at least I did, and he seemed happy too. We did not kiss goodnight, that being the usual mode of behaviour in those days, much more subtly romantic and intriguing than the immediate attack that passes for romance today.

We had one more date, then I was due in Scotland for my concert party, a summer-show season of four months — my second one at Barrfield's Pavilion at Largs. Mother seemed to be calm about my new boyfriend, saying only, 'He's very funny and he dresses well, but he's Yorkshire, isn't he!' It was true, my friend always dressed immaculately. He was beginning to seem very handsome to me and he had beautiful hands. However, work came first and off Mother and I went to Largs. Then I had regular telephone calls and one or two letters, together with a photograph of him, which I kept on my bedside table. I knew nothing at all about sex, nor where babies came from, except for a few garbled and completely inaccurate stories from some of the girls at Levenshulme High School.

When I told Mother about these comments she dismissed them with a little laugh, saying they were quite wrong and I must not bother my head with such nonsense. She did not enlighten me though! All I knew was how to walk onstage and do my act — just pointed in the direction of the stage and left to get on with it. Now, though, I had something else to think about, my 'knight in shining armour', as I called him to myself, and he was ever in my thoughts, except when I was in the theatre. I had always been romantically inclined; the Walt Disney films were my favourite and I saw all of them. I sat through *Snow White* many times. The song 'Some Day My Prince Will Come' always made me cry, as I never thought this would happen to me.

In the middle of the summer season 'my knight' telephoned our digs to say he was coming up to Largs to see me. What excitement; I was transported to Disneyland and Mother was very cross and worried. She telephoned my father, who prised himself away from his beloved office and came up, not best pleased but ready to do his duty whatever that turned out to be. Then *he* arrived and I ran from the digs at top speed — I had seen him from my bedroom window — and nearly knocked him over. I was mortified that I had a large red blister on my nose, caused by the sun, that I was wearing old navy shorts and a striped shirt. 'Well,' he said, 'you look about ten years old,' which was not the kind of greeting I had imagined. Then he met my father, who was cool and cautious but shook hands with him, for which there was an ulterior motive, which I found out later. John was staying at an hotel in Largs, so he went to get changed and then came back to our digs for lunch. Afterwards, we went for a drive in a car he had hired. He kissed me for the first time, but I did not enjoy it as I had dreamed of doing; I felt awkward and shy and conscious of my sunburned nose. I was also a bit scared, for we were miles from anywhere, out in the countryside, and I wanted to go home! I felt numb and did not know what to say. It was Sunday and we were not working at the Pavilion. The afternoon was giving way to evening. He tried to kiss me again, but I refused crossly and so we went back to Largs where Mother and Daddy were waiting, the latter looking meaningfully at his watch. We said goodnight and I went into the house after promising to go out to supper with him after the show the next day. My father did not seem at all worried and told Mother and me that he knew that I was safe with this young man, as he had discovered that he was a Freemason like himself; that was the reason for the handshake, to find out if he was one, the mysterious and secret handshake that was the guarantee of honour and discretion. So we were all happy and went to bed.

The very next night after the show John took me to a quiet nook in a wood and attempted to deflower me. In spite of the sylvan, romantic setting, his efforts were unsuccessful, partly because I was standing against a large tree at the time and surrounded by ferocious midges. I imagined them to be my protectors alerted by a good fairy! I was so naïve still that I really thought I had been 'seduced'. I looked in the mirror the next morning to see if I appeared any different, but no such luck — the same boring face stared back at me. So I went and had my plaits chopped off and emerged with a short page-boy hairdo, as a mark of my new womanhood. Mother was apoplectic at this heresy, as I had not confided in her. All was well, however, for the reaction of my colleagues was firmly on my side. The new look was an enormous success and worked well onstage as well. My hair, then, was shiny and very dark, near black, and the lights onstage created a dazzling effect. John, when he saw me, was delighted and called me his 'little beauty', and I was thrilled to know that I was finally a mature and sophisticated woman secure in my worldly wisdom. We were engaged the following year. Mother was distraught and we fought constant battles, but the more she disapproved of the liaison the more determined I became not to give up my knight whatever happened. I was hopelessly in love and he was my whole life, I thought. Various people tried to talk me out of our relationship, especially Aunt Pop. Even my love's best friend, Eric Hargreaves, warned me against him and advised me strongly to give up all thoughts of marriage, as he was a notorious womanizer — actually the word he used was altogether stronger, 'whoremonger', a word with which I was not familiar. I had heard of fishmongers and ironmongers but not this kind. I asked Mother what 'whores' were and she replied 'bad girls who go out at night,' which hardly explained matters. It was all to no avail.

Whilst playing the Grand Theatre, Bolton, I had a message from Don Ross that George Black was holding auditions at the Palladium for a new show the very next day. Also Edward Black, his brother and head of Gaumont-British films, was looking for a new leading lady for a film and would also be at the Palladium. George Black, apparently, had asked for me to audition, in spite of the fact that he had seen me work before many times. Mother and I travelled to London by train after the show at Bolton. Jack Hylton had kindly arranged for Bryan Michie to meet us and the three of us stayed up all night in the Cumberland Hotel lounge as we could not afford a room. Next morning we arrived at the Palladium, where there seemed to be dozens of girl singers including two from Jack Hylton's band, who were playing for the audition. One of the Hylton singers was already dressed and made up and looked gorgeous in a superb evening dress. They all did. Except me. I only had what I had travelled in, a summer frock. I don't stand an earthly, I thought to myself as I started to make up in the crowded room. Suddenly I was called onstage, with my make-up only half finished, but I flew down the stairs. I walked onstage in front of the waiting band and they struck up the introduction to my song, 'It Never Rains but it Pours'. The stalls were crowded with artists, directors, including Wendy Toye, the dancer and choreographer. When I stopped there was a pause. This is the end of me, I thought. Then O joy, tremendous applause from the stalls. It was a thrilling experience and such a relief. Don Ross came round in high excitement and Jack Hylton beamed and said, 'You've got it all, kid, a show with George Black, a film for Edward Black and a contract.' Apparently he had been sitting with the two Blacks, letting his deputy conductor take over onstage.

We travelled back to Bolton on a pink cloud . . . but nothing seemed to come of it. Oh well, a return to variety was on the agenda — then suddenly something did happen. I was offered the junior lead in the film *Band Waggon* so, at least, Edward Black came through at last. It was a good break, as I had two songs to sing and some nice clothes to wear, for the first time. Arthur Askey, a kind soul with a good 'head' on him as well, was starring, so too was Dickie Murdoch. We had a wise and tolerant director in Marcel Varnel, a plump and jolly Frenchman who guided me through the intricacies of film technique, much of which just rolled off me, I'm afraid. We used to have delicious toasted sandwiches on the set for breakfast, which I made the most of, becoming 'rounder by the day' as Mr Varnel warned me with a grin. Arthur and Dickie promptly named me 'Madame Gutzy', which they called me for years afterwards. It was an enjoyable film. Arthur always had the gift of making his colleagues happy, as opposed to some comedians I have worked with.

6

Black Velvet

Cinderella came round again, this time at the Theatre Royal, Newcastle, where I reprised my Dandini role. Again the audience was wonderful to me and altogether it was a sublime experience with a cast that was a joy to work with. Pantomime in those days was an experience to be cherished and remembered for years afterwards. When, later, it was invaded by pop singers and desecrated by 'blue' comics the spirit of this joyous Christmas show was ruined for ever and no longer enraptured children nor, indeed, their parents. The magic and innocence was dragged in to the mud and left to die. I was lucky to experience pantomime in its true form for some years. One of the most delightful traditions, in the provinces anyway, was that whole families, including grandads and grannies, would book seats for every week of the run and on the last night, as they knew the show by heart, they used to say the lines with us, amid great hilarity; the artists would dress up in disguise to try and confuse the children, but never did as they knew us so well by then. A lot of ad-libbing and tricks were played and the audience would applaud every diversion from the script. It was a Christmas party which we all enjoyed; presents from the families poured onstage after the finale and flowers almost buried the performers. Tears flowed with the laughter, because this was the last night of the show, and we had to say goodbye to our friends and fellow performers. These were great shows with breathtaking clothes, glorious sets and Emile Littler's own interpretations of the traditional fairy stories.

One morning I had a telephone call from George Black of Moss Empires, at that time Britain's leading impresario, who had persistently refused to offer me a date. It was a summons to appear at Cranbourne Mansions at eleven o'clock. Seated there were George Black, Robert Nesbitt, the producer, and Joan Davis, the choreographer. George Black was a tall robust-looking man with silver hair, a pink, healthy face and a small silver moustache. He managed to look fatherly and fearsome at the same time. 'We are putting on a show at the London Hippodrome,' he stated and then paused. 'Would you like to be in it?'

I drew a deep breath, to see if I could still do it, then answered, 'Yes, Mr Black.' He asked me how much I was earning, though I suppose he knew, so I told him: 'Twenty-three pounds and ten shillings.'

'Do you think you should have more than that?' he asked with a twinkle.

'Oh yes!' I quickly responded.

I was flummoxed by his reply, which was, 'Why?'

At this, I tried desperately to find the right answer, to avoid sounding big-headed; so I said lamely, 'Because this is the West End.'

He laughed benignly. 'Then what do you think you should have?' Of course he must have been ribbing me and probably thought it all very amusing, but I was trying to estimate a figure that would not put me out of the door. Finally I blurted out, 'Twenty-five pounds.'

'Settled,' he announced jovially. Then I was given the times of rehearsal and other details of production, and Mother and I floated out into Leicester Square on our beautiful balloon.

On the first day of rehearsal I was so nervous that I asked Mother to come along with me. It was my first West End revue and everyone knew each other and seemed so confident and sophisticated. I tried to guess what I would be given to do and came to the conclusion that I would be in one or two production numbers with the other artists and, if lucky, would have one song on my own. That was hoping for too much, I thought. The producer, Robert Nesbitt, read out the routine and outline of the show, as well as what each artist had to perform. It was an amazing example of organization and planning. We were to have only twelve days' rehearsal, which was unheard-of for a big London show; but the planning had been so meticulous that all ran smoothly and there was never a moment's panic.

This first rehearsal was attended by Vic Oliver, whose suave and charming presence dominated the room; Roma Beaumont, looking delicately beautiful and cool; Carole Lynne, blonde and ravishing; Iris Lockwood, elegant and poised, with a tigerish beauty; and Roberta Huby, who literally glowed with life and looked stunning. Then me, feeling I should not be there and wondering how I could possibly fit into all this glamour. We were soon informed by George Black that there were to be five leading ladies, including myself. I shall have nothing to do, I panicked; there'll be nothing left. I looked towards Mother, who smiled encouragingly.

Robert Nesbitt read out the show's routine. 'After the overture there will be the opening song sung by Miss Pat Kirkwood.' Oh good, I thought, at least I have one song. Then there were a few more items that I scarcely heard as I was listening out for my name. 'Next item is the song 'My Heart Belongs to Daddy' sung by four of the leading ladies.' I held my breath, for one of us was out — but not me, I was relieved to hear. The next scene was set in a beautiful replica of the Café Royal from Victorian times. I was delighted to hear that I was to represent Vesta Tilley in her song 'The Army of Today's Alright'. By this time I was speechless and we had only reached the interval. Then came the best and most surprising news of all. I was to have a single spot on my own in the second half, with two songs by Cole Porter, 'Get Out of Town' and 'Most Gentlemen Don't Like Love' — neither of which I had ever heard of. Then George Black announced that the dresses would be by Alex Shanks and Norman Hartnell. I was, finally, in a coma of delight.

Rehearsals were to start the next day, with fittings and discussions about clothes. Norman Hartnell arrived and I was shown the sketches, which were unbelievably glamorous and beautiful. For the opening number called 'Bubble, Bubble' I was to wear a black velvet dress, an enormous white Arctic fox-fur Cossack hat and a large white fox-fur muff to match. GB explained that they had chosen the title *Black Velvet* to imply that the show would be a mixture of Guinness and Champagne, like the famous drink of that name. I came to hear later that I was supposed to be the Champagne — hence the opening song 'Bubble, Bubble' — and Alice Lloyd, the great Marie's equally great sister, who was to sing 'Good Old Iron' in the Café Royal scene, was the Guinness. She was a great old girl and wonderful artist, who shone like a beacon and filled the theatre with laughter.

For the 'My Heart Belongs to Daddy' number we four were to be dressed by Norman Hartnell, who designed for us four suits: a dress and short bolero jacket with a hat to match, with fox-fur trimming to match the fox-fur on the cuffs of the jacket. So there was a white outfit, a rust one, a black one and a pinky-beige one, all with fox fur dyed to match. Then there were the chunky diamond bracelets and rings, which clunked merrily as we moved. The whole effect was fabulous.

For my own spot I was to wear an off-the-shoulder burgundy satin dress by Norman Hartnell, which had a crinoline skirt and a fitted bodice. The dress was heavy, the skirt seeming to have miles of material which reached to my ankles, and the crinoline wire gave the effect of a large circle. This was a long way from my white skirt and red jumper, and I hoped that I would not fall over on my first night. Ah yes! The first night loomed like a great shining beacon. Excitement and terror combined, the terror beginning to win as the time drew near and I would have to step on to the stage of the London Hippodrome. The worst moment would be my single spot in the second half, when I would be alone onstage without a safety net. We were living then in Clarence Gate Gardens, in a rented basement flat, which was cosy and warm. I had my own bedroom for the first time, so I could toss and turn and say my prayers in peace, falling to sleep at last exhausted. But then the dreams started. One, in particular, kept coming back. I was centre stage and had forgotten the words of my song. Then my dress fell off and the audience booed and shouted. I was experiencing the 'bird' at last, but as I was about to recite my response the safety curtain came down and I woke up.

The show opened in November 1939. We managed to get through the day and to the theatre where Mother, looking pale, left me. Strangely my nerves left me then and I began the chores of making-up and dressing. My dresser was a Scot, Kathleen MacRobbie, who was a cheerful, motherly and calm jewel of a woman and a great comfort to me. The great sweep of the overture obliterated all else and like racehorses at the starting post the artists were ready to go, eager to be onstage. All being so young, we were bursting with energy, fear

112

forgotten. It was a sparkling and impressive audience which greeted us, resplendent in full evening dress and tiaras, diamonds twinkling and white ties to the fore. We had opened in Brighton the week before to a wildly enthusiastic audience, but this was different. Vic Oliver had warned me. 'Hippodrome audiences do not call out 'encore' or 'bravo', but do not be put off; they will be warm but restrained. Do not be shaken, you have nothing to fear.' That was kindness itself — I had never spoken to him before, except to say 'Good morning, Mr Oliver' at rehearsals.

Vic Oliver was different from any other comedians we had. He was tall and soigné, for one thing, had an endearing 'lived-in' face that crumpled delightfully when he smiled or laughed, which was often, and a thick croaky Austrian accent. He played the violin in between his patter. He married Sarah Churchill, and thereby acquired Sir Winston Churchill as a father-in-law. I was rather overawed by him as he was so sophisticated and self-assured, but I soon discovered how human he was. Another kindly act of his was unknown to me. He approached my mother during the week at the theatre and pleaded with her not to allow me to marry John at any cost, because he would 'peddle her for what he could get and ruin her career'. Mother told me this later, saying that Vic was deadly serious, although I did not know how he came to hold this opinion of John. Of course, this had no effect on me, although I appreciated his concern. My reaction was: poor John, everyone is against him, except me! Youth is often stupid.

When we opened at the London Hippodrome I was prepared. 'Bubble, Bubble', the opening number of the show, went well. 'My Heart Belongs to Daddy', the quartet, was next. I was lucky to have been given centre stage, so I made the most of it. Then before the interval came the Café Royal scene, and I sang my Vesta Tilley number, 'The Army of Today's All right', dressed in grey trousers, cyclamen jacket — known in the business as a 'bum starver' — and pill-box hat above a man's wig, into which my long hair had been bundled. I carried a swagger cane. This went down tremendously, and I received the first music-hall type of applause of the show. I was floating on air throughout the following interval.

Then the big crisis, my single spot in the second half, arrived. I sang 'Get Out of Town' by Cole Porter. The interesting feature of this first song was the utter stillness and quiet of the audience. Of course it was a sophisticated number, so I acted my head off and sang my best, the result being a rush of lasting applause that washed over me like warm syrup and gave me an appetite for the second Cole Porter song. This was the complete opposite, a witty attack on the male gender called 'Most Gentlemen Don't Like Love'. I was more at home with this though it was much too sophisticated for my tender years and some of the words were far beyond me. During this song I had to walk across the stage down some steps at the side on to the apron, a large half circle above the orchestra, and continue the song walking back up the other side. There I had to sing the second and last chorus.

As I stepped down, singing away and clutching each side of the enormous skirt of the dress, there was a terrifying noise behind me. It rang through the theatre. I stopped. I knew what the noise meant. The skirt of my dress had caught at the back on something onstage and ripped. The orchestra stopped. The audience gave a loud gasp of horror. I did not know what to do as I was caught fast on whatever it was onstage. Suddenly through my head went a quick thought, Who do you think you are, Kirkwood, wearing a Norman Hartnell dress? You had better go back to your white gymslip and the bobbly hat. I laughed, threw back my head and laughed out loud and long. Then the orchestra laughed and, at last, the audience did as well. We all laughed heartily. I turned and tugged with all my might, the dress came away and I folded the skirt on my arm. Then I continued the song, walking round the apron up the steps at the other side of the stage, and bowed. The applause was tremendous and laced with hilarity. That such a misfortune should turn into such a joyful experience was a small miracle. This near-disaster turned into a triumph; the press was delighted and gave me fantastic reviews. I had 'behaved like a 'veteran' and showed no panic — it was a victory,' said one critic.

My next entrance was a scene with two of the other leading ladies, Carole Lynne and Roma Beaumont with each of us singing a different song. Mine was 'It's a Lovely Day Tomorrow'

— a cracker, I thought. We all wore large lacy crinolines, which looked like wedding cakes; one white, one blue and mine, pale pink, another triumph for Norman Hartnell. The wonderful thing for me was that when I made my entrance the audience applauded loudly, and at the finale they were stirred to excessive applause and bravos, some even on their feet and clapping furiously. What an evening to remember! Backstage there was pandemonium, and the press was there in full force. I went back to Clarence Gate Gardens, had some supper and went to bed. Daddy was a great hit with George Black, it seems, as he was supremely unimpressed by it all. He had watched the show until the interval, then went to the bar for a drink and met up with 'GB'. 'Well, Bill,' said GB, 'what do you think of the show and what about your daughter! — aren't you proud of her?'

Daddy's reply to this was, 'I've had enough of all this. I'm going back to my office tomorrow!' GB was a fan of his forever.

The next morning at ten o'clock the telephone rang. It was Alfred Black, George Black's son and stage director. 'Have you seen the papers?' he asked breathlessly; I was half asleep. 'No,' I answered rather crossly. 'Well get 'em,' he shouted 'You're a star!' then hung up. So I had a cup of tea and breakfast and thought a bit. Of course I didn't believe him or, rather, was too dazed to take it in. So I dressed and went into the sitting room. By this time it was after eleven, but what a spectacle greeted me. There were flowers everywhere; Grandma, who was staying

116

with us, was drinking champagne and had two pink spots on her cheeks. The reviews were ecstatic and I was relieved and thankful that I had some marvellous personal notices. 'Britain's First Wartime Star' was the headline in the *Express*. I was eighteen.

I had determined to find out what had nearly ruined my first night and went to see the stage manager. I suggested there must be a nail on the stage just by the steps on stage right. He was horrified. 'A nail on the Hippodrome stage — impossible,' he puffed. 'Well, come over and have a look,' I suggested firmly. Sure enough there it was — a large rusty nail sticking up at exactly the spot where I stepped down. He went white. 'We'll have it removed straight away,' he said. 'I can't imagine how it got there!' I had a quick flash-back to the cut microphone cable at the Metropolitan theatre, Edgware Road, some years earlier.

Black Velvet ran for two years at the London Hippodrome and two more years on the Moss Empires tour with a different cast. Whilst in London we had full evening dress every night in the stalls — tiaras everywhere! One night King George VI and Queen Elizabeth with the two princesses Elizabeth and Margaret came to see the show, not in a box but sitting in the centre stalls, so near to us. What a thrill that was for us all, but every night there were famous names in front, so we became quite used to it and were rather cross if there was only one. *Black Velvet* was the last of the glamorous shows we were to see as war had broken out in September 1939 and we had opened in November. There was not a show like it in Britain for many years to come. People seemed to sense this and came in droves; we always had a full house and as we were playing twice nightly, with two matinées a week, the numbers involved must have been staggering. The show was the hit of the war and long remembered.

Backstage it was rather like being in school; we were all very young. I was the 'baby' and sometimes irresponsible. The Hartnell fox hats we wore in 'My Heart Belongs to Daddy' were all very beautiful, but mine seemed to hang over my face, like a large brown cat sitting on my head. I could sense that my face was partly hidden from the gallery, or upper circle as it was called at the Hippodrome. This bothered me, so at one matinée I persuaded Kathleen to get me a large pair of scissors and, to her horror, I snipped away the fox fur that lay on my forehead, quite a bit of it; that was better. But as I was waiting to go on for the number, one of the leading ladies noticed this operation and was horror-struck, in disbelief that I had cut my Hartnell fox fur hat. I did not reply to this as it was time for us to walk onstage. I was very pleased with myself because I could see the gallery and they could see me. I was less pleased later when I was fined for my desecration and had to pay up. Apparently I had been reported to the management. I was always being fined for something or other. The second time I was only half to blame. In the Café Royal scene, closing the first half, all the girl artists had to come down the steps into the stalls, walk down the aisles and ask the men to polka with them. Mostly the chaps were frightened to death as they had their wives with them, but some of them joined in the fun and we danced up and down the aisle. This was an awful chore for us as the aisles were too narrow and the men couldn't polka. Worse, we sometimes had to ask three or four before one got up. When I asked one fellow, with a flat cap on, sitting in the back stalls, the usual 'Will you polka?' he replied in a broad northern accent, and with a look of great disapproval, 'Not just now, thanks!' Did he expect me to come back later, I wondered. The upshot was that Roma Beaumont and I got together and devised a plan. We will ask 'Will you polka?' twice, and if no one agreed we would go round the back of the stalls, down the other side, through the pass-door and to our dressing rooms, where, Roma said, we could 'put our feet up and have a nice cup of tea.' This we did, which was most enjoyable, and we felt clever and superior to the rest of the 'leading ladies' left coping with their recalcitrant partners. This euphoria, sadly, did not last long. The leading lady who had reported my injured hat repeated her performance, spilling the beans about Roma's and my escapade through the pass-door. So we were fined, me for the third time. She must have had eyes like a hawk. She later became a great friend of mine: wild horses would not drag her name from me.

One evening when I was ready for my first entrance I went down early to the side of the stage to see the opening spectacle of the show, for the first time. It was so utterly beautiful: the gorgeous show-girls, tall and slim and the pretty doll-like dancers, the music, the lighting — all fascinated me. Suddenly onstage everything went very quiet, the music was subdued to an 'umpty-tumpty' ad lib, and the dancers and show girls were standing with their arms outstretched pointing to the centre of the stage, but no one was there. Horror! They were pointing at where I should have been but wasn't. My entrance was from a high platform, about fifteen feet, and to reach it I had to climb a steep set of steps and then trip lightly in time to the introductory music down the curved staircase at quite a speed. Somehow I scrambled up the steps and leapt, at the risk of my neck, and with a fixed smile, down the curved staircase where I began the opening song 'Bubble, Bubble' at last. I was fined again, naturally, but thankfully, that was the last time. All fines went to the Actors' Orphanage, so at least I was a regular contributor to this worthy charity! The orchestra and our musical director, Debroy Somers, enjoyed the whole event — I think it made their evening. But GB was not pleased!

The music for my entrance down the staircase began to get quicker and I asked Mr Somers to slow it down as I was in danger of falling. Nothing happened. I asked again. Still it was too fast and, inevitably, one night it was so fast I could not stop and fell full length at the bottom of the steps, my muff rolling away and my large white hat askew. More seriously, my right ankle hurt badly and I hoped it was not sprained or broken. The audience gave a loud tearful groan, but I began 'Bubble, Bubble' whilst I was getting up, collected my muff, still singing, straightened my hat and finished the song. My foot turned out to be only slightly hurt and I continued the show. I was furious with the musical director and surprised because he seemed such a cheerful and nice person. I thought of reporting him to GB but decided to wait until the next performance. The music was back to normal and remained so for the rest of the show so I guessed that GB must have seen the incident — he often watched from the back of the stalls.

Mother would not allow me to receive telephone calls at the theatre. She said, 'There are some very funny people about in London,' and also that some 'nasty men' would go to any lengths to 'obtain their ends'! But one evening, Dick, the stage doorman, knocked on my dressing-room door and said there was a call for me. I thought it must be something extremely important for Dick to let it through, and bearing in mind Mother's advice I went downstairs prepared. 'Hello,' I intoned in a discouraging way. 'Good evening, Miss Kirkwood,' was the reply. 'This is Prince Obolensky speaking.' In a flash I remembered reading in yesterday's newspaper that Prince Obolensky had been killed in a racing car. 'Oh, have you been resurrected?' I said. 'You were killed in a racing car yesterday.' That will settle this impersonation, I thought. 'That was my brother,' the voice replied, quietly. I felt dreadful and apologized immediately, wishing I could sink through the floor. Then, 'It would give me great pleasure if you would agree to have dinner with me one evening' the prince said. 'Thank you for asking me, but I am afraid I cannot accept your invitation. You see, I am engaged,' I heard myself say. 'I am sorry, I quite understand,' he replied. Just think I might have been Princess Obolensky one day! I wondered why Dick had let the call through, but he must have been more trusting than I. I have often regretted not accepting the invitation, for he had such a lovely voice. As my favourite song was 'Someday My Prince Will Come' I felt I had missed something that might have been fated. But I was engaged after all, was I not!

Much to my disgust I had to leave the show for eight weeks' pantomime at Christmas, to play Dandini again at Manchester, as I was still under contract to Prince Littler. This was the last pantomime of the three for which I had been contracted. George Black tried hard to persuade Prince Littler to release me from the contract, but he was adamant and would not. Although I was sad to leave my first big London show I could not blame Prince Littler. After all, he had put his faith in me and given me my first break in London when I first played Dandini at sixteen. So, a notice was put in the programmes saying that I was leaving the show for a while owing to a former commitment, that Gabrielle Brune would take my place, and that I would be returning in the

New Year. What a fuss. I was flattered to bits. When I returned to *Black Velvet* I was given new dresses — no more crinolines — and new songs. One of them, 'Oh Johnny', I loathed from the start. There were photographs in the press, with 'Pat's Back' in the headlines. All this made me rather nervous, as I was not sure whether the songs and dresses would come up to the first ones. But everyone seemed to like 'Oh Johnny' except me, and as the dresses were much simpler and more youthful-looking all was for the best.

I was thrilled when *Picture Post*, the most famous magazine of the war years and after, had me on the cover, with two full pages of photographs inside. Then *London Illustrated*, also a powerful and long-standing magazine, had a full-page photograph of me in the centre with the headline 'Britain's First Wartime Star' and 'Here She Is'. Even more exciting, the American magazine *Life* had a whole page inside with photographs, this page having been transferred from *Picture Post*, which also named me 'Britain's First Wartime Star'. The photographs showed me visiting Oxford University, blithely walking round the hallowed precincts, unaware of the fuss this would cause. Also, the cover picture in the *Picture Post* had me wearing a mortar board. Heresy! In *Life* magazine, there was one taken with the chaplain, walking through an archway. The caption read, 'Pat and the Parson help guarantee there will always be an England.' An immediate reaction came from the University hierarchy and the religious groups as well. 'Why was an actress allowed into the most sacred areas of the University?' and 'Why was she photographed with a man of God?' There were even letters to the press.

7

Top of the World

I had now been engaged for two years with no sign that my fiancé was eager to marry me. However, once I opened in *Black Velvet* in London, he suddenly became most pressing that we should be wed immediately. I was less than enthusiastic about this, as my time in the Manchester pantomime had given me breathing space away from him and, during the eight-week run, he had never made the effort to come and see me. Father was still firmly against the engagement and even more so about the marriage. He gave me dire warnings about the future if I continued with this 'disastrous relationship'. In any case, as I was still a minor, nearly nineteen, he reminded me that I would need his permission, which he would never give. I wondered at the time why it was that I was not as upset about this as I should have been. The result of all this brainwashing was that when I returned to London, I informed John that I wished to break off the engagement, giving the reason that I had 'met somebody else' — which I had not. The effect was dramatic. A few nights after I returned to *Black Velvet* he appeared from a corner behind the door of the dressing-room where he had been hiding, and began a tirade of abuse and anger which was quite frightening. I stood firm and gave him back the engagement ring, which he had told me was an emerald set in diamonds but which I subsequently discovered was paste. He threw it violently across the room saying, 'That's no good to me,' but he picked it up and left.

All this took place in 1940 and John, who was nothing if not plausible, soon talked me round, saying that he had been deceived by a friend who had sold the ring to him. He then gave me another, much smaller one, with what looked like an emerald, but by now I really did not care. After the scene in the dressing-room, there were telephone calls, and letters expressing his love for me. His persuasion was so effective, and I wanted to believe him so very much, that we resumed our engagement. As he was the first and only man in my life, fifteen years older and so experienced with women, I really did not have a chance to escape, although I tried.

After *Black Velvet*, George Black had a new production, *Top of the World*, a 'book-show', as it is called in the theatre, meaning a musical play, the accent being more on the story-line than the music. He offered me the younger lead, but insisted that I take a holiday before rehearsals started. So where else could Mother and I go other than Blackpool? John followed us — his family home was there and he was born and brought up in the town — and told me of a plot he had designed to allow us to marry at once. It was a nasty, deceitful and untrue plot which I was to regret the rest of my life. At the time, though, it seemed a great adventure and marriage a romantic dream come true. Also, I had become restive under Mother's rigid control and wanted to be free. How ironic.

We were married in the Actors' Church in Blackpool. I wore a grey suit and hat, as there had been no time to collect a trousseau, nor anything else. There was no one to give me away so I walked down the aisle alone, thinking of the white wedding I had always imagined but which I would never now have. I was terrified and wanted to flee from the church, which I should have done. Daddy had refused to be there, as he had telephoned Mother and found out that she had never agreed to the wedding. He was dreadfully angry and hurt.

I was upset and miserable when I heard this, and as I walked down the aisle my heart was full of foreboding. Thankfully something happened to lighten the gloom. Reginald Dixon, the organist at the Winter Garden, Blackpool — a national institution — played 'Ain't She Sweet' instead of the standard Wedding March. This revived my sense of humour and I almost laughed, but couldn't as there was a lump in my throat. We went to a hurried reception at the house of my husband's parents. Mother's face was ashen. We stayed about half-an-hour, then Mother drove off back to Manchester and Daddy, thinking that she would be there to stay and that it was the end of her happy days in the theatre. John and I drove to the Midland Hotel, Manchester, where we had two days' honeymoon. We were married on 10 August 1940.

I was completely unprepared for marriage.

Mother had never told me what to expect, which was the usual way in those days. Also, I was still being given pocket money and I knew nothing about managing finances or a home; cooking and sewing were strangers to me. Looking back, marriage should have been the very last experience to enter into. I had no friends except the actors in the shows I was in, and most of them were much older than I. Those who were not were isolated from me, because they were playing minor roles and they treated me with a kind of awed shyness. I, too, was shy, except onstage, which did not help me make friends. In fact there was no one in my life except Mother, until John came along. Mother and I never went out anywhere, so I never met anyone. It was simply the theatre and the flat that made up my life. Although I did not realize it, I was lonely, my only 'friends' being the audiences. I was dangerously vulnerable.

In the past year we had really felt the effects of the war. Food was rationed and we had had some air raid warnings but no severe bombings. Also, of course, there was the black-out to contend with. But now, during rehearsals for *Top of the World* underneath the roof of the Stoll Theatre, there were frequent air-raids, so much so that Bud Flanagan, a member of the Crazy Gang, suddenly disappeared. It was said that he just walked out of the theatre, hailed a taxi and said 'Blackpool'. George Black was very cross and it was three days before Bud returned.

As the south coast was being shelled the week we should have opened at Brighton, we could not open there before the Palladium, so GB decided we should 'open cold', as it was called, straight away in London. This was unheard-of, as West End shows always ran for at least a week out of town to get the show ship-shape and polished for London. The press was asked to abstain from attending our opening week at the Palladium, to give us time for alterations or whatever needed adjusting before the first night opening. In those days the press were more sympathetic to the theatre, and they all kept their word and stayed away for our first week. They were always referred to as 'the gentlemen of the press'. And they were then.

The first night was a tremendous success. I had two great songs, one closing the first half, called 'Rhumboogie', an American number, with the whole company onstage, and with me leading them in a hilarious dance routine; the Crazy Gang, dressed in embroidered and sparkling caftans, were enjoying themselves energetically, and the whole enormous stage was alive with colour, dance and song. The plot of the show was imaginative and different from any previous musical show for some years. I had a great song in the second half, all about the things we loved in London. The chorus line behind me consisted of a host of London characters — policemen, firemen, nurses, ARP men, newspaper sellers — all doing a soft tap step in tune to the music with straight faces. The orchestra played a subdued rhythmic accompaniment while I, dressed in a plain yellow suit, sang the wonderfully evocative lyrics with all the stops out. The song was called 'My Kind of Music' and ended with the words, 'The top of the world is London Town, the top of the world is town'. At the end of the song the audience, which included, besides civilians, many members of the armed forces, rose in a body and cheered themselves hoarse, the ovation seemingly going on for ever, tears mixed with cheers. It was something to remember.

I recall that about this time Glenn Miller and his orchestra were in London for a concert and I sang this song to their accompaniment. At the rehearsal I was amazed at the musicians' reaction — they all threw their instruments into the air in a spontaneous demonstration of applause! Bing Crosby was there and he too sang a song. Afterwards photographs were taken of Bing and me together.

To return to the show: air-raids had started and the sound of bombs falling added to the emotion. We had raids every night, and we never knew who would be onstage when they dropped. Tommy Trinder had a side-bet arranged, based on which of the comics would be on when one dropped. It was always Tommy! Bud Flanagan said it was poetic justice. I had my turn too; one night in the middle of singing 'Rhumboogie' a bomb fell so near to the theatre that all the stalls' heavy double-plated doors burst open and the whole auditorium shook. Everyone onstage carried on regardless and the audience never moved. This happened on the Saturday night of our first week at the Palladium.

On Sunday morning I had a telephone call

from Charles Henry, GB's second-in-command, to inform me that the show was closing and that all theatres would be shut down until further notice. I was broken-hearted. It was the best part I had ever had. I was washing my hair when the call came and I remember the shampoo running down my face with the tears. What we were not told was that on the Saturday night a landmine had landed on the Palladium roof and become lodged in the chimney. The bomb disposal men had defused it then carried it out through the stage door on Sunday morning. All that brilliant cast, the Crazy Gang, Chesney Allen, Bud Flanagan, Jimmy Nervo and Teddy Knox, Tommy Trinder — all of us — were devastated, but none so upset as I. The show was even better for me than *Black Velvet* as it had some acting in it and the songs were superb. I always had an ovation after 'My Kind of Music'. Parts like this do not grow on trees. Joan Davis, our wonderful choreographer who had devised the routine for 'My Kind of Music', was also shattered. What a waste and what a loss financially for George Black. The horrific memory of Bud calling the cast up on to the roof of the Palladium in the interval to see the sky a mass of flames, as the Surrey Docks burned to ashes, has always stayed in my mind. So we opened on Tuesday and closed on Saturday.

It was not long, though, before the theatres opened again and George Black was determined to reopen *Top of the World* at the Palladium. This proved impossible, as the Crazy Gang refused to return to the show. Bud Flanagan explained why. First, the Gang were not happy being dressed in gorgeous caftans and playing parts instead of being themselves. Bud said that they did not feel that their parts were sufficiently important for their name. Also, there was another reason for their refusal, which I learned sometime later from GB's office. Bud had said, 'Anyway, it's the kid's show.' Me! What a tragedy. GB was naturally furious and frustrated. It was a disastrous decision for them to have made.

Life perked up again when I was invited to appear in a command performance before the King and Queen and Princesses Elizabeth and Margaret at Windsor Castle. I was informed by 'one who knows' that this was the real genuine Command Performance as it was the only one where the artists were personally chosen by the king and queen, rather than relying on agents' recommendations. What a magnificent experience it was. When we first arrived we were shown into a large banqueting hall, where the tables were laid with a feast. We were waited on by footmen in livery and powdered wigs. Afterwards we were shown into the hall, where we were to perform, and the dressing-rooms. After the show we were summoned to the throne room, where we were to be presented to their Majesties and, first, given instructions as to what and what not to do. We were not to give a full curtsey, simply a 'bob of the head' and must not speak unless spoken to. We were presented individually and it was all most impressive.

When it came to my turn, I was so delighted and thrilled that I just stood there smiling and waiting for something to happen, instead of simply curtseying and moving on. There was a silence. I smiled delightedly at the two princesses, who looked so attractive, but they did not smile back. Then the King spoke to me, as he must have thought I was never going to budge if he did not. 'Well, what do you think of our hall?' he asked me, meaning the small theatre where we had played the show. It was quite unremarkable, rather like a village hall, and I could not think of what to say. Not wishing to be critical, I simply said, 'It's very good for sound, your Majesty.' This seemed to amuse him, as he turned to the Queen and said, 'Well, that's something, isn't it!' I moved on quickly after that, not forgetting my curtsey.

Then an offer came soon after *Top of the World* had finished for a show called *Lady Behave*, starring that great artist comedian Stanley Lupino, with Sally Gray. It was to be put on by Jack Hylton, and was set to open in Manchester before coming to His Majesty's Theatre, London. Whilst rehearsing in Manchester for *Lady Behave*, my parents took me out to lunch. Father looked grim. He proceeded to produce documents which proved that I had been paying John's income tax as well as my own. He had done quite a lot of research. I was shattered. Mother's contribution to all this was to relay the news that my husband had been heard trying to make a date with a barmaid at the Palace Theatre, or so a friend had informed her. I remember going back to the hotel and walking down the long silent corridor to my room with tears streaming down my face. Later, when I challenged John about all this he produced some complicated explanations which were not even well thought out and obviously untrue. But rehearsals and the opening at the Palace were enough to take my mind off everything but work, as always, and how thankful I was for this.

Lady Behave at the Manchester Palace was a tremendous success. I had some good numbers, the title song as well as my own spot of two numbers in the second half. On transferring to London our success was repeated, which gave me a tremendous lift — an audience can cure any problem, for a time. We had a brief respite from the air raids, but not long after we opened there they came back again. In order to counteract this, the times of the shows were changed to matinées and even morning performances. I celebrated my twenty-first birthday during the show and Stanley presented me with an enormous silver key with a large satin bow during the finale line-up. The audience loved it and so did I.

John decided that we should move to the Selsdon Park Hotel, a splendid country hotel outside Croydon. It was only fifteen minutes by train from Victoria and in view of the fact that my talent for domestic life had not yet been discovered, it seemed a sensible thing to do. The curtain at His Majesty's Theatre came down at 8.15 p.m., and we used to catch the 8.24 from Victoria, thanks to the wonderful London taxi drivers. I had now been married for a year and was happy with my work and still very much in love, except for one thing that kept worrying me. There was a woman, living with a theatre impresario, who was a close 'friend' of John. It was quite clear to me, naïve though I was, that she had determined designs on my husband. She was much older than I and extremely glamorous in a 'hit-em-in-the-eye' way, very sophisticated and expensively dressed. She was also a foreigner — Austrian, she said. My husband, who always clung to anyone influential, was detailed by this 'friend' to look after his mistress whenever he had to leave London. I could never learn from John what exactly his duties in this respect entailed. I only knew that there was much running about after her and dinners together whilst I was working.

On my twenty-first birthday, to my surprise, an enormous party was arranged at the Savoy Hotel. Nearly all my friends were there: Vic Oliver, Bebe Daniels, Ben Lyon, Arthur Askey, Stanley Lupino, Sally Gray and Aunt Freda, who enjoyed herself enormously for once. I was informed about the party only the day before, and as I did not possess an evening dress there was a rush round to find one suitable, a gold lamé number, much too old for me and too long. But there was no time for alterations, so it was a miracle I did not trip up and fall flat on my face on entering the Savoy. John's friend and the *femme fatale*, who I shall call Colette, were there, she resplendent in a shimmering close-fitting dress and obviously ready for battle. I turned to my husband, who had arranged the party, and entreated him, earnestly. 'Please don't dance with Colette tonight, not tonight, please.' He said he would not. He had engaged the River Room for drinks before dinner and a large room with double doors opening from the ballroom for the meal — it was all splendid. As soon as the orchestra struck up after dinner, my husband asked Colette to dance, not me, although it was the first dance. I was too upset to be angry — that came later.

Dear Ben Lyon came to my rescue and asked me to dance and I walked on to the floor feeling utterly miserable. Poor Ben — my entire attention was on Colette and my spouse, although Ben tried to talk me out of this, but to no avail. I determined not to leave the floor before they did, but it was a marathon, as they continued dancing and laughing and talking intimately for what must have been an hour, although it seemed much longer to me. Finally we had to stop, as I had done two shows that day and with all the pent-up emotion I was experiencing I had to give in. Ben was sweet and obviously knew what was going on, but ignored it all and chatted away gaily to me. His words fell on stony ground. He was so kind and I was behaving disgracefully, but I was young and naïve and not able to keep my feelings under control. Two minutes after we left the floor my husband and Colette came back to the table, the latter breathless. She was much older than I, and gave the continental version of 'whoopee' as she sat down.

Worse was to come. When the speeches were

over, my own short but steady — I was in control of myself by then — my husband came over to me and announced brightly that he had some business to talk over with his 'friend', so would not be able to drive Mother and myself home but would be leaving with him and Colette. He followed this by saying that he had arranged with Bill, one of the guests, who was living at our hotel, that he would drive us back instead. So Bill drove us home, bade us goodnight, thanked me for the party and disappeared. Mother, who was furious, and I waited until nearly 4 a.m. in the hotel room that I shared with my husband. Mother was determined not to go to her own room until John arrived. By this time I was numbed. My twenty-first birthday party ended in a damp pillow after a useless confrontation with my husband. I thought everything would seem better once I reached the theatre.

Another great consolation was the fact that I had managed to persuade out of ostensible retirement a most wonderful woman as my dresser. Bessie was unique: a large lady with a heart to match; she had a marvellous sense of humour and was a complete professional in her work. She was my surrogate mother and I loved her dearly. During *Lady Behave* I travelled up from Croydon alone each day and went straight to the theatre, so on matinée days Bessie would bring me a delicious hot lunch cooked by herself from her home. She lived in Charing Cross Road above the book shops, in a large flat on the top floor, so in order to bring me my lunch she would walk down innumerable flights of stairs, clutching the lunch on a plate covered by another one, hail a taxi and arrive in a state at the theatre stage door, before climbing up two more flights of stairs to the dressing-room. No matter what the weather, the food was always hot and Bessie cool. She was married to a nice chap called Frank Porter, whom she tolerated more or less kindly. She had neat black hair, always wore a black dress and her face was extremely pretty, with beautiful white skin, dark brown eyes and small white teeth. She always dressed Alfred Lunt and Lynn Fontanne whenever they were in London, and in fact never dressed anyone else. So I therefore felt quite flattered when someone in the theatre informed me that Bessie had declared to all and sundry, 'I only dress the Lunts and Miss Kirkwood.' She was an indomitable Cockney and in all the years, no matter what crises occurred, I never saw her fuss nor panic nor move quickly, but calmly resolve the situation. Bessie was the top dresser in London for many years. Her mother had been a dresser before her and her daughter certainly knew her theatre, too. She had a golden and wicked sense of humour, and we shared many laughs together.

This is a typical Bessie story. When the Lunts were playing in London during the air raids, they used to live in the country and drive to the theatre each day. They were concerned about Bessie being in the centre of London, high up in her flat at a time when the bombing was really bad, so they invited her to stay in their country house so she could get her sleep. Bessie agreed to this, so off they went on Saturday after the show. On Tuesday her husband Frank was surprised to see his wife walk into the flat, complete with suitcase. 'What happened?' asked a bewildered Frank.

'Couldn't sleep,' Bessie announced firmly.

'Couldn't sleep,' repeated Frank, 'in the beautiful quiet country with no raids? Why not?'

'The bleeding birds!' replied Bessie.

The war was beginning to pinch hard by now. We lived on our rations and although we heard a great deal about the 'black market' none of it came our way. It is doubtful whether we would have taken advantage of it anyway, even though the temptation would have been great. So we were stuck, like nearly everyone else, with one egg a month, two ounces of butter, spam, snook — some sort of fish — and salad. I used to eat my butter in one go, on toast, and it was gorgeous. I did not see the point of a small scrape of it to 'make it last', as it would spoil the joyful treat of the wonderful taste. Mother made her butter last for two weeks, but she did not seem to enjoy it much.

When John and I were married I thought my life would be different, that this was a new beginning. My life would be freer than the life I had lived with my mother, I would have someone to talk to and laugh with — a companion. But I found I had exchanged one guardian for another. Then something happened which changed everything. John was called up. He was devastated, but his influential friend, the impresario Jack Hylton, who had made him his manager, intervened and arranged for him to work for Entertainments National Service Association (ENSA) and to gain a commission at the same time. So I experienced what thousands of other women were going through and stood at the door of the hotel watching my husband in his smart new officer's kit walk away from me down the long drive. Where he was going I knew not. I supposed he would go to London to ENSA's headquarters, staying with his friend until he knew where he was to be posted. I walked back to our room. To my surprise I was told I had been moved to another room on the same ground floor. When I opened the door I found the room was the size of a walk-in wardrobe, containing one single bed, a wash basin and my large cabin trunk, already packed with my clothes. There was barely room to climb into the bed. The room we had before John left was a large double room with a bathroom and a spacious hanging space for clothes. There was not even a wardrobe. There was nothing to do but have supper in the hotel dining room, though the thought of it sickened me.

Many questions ran round my head. Why didn't John tell me all this? How is it my trunk was packed without my knowledge and moved to the new room. I determined not to think about it as there was obviously nothing to be done. I had some scrambled eggs and then went to my mousetrap room. As I opened the door a gust of wind almost shut it again, for the window was wide open. A suitcase had disappeared; my room was on the ground floor and I had been burgled. The suitcase was found later in the shrubbery, but it had only contained some soiled linen so the thief must have thrown it away. The next morning I rang Mother and told her the news. I also rang for a taxi to take me to Croydon station. Miraculously I did not lose my ticket — a frequent occurrence, as I was and always have been absent-minded about inanimate objects, but seem to 'spring to' when there is a crisis. I once lost my season ticket and I was always losing my gloves. When Bessie put the gloves on a cord round my neck, I managed to lose both gloves and cord! Mother was with Daddy in Cheshire but in a flash, it seemed, sped to my side, having collected Aunt Freda as well. In no time I was out of the hotel and back to London with Mother and I together again in a flat.

Just before John was called up something else disastrous had happened. HMV, with whom I had a recording contract, wrote to all its artists saying that the shellac used in making their records was in short supply due to the war effort, so they were asking all their artists under contract to accept a substantial cut from their royalties. John replied to HMV by letter refusing the request, flatly. I was not told of this until my contract with HMV was cancelled. I asked John why this was and he told me, quite proudly, what he had done. I was shocked and knew then that this was a highly damaging blow to my career. I learned later that I was the only artist who had refused their request, even though I knew nothing of it. All this happened before I was twenty-one.

8

Let's Face It

Mother and I were settled in London again after John's call-up. I wondered how long we would be there, together in this rented furnished flat, as previous experience had shown that when the Blitz eased for a time, the owners of these flats wanted to come back, so we would have to find another one. It seems that we never had a written agreement nor a contract with the owners. Another thing was that Mother never agreed to pay rent when we were on tour, so each time we came back to London we had to find a new place. Since *Black Velvet*, however, Mother had accepted that we would be in London for some time and relaxed her economic vigil somewhat. So we had a permanent place at last. John had been posted to the Orkneys, so Mother was happy. I received one letter from him saying where he was going.

I went to see a show at the Hippodrome, *The Lisbon Story*, and I met George Black in the foyer. He told me I should not have done *Lady Behave*, that it was not right for me. He seemed quite cross, but I could not think why, as he did not have a show for me at the time and I had to keep working. Not only was I a workaholic but I needed the money. If a show closed, I used to walk into my agent's office and say, 'What do I do now?'

He used to look at me in amazement. 'But you have just finished a big show. You are supposed to be resting.' 'Resting' was not on my agenda, however, which is why I often made a mistake in choosing the wrong show instead of waiting for a better one — the main thing was to get on stage again, then I was happy!

The next show I did was one from America called *Let's Face It* in which Danny Kaye had starred in New York. It was the leading lady part, but not much of one as the show was a vehicle for Danny. His part was taken by Bobby Howes and I regarded working with Bobby again as a happy arrangement, so I took the offer. We toured for thirteen weeks, as the management could not find a theatre for us in London. It was not a happy time because the director was not 'Kirkwood friendly' and neglected me in order to direct his wife, who was also in the show. I felt isolated and unhappy. John had not yet left London for the Orkneys, to my surprise, and telephoned me once or twice, but he never came to see me. He advised me to walk out of the show, but of course I did not follow this disastrous advice. The tour dragged on.

On our thirteenth week the management announced that *Let's Face It* had been taken over by George Black, as they could not get a theatre, and we were to open at the London Hippodrome. What joy! The show was to be re-dressed and re-produced by George Black and Robert Nesbitt. Wonderful! We began rehearsals at the Hippodrome and, to my delight, I was given a new song before the interval at the end of the first act, a Cole Porter number called 'Just One of Those Things'. This had not been heard of before in London, so I was proud to be the one to introduce it. It was a classic Porter song and a show stopper. After the first night, which was surprisingly successful, there was a first-night party at the Savoy for the cast and production. The party had just begun when an American army officer came over to our table. 'Hope I'm not intruding,' he said. 'My name is William Wyler' — gasps all around the table, as this was one of the greatest, if not *the* greatest, of film directors in America — 'And I would like to say how much I enjoyed your show.' Then, turning to me, he wagged a fatherly finger at me. 'And as for you, young lady, you will be in Hollywood next year.' I was thrilled at this compliment from such a famous director, but thought later that it was simply 'pie-in-the-sky' because the war was still on. Two years later his prediction came true. In the meantime the raids began again and poor Mother was petrified, going to the shelter every night from our flat in Curzon Street, above the Mirabelle. I refused to go as I needed my sleep and used to plug my ears with cotton wool. We were then playing *Let's Face It* twice daily at the Hippodrome, which was tough, as it had been geared for once nightly only, as we had been doing on tour, and it was a big production with many changes of clothes and scenery.

When the show finally closed I was required to do my compulsory ENSA stint of ten weeks, although I knew of some artists who never seemed to do any. We toured all over the country in a large coach, staying at abandoned stately homes, unheated, small rundown hotels in towns, wherever ENSA could put us. We were a tiny company, about six of us altogether. We used to set off late afternoon in our coach, the army camps were nearly always a considerable distance away and it always seemed to be winter whenever I toured with ENSA — every year during the war. Everything was worthwhile after we arrived at our destinations; the 'boys' were a wonderful audience having been starved of any entertainment and billeted in remote isolated camps miles from civilization. It was a joy to play for them. On one ENSA tour we also visited Sir Archibald McIndoe at East Grinstead, his famous 'guinea-pig' hospital, where he operated on the injured RAF pilots and crew who had been badly burned. It was a shaking experience to walk among these young men, some blinded or without a recognizable face at all, others with no mouth, just a hole, or no nose. Their spirit was something to marvel at and I remember signing the plaster casts for those boys who had leg or arm injuries. To see those brave but disfigured heroes being so jolly and, those who could, actually laughing, was heart-rending and unforgettable. It was an effort not to crack emotionally, and afterwards I felt utterly exhausted, yet so proud of our RAF heroes. What a lesson to all of us who grumble about our lives or frustrations. How trivial our problems seem when we come up against the true horror of war and ruined young lives.

On my last ENSA trip I was given what was called a 'B tour', performing for the Pioneer Corps, which was tougher than the others, and playing camps many miles away from our base amid primitive conditions. Our audience was, at first, far from friendly when we arrived in our coach. They had been so neglected in the way of entertainment, being so far away from any town or even a village, that they were all thoroughly 'browned off' — in the language of the army then — and could not believe that our small company was going to lift their spirits. We had a fine little company, all good troupers who were determined the troops were going to enjoy our show, come what may. We all worked like madmen, and after the first ten minutes our audience thawed out and became enthusiastic and responsive, much to their own surprise, I think. When the curtain came down the applause was tremendous — what a glorious row. Whistles, cat-calls and stamping feet nearly deafened us. The colonel made a speech, which suffered from the fact that he had obviously been celebrating our arrival with gusto and got a few things wrong. 'Now remember Pat Kirkwood,' he hollered, 'remember her show at the Hippodrome. *Blue Velvet* — what a show!' I do not suppose that any of our audience had been within miles of a West End theatre. He then continued, 'It was a George Black show.' He got that right, then ruined it all: 'What I would like to know is where would George Black be without Pat Kirkwood!' I wanted to sink through the floor. The audience sat in a puzzled silence but decided to ignore all the waffle and gave us a great ovation as we left the stage. It had all been worthwhile. The 'B tour' was rough and very tiring. Mother travelled with me and bore up well, as she always did, but when we returned to London she was diagnosed as having bronchial pneumonia and had to go to hospital for a while.

I saw no more of John after we arrived in London, but a source close to him informed me he had been moved from the Orkneys to Croydon. This was because he had been about to be court-martialled for helping himself to the mess funds, but his 'influential friend' had managed to get the case waived and he was posted to Croydon instead. He had set up an establishment with a girl who worked in his office at ENSA. She was married and her husband was abroad in the army. I remembered the girl as I met her once when I went to the office some time ago, nearly two years previously, and noticed how close they were. This I discovered much later. By now I was immune to shock from John's way of life, but I was always hurt by it. Now that I knew that he did not love me and had married me only for his insatiable ambition I was too deeply hurt to contemplate a reconciliation, although he had not suggested it himself nor made any great effort to persuade me — after all his time was filled.

In July 1943 I starred in *Happidrome* at the Grand Theatre, Blackpool, and in December the same year I played principal boy at the Coliseum, London, in *Humpty-Dumpty* for

148

Emile Littler. I played Prince Rupert and loved every minute, as the clothes were beautifully designed and made in Emile Littler's own headquarters in Birmingham. He had a genius of a designer/costumier called 'Physhe' and my costumes could not have been finer. I wore French panne, purple velvet and hand-embroidered satin coats, the hats — made by Emile's milliner, Sacha, who worked alongside Physhe — were equally magnificent, and clever too, as they were tall hats and increased my apparent height. The scenery was superb and filled the huge stage at the Coliseum with colour and beauty. We played two shows per day, 3 1/2 hours each, so it was hard work but so enjoyable that it was not tiring. We ran for twenty-two weeks, unheard-of for pantomime, and the theatre was packed throughout the run.

Thankfully, I was back to choosing my own songs instead of, as in *Black Velvet* and the musicals I had done, performing whatever was given me. The songs in *Black Velvet* I would never have chosen. 'Oh Johnny', for example, made my flesh creep; 'Get Out of Town', a practically unknown song by Cole Porter, was far too sophisticated for an eighteen-year-old. I did, however, like 'It's a Lovely Day Tomorrow' and 'Bubble, Bubble,' which opened the show. Strangely 'My Heart Belongs to Daddy' became linked with me, because I had supposedly 'introduced' it to England. This was not true as I sung it as part of a quartet in the show, consisting of Carole Lynne — later Lady Delfont — Roberta Huby, Norma Dawn and myself. I did make a rather mediocre record of it, but I certainly did not sing it on my own until 1993 when I sang it in my one woman show in Wimbledon.

After *Humpty-Dumpty* I made a film — *Flight from Folly* — at Warner Brothers' Teddington studio, as there did not seem to be any activity in the musical theatre. It was directed by a fine film-maker, Herbert Mason, cheerful, witty and an altogether good sort. So the experience turned out to be pleasant, at first. We had been filming only a short time when the raids began again. The first night the explosions were pretty frequent. All the guests at the hotel, the Lawrence Hall Hotel at Ham Common, and some of our cast, came down to the large lounge with french windows. We could see aeroplanes clearly from there. Suddenly a small fat man, with a round pink smiling face, exclaimed loudly, 'Hush, wait a minute and listen.' We did. 'Those are German planes,' he said firmly. We had all thought they were ours because they were flying so low.

'German?' we echoed fearfully.

'Yes, the engine has an entirely different sound,' the fat man declared.

We all watched the planes — they were coming singly — then we saw a large flame coming from the tail of one and it plunged to earth with a terrific explosion. 'Hooray!' we all shouted, 'another Jerry down.' But we were not mentally alert enough at that time of night and did not catch on to what was really happening. Another plane came in view and the same routine followed: a flaming tail, about twenty seconds after the engine stopped, then a tremendous explosion, which seemed nearer to us this time. But we all cheered again in our ignorance. Two or three more appeared with the same flame, a pause and a bang. Our nice fat man began to organize us, for he must have guessed something was wrong, and he ordered us to hide behind the chairs and sofas. We waited for about half an hour but no more planes appeared. By now it was in the early hours of the next morning.

The all-clear went and we all trailed upstairs to bed, rather bedraggled. I had to be at the studio at 7.30 a.m., so wheeled my bicycle out of the hall and started to cycle to Teddington Lock. A plane appeared with the same engine sound as last night, but I kept on cycling. There was no air-raid warning. Then I saw the flame at the tail end and heard the engine cut out. I threw my bicycle down and leapt against the pavement wall just before the explosion, which sounded as if it was only 100 yards away. The night before we had not been able to hear the ominous cut-out of the engine, which meant that in a few seconds the plane would hit the ground and explode. I was scared stiff, but a few yards along the wall I spotted a small boy with his school cap on at a jaunty angle, looking just like Richmal Crompton's William, but his small face was white. He was standing pressed against the wall, like me. 'Are you scared, Miss?' he asked me.

'Yes, I am' I answered truthfully.

'S . . . s . . . so am I,' he stammered.

151

'You'd better go home to your mother' I told him as firmly as I could, wondering if all was safe at the hotel and if my mother was. I cycled back to the hotel. There was utter chaos as I reached the entrance, and people were flying all over the place. Mother was on the landing in her nightdress, pale and worried about me. No one seemed to know what to do or what was happening. Apparently one of the guests had heard on the radio that these planes could not yet reach London, because of inaccurate calculations, but were being piloted up the River Thames to Teddington, Shepperton and so on. I wondered about little 'William' and whether he was safe.

In the middle of this nightmare a plump figure descended the staircase, wearing a bowler hat, striped trousers and black morning coat, complete with an immaculately rolled black umbrella. 'Good morning,' he said cheerfully. It was the same man who had taken charge of us all the night before. I simply stood aghast as he walked briskly down the stairs of the entrance, turned right and walked to the bus stop, about 100 yards away. He stood alone at the stop with his umbrella in a dignified pose and one foot in front of the other! I found the receptionist, who had been watching all this, and asked her who he was. 'Oh,' she whispered, 'he has been a resident here for years. His nickname is 'Mr Tough!' We learned that these machines were flying bombs, popularly referred to as 'doodle-bugs' — later officially designated V1s — and not long after I reached the hotel they started coming over about every fifteen minutes.

Our director, Herbert Mason, appeared at the hotel, looked at me sternly and then announced, 'I'm not shooting you today; you look awful. You and Norah' — my mother — 'had better come and stay with us at Chorley Wood.' It was quiet and peaceful when we arrived at the house, a pretty country dwelling covered with creepers and with a large garden full of flowers. No other house could be seen. Herbert's wife was a gentle, shy creature. His daughter was working in a munitions factory. These dear people took us in and in spite of the shortage of food shared everything they had with us. We were so thankful to be there, for it was a lovely spot, but our film was waiting to go on to the floor at Teddington and every wasted day added more to the budget.

There was some relief from the flying bombs, so in a few days we returned to the studio. But first we went to the Lawrence Hall Hotel. What a disaster met our eyes. The night after we had left for Chorley a flying bomb landed in the garden, the explosion hitting the back of the hotel and a small lodge where some staff lived. Sadly, two of them had been killed. The garden was a wreck with a large pit where the bomb had hit, bits of which were still there. In the bedroom Mother and I had occupied, the windows had been ripped out, as had most of the wall facing the garden. The most scary thing of all was a large shard of glass which had embedded itself in the centre of my pillow.

When the film was finished we packed up to go back to London. On leaving Teddington we drove through a beautiful small forest; it was a lovely morning, with the sun filtering down through the trees; a blackbird sang, making us feel that life was good after all. We relaxed. Then we heard that dreaded ominous sound, a flying bomb, which seemed to be directly above us. Our driver put his foot down hard on the accelerator, though that can hardly have helped us, as by now the bomb, though we could not see it, sounded as if it was directly above us. The engine cut out, the driver stopped the car and we all waited breathlessly. The silence, though it was only seconds, seemed to last forever. Then the explosion came, an enormous one. The car shook and trembled; everything shook, including us. Mother fell to the floor. The driver turned his white face to us, 'That was a near one,' he stammered.

We drove on and eventually Mother spoke. 'We are not going back to that flat,' she announced. 'There is nothing above us but the roof.'

'Well, where are we going?' I ventured.

'The Grosvenor House Hotel,' Mother informed me.

'We can't afford to go there,' I gasped.

'We can't afford not to,' was Mother's final word.

Two weeks after the film was finished the Warner studio was blown to smithereens, killing the studio manager.

After *Flight from Folly* — an apt title in the circumstances — there was quite a shake-up awaiting me. I received a telephone call from my agent, urgently asking us to come to the office as there was a great surprise for us. He was beaming all over and pointed at two documents on his desk. One was a seven-year contract with Metro-Goldwyn-Mayer, the other, a similar one from Twentieth-Century Fox. 'Well,' he said, 'it seems you only have to choose which studio you would like to work in.'

Part of me was delighted, but something niggled me. I had never enjoyed making films, beginning with the traumatic experience I had when I was very young; the only one I had felt relaxed working on was *Band Waggon*, directed by Marcel Varnel. This cosy, plump Frenchman was capable, sympathetic and knew what he was doing, unlike the chauvinistic, untalented directors who made my life a misery when I was sixteen. They pounced on my inexperience and lack of confidence and bullied me in front of the entire cast. I made three films, and at the end of the last horror my contract was mercifully dropped. Mr Robert Clark, the Scottish head of the company, who had signed me in the first place, sent for me and told me the fault did not lie with me but with them. He made me feel better by saying, 'We just don't know what to do with you; we have let you down.' I was relieved but never forgot the nightmare of those three films.

So now here was my agent and my mother looking at me to know which film company I was going to join. I did not want to sign with either but my agent pointed out to me the generous financial offer and the beautiful climate of California. I thought of all the stars I had idolized for so long — Joan Crawford, Bette Davis, Ginger Rogers — and was thrilled at the thought of actually meeting these wondrous creatures. So I asked my agent which was the better studio of the two. He replied that MGM was the most important and successful and suggested I sign with them. So I did. I have often thought, as I did then, how wonderful it would be to have someone to advise me what to do; someone whom I could trust and who would help me not to make mistakes in choices of shows, of songs; someone strong, who cared for me and was on my side. That never happened. It was always a lone battle.

In the meantime MGM were waiting for me to go to California, which I could not do as the war was still very much in progress. So I had no work, as I now belonged to MGM. The press was full of the news. One headline read 'Pat Kirkwood Signs up for £250,000.' Well, that was all tarradiddle, as the contract had me 'on option' for seven years, but I had a firm contract for one year only. True the earnings went up each year, provided the option was taken up by the studio, and in larger amounts, and my starting salary was substantial as well. But the war was on and I could not leave Britain nor work.

After cooling my heels for two months I was desperate to get back to work. Suddenly Emile Littler asked me to play principal boy again in *Goody Two Shoes* at the enormous Coliseum — Robin Goodfellow no less, but no princely title this time. Mother could not understand why I wanted to do this, as I was now contracted to MGM and consequently on the pay-roll at a high salary. Why work two shows a day at the Coliseum? I informed my agent that I wished to do the pantomime. MGM was alerted and an arrangement was made that satisfied all parties. MGM would continue to pay me, but Emile Littler would reimburse the same amount to MGM. This was fine by MGM, but Emile Littler had to raise my salary for the pantomime. I was nevertheless working in the pantomime for nothing — and happy to do it.

We had returned to the flat but the raids continued to be fierce and we had many incendiaries on the roof. Mother repeated there was nothing above our flat at Clarewood Court except the flat roof, so we went to Grosvenor House again, where we had a room on the third floor facing the ack-ack guns in Hyde Park. On our second night at the hotel we were sound asleep when there was a most tremendous explosion which rocked the hotel. We both leapt out of bed, one on each side, at the same time. There had been no air raid warning so we didn't know what it was. The corridor was full of guests in their nightwear, all looking anxious and bewildered. 'What was it?' Mother and I stuttered. It was a V2. Mother was shaking with fright and I was scared to bits. The explosion was enormous, heavier than any previous ones. The next day Mother decided we would have a really good lunch for a change, so down we went to the dining room. The menu was a gallant effort with the spam and 'Woolton Pie' written in French, but even so it was sparse. Then my eye lit on something that sounded delicious 'Roast Kid! We ordered and waited with great anticipation. The waiter set the plates down and I cried, 'No — no, no, no Lewis!' The waiter was shaken. 'Tell me, please, this is not kid, is it?'

'No, madam,' he replied, looking ashamed, 'it is goat.' I could never ever mistake that dreadful pong I had endured for weeks from the goat Lewis in *Band Waggon*, and how the studio had to be fumigated after we left. So it was 'Woolton Pie' again, after all.

After lunch Mother disappeared, saying she would be back soon. She seemed rather mysterious. When she returned she was all smiles. 'I've found the most wonderful place to shelter tonight,' she announced. 'It is in the basement, with proper beds and bedclothes, and heavy curtains sealing it off. It is so quiet we must go there tonight.' That evening, at about nine o'clock, we took the lift in our nightclothes, clutching a pillow each. The lift stopped at the first floor and into it entered two beautifully dressed couples, the women in full evening dress, complete with masses of jewellery, and the gentlemen in dinner jackets. They had obviously come from their suites to go down to dinner, but when they encountered Mother and me in our dressing-gowns and bedroom slippers, clutching our wash-bags and pillows, they froze with shock. Not a word was spoken as we descended to the dining-room floor, where the four left unsteadily. We carried on to the basement, I hoping that no one had recognized me and that one was not a journalist.

Mother's 'shelter' was indeed a haven of quiet, with many beds all in a row and made up in Grosvenor House style. Mother gave me a triumphant smile. There was a soft low light from the basement beyond the curtains, so it was quite dark with just a glow. No one was there but us. I could not believe our luck. So we went to bed and to sleep, sighing gratefully, not a sound of the war going on outside. I was suddenly awakened by a female voice, shouting desperately, 'Stop snoring, stop snoring.' I looked over to Mother's bed where a woman in a nightdress was shaking her mercilessly. I leapt out of bed and went over to Mother's, about to remonstrate with the woman or push her over, I had not decided which, when I saw that all the beds were filled with people; I could not see if they were all women or not, but I reached the female who was giving mother a bad time. 'What do you think you are doing? Stop that at once,' I bellowed.

The woman stopped all right, then turned to me; I could see a white, tired face, near to tears. 'Who are you and what are you doing here? This is for the ARP wardens on duty all night, to give them a place to rest,' she whimpered — obviously an air raid warden herself. I felt dreadful and offered an apology instead of a reply to her question. So, looking and feeling completely crushed, we returned to our room — it was 5 a.m.

Of course we could not continue to stay at the Grosvenor House, so began to look for a flat. We

159

eventually found one in Duchess Mews, Portland Place, about a hundred yards from the BBC. This was not a strategically good place to be, as it was one of the prime targets of the German bombers. I shall always remember Duchess Mews for a most beautiful experience in the middle of a violent raid. In a merciful moment of silence in-between the bombing we heard someone playing the piano, so wonderfully that we held our breaths. It was a Sunday night, very dark and windless with a fine rain. We opened our window on to the mews and saw a lit, open window in the house opposite us. An elderly man was sitting and playing as if there was no raid, no war, no fear, no grief nor pain. The music poured out into the mews like a benison whilst we watched and listened, enthralled. It was an awe-inspiring moment. Who was this great musician, we wondered. The next day we found out. It was Paderewski.

The Coliseum pantomime ran twenty-two weeks, and not long after, the war in Europe was over. On VE Day 8 May 1945, London came alive. Mother and I were packing to go to America three days later. As we carried our clothes from one room to another we had the radio on, and what joy and relief flowed from it. We were alternately laughing and crying: laughing as we heard the people singing in the streets and cheering in Trafalgar Square; crying when we thought of our leaving at such a time for a far-away country. I had never been out of England before, nor ever thought of it. The telephone never stopped ringing and though I really did not wish to go out — I had a marathon of packing to do — two old friends of Mother finally persuaded us to go off to Trafalgar Square. This was a sight to behold. Even the pigeons seemed subdued by this wonderful spectacle of happy people, freed from their fears and griefs for a time, all as one in their relief and thankfulness.

What a glorious day it was. Whilst we were in Trafalgar Square a group of young people began to walk round with an enormous photograph of me that they had taken from a poster outside the Warner Cinema, in Leicester Square, which was showing *Flight from Folly* that week. What a thrill that was for me, and how I wished I could stay forever in Trafalgar Square with all these lovely people who had been through so much.

9

Hollywood

Three days after VE Day Mother and I flew to America in the first civilian aeroplane to take off since the war began — an old Atlantic clipper, the last of her tribe. We touched down in Shannon, Ireland. On board there were many high-ranking officers in uniform. When we landed, however, they all had to change into civvies before they were allowed to leave the plane, as Ireland was neutral. They made a most odd picture in their pre-war suits, some with trousers too short, jackets too tight and altogether creased and worn out. Such a shock after their splendid bemedalled uniforms. At the airport a marvellous English breakfast greeted us, with masses of eggs, bacon, sausages, hot toast and butter. We set to with enthusiasm and felt ready for anything, which was just as well as the journey took sixteen hours. Although we had bunks, we did not sleep much. After landing in Newfoundland for refuelling we proceeded to Baltimore, in Maryland, where the old clipper came to rest. Then we had to pile into a small boat and be delivered into the hands of the customs officers, who treated us very brusquely — not a pleasant experience.

We had a warm reception by two representatives of MGM. By now it was late evening and all the lights were on. We were both ecstatic; it was like fairyland after our black-out at home, and the two MGM chaps were highly amused at our reaction. 'Hell,' one said, 'if they think Baltimore is so great what are they going to do when they hit New York!' We were driven to the Statler Hotel in Washington first and shown to a luxurious suite next to the top floor, but we were so tired we just fell into bed and slept. The next morning Mother rang for room service, which came immediately. 'What would you like for breakfast?' asked the smiling waiter. 'Everything,' Mother replied and got it. An enormous trolley arrived with bacon, eggs, brown muffins and so on. I had waffles with syrup and sausages; then we switched on the radio to hear the news. 'Well, it looks like one hell of a morning, my friends, so you might just as well go back to bed,' the gravelly, relaxed, sleepy voice announced. We were stunned.

'That's it,' Mother said firmly, 'I am never going to leave America.'

During the long flight from London I had time to think over what I had left behind. Emile Littler had offered me *The Quaker Girl*, a musical play, originally American — a storming success in the thirties — about a Salvation Army girl who goes to New York and becomes the toast of the town. It was a wonderful part but I could not accept it as I was now tied to MGM and about to leave England. I felt really sad about this and was right to be so — a regret I never banished. Then I remembered Mother and I going one evening to the Hippodrome to see a

163

show and meeting George Black. When he saw us he came quickly towards us, looking grim, which was not his way; then, with great force, he weighed into me. 'You should not be going to America — it's much too early, a bad decision. You should stay here and consolidate.' He was really upset, I could see, and he certainly put the wind up me. My trepidation was tempered somewhat by the memory of one lunchtime in a restaurant near the Hippodrome after the first night of his show *Strike a New Note*. George Black and his wife entered, GB looking stormy. He walked over to our table, patted me on the head and announced, 'Don't worry, dear, we haven't found anyone to replace you — yet!' I felt a cold chill run through me. Dammit, I thought, I've only just arrived. I had done only three shows in London and was playing at the Hippodrome in *Let's Face It*. I think he had not forgiven me for signing up to do *Lady Behave*, my second show, instead of waiting for him to offer me one.

I think, really, that as he had given me my first break in London, and in a wonderful showcase, he looked on me as his 'discovery', and if I worked for any other management I was being disloyal. Well, I was not; I had always enjoyed working for GB; he knew his theatre and had complete knowledge of all the mechanics behind the scenes, but he never interfered with an artist's performance unless they needed it. I have seen him take off his jacket, climb on stage and teach a performer how to make an exit. He had great taste and style and everyone, artists and

164

staff alike, enjoyed working for 'GB', or 'the Guv'nor', as he was affectionately known. He was the last of the great impresarios.

In New York we were wafted into the Churchill Suite at the Waldorf Astoria Hotel where unbridled luxury surrounded us. We were on the twenty-fifth floor, and the lights of Manhattan were below and round us, twinkling their welcome. We had a wonderful few days there and were taken to the Stork Club, the 21 Room and all the other glamorous places; MGM certainly knew how to welcome newcomers to their company. Crumbs, I thought, I hope I can justify all this. We were taken to meet the big-wigs at the William Morris Agency, then the most powerful agency in the world, which was to represent me in America. They also had offices in Beverly Hills, Hollywood, and would assign one of their representatives to me there. It all seemed like a glorious dream. We had invitations galore from celebrities; we met Irene Dunne and her husband at one cocktail party, where, sad to say, Mother was too much of a success with the aforesaid husband. It is strange how daughters never consider their mothers to be attractive; they are simply 'mothers'; so it is quite a surprise if they are considered attractive by members of the opposite sex. In this particular instance Mother was completely innocent and rather embarrassed, as this husband devoted his entire attention to her, ignoring everyone else and making it impossible for Mother to meet anyone else in this scintillating gathering. He was obviously flirting like mad and his glamorous spouse was getting crosser by the minute. I was having a quiet fit, as Irene Dunne was a major star at MGM and had a great deal of influence with them, so here we were 'putting up a black' as soon as we arrived. Strolling up to Mother and patting her on the arm, I said, 'Excuse me for interrupting,' to the husband, and 'I think we had better leave now, Mother. Remember we have an appointment at eight o'clock for dinner at the Waldorf.' Mother looked relieved and extricated herself from the tight corner she was in and we took leave of our hosts and left. I glanced at Irene Dunne and saw that she was ready to go to battle with her recalcitrant husband, who obviously was not going to win.

Our next social engagement was with Eddie Hillman, the car magnate, and his wife June, who had been an enormous star in London during the twenties and thirties. She then married Lord Inverclyde who later divorced her in a sensational case, and a while afterwards she became a columnist in a daily newspaper. She was still a very beautiful woman and she and her husband were wonderful hosts, eager to hear about London and how we had all survived. I had my new hat on — cocktail hats were the rage in those days — and one of the guests came up to me and said, 'Gee, what a lovely hat; it suits you so well. You should always wear that style.' This pleased and surprised me, as I could never imagine being complimented by an English woman at a cocktail party.

In a few days we caught the Twentieth-Century train to California and what a train! We had a suite consisting of a sitting room, bedroom and bathroom, all beautifully furnished and decorated. Even the *Brighton Belle*, then the pride and joy of the British rail network, could not compete. We passed through the most beautiful scenery, some wild and bleak, some leafy and fertile, before reaching California. On arrival at Los Angeles we were greeted by two more representatives of MGM and driven to the Beverly Hills Hotel, the meeting-place for most of the stars of the day. The hotel had a slightly old-fashioned look, in spite of the swimming pools and all the other paraphernalia of healthy luxury living, but had a comfortable feel to it. As we drove up the drive a figure appeared, a male who was weaving his way rather unsteadily towards the exit. I recognized him immediately, Spencer Tracy. Though he was a little the worse for wear, I was thrilled to see this splendid actor, whom I had admired for many years, suddenly appearing before my eyes.

I had been informed months before that I would be making a musical film in Technicolor and that my leading man would be Robert Walker. This delighted me, as I had seen him give a splendid performance in *The Clock* opposite Judy Garland and admired his obvious talents and charm. In fact he was brought to the hotel to meet us the day after we arrived. I was so thrilled I could not say a word. Mother was no help either, so he must have thought I was a real dumb-bell and left after a few pleasantries. I was then informed by an MGM big-wig that it had been decided that Van Johnson would be the leading man. I had never heard of him, as none of his films had yet been shown in England, but he was the number-one box-office draw in America and a hero of the 'bobby soxers'. The man who told me all this was highly amused I did not know of him, as he had been certain that I would be most impressed and excited that he was going to be the leading man. 'But I thought that Robert Walker was going to play the leading man,' I protested.

More laughter from the exec. 'But he is not nearly as big a star as Van Johnson,' he chortled. 'We thought you would be thrilled.' Well, I wasn't — at first.

I then met the member of the William Morris Agency who was to represent me. I entered the office to see a rather handsome man with broad shoulders sitting behind an enormous desk. He was pleasant enough, but he remained seated when I entered, which surprised me — but this was America and manners were different. I asked him when the film was to start shooting, as back in England my agent had been pestered with calls from an impatient MGM, demanding to know when I could start. My new agent, called Johnny Hyde, assured me that I would not have long to wait but that certain things had to be cleared up before we could start shooting. So I started to take my leave and he then rose from behind his desk. He was no taller than five feet, yet one of the most powerful agents at William Morris; he represented many big stars including Marilyn Monroe, who was then beginning her rise to stardom. It was a shock to see him leave his desk, but Mother and I made no reaction. His face was quite impassive, but what suffering he must have endured and what spirit he must have had to conquer his cruel disability. I asked him if I could see the script of the film I was to make and he promised to send it to the hotel the next day. He also asked Mother and I to have dinner with him and his wife at Romanoff's restaurant the next evening, which we accepted. I could not wait to see this famous establishment, which all the big stars patronized and which was always packed with the film colony's most powerful talents, be they directors, top executives, writers or actors.

So off we went to Romanoff's to meet Johnny and his wife Moselle. When we were all seated the waiter brought the menus. These were enormous, the size of a wall mirror, and packed with a choice of French and American dishes. Having chosen, Mother and I did not know where to put these large white cardboard sheets; we could not lay them on the table and the waiter had disappeared. 'Put 'em here,' snapped Moselle, rather crossly, laying them on the chair of the next table. It soon became obvious that things were not too rosy between the two Hydes, and as dinner proceeded Moselle's face grew ever more stormy. I could see that the dinner invitation had merely been a duty on Johnny Hyde's part and that Moselle could not wait to get out of the restaurant. Some time later I heard that Johnny Hyde was madly in love with Marilyn Monroe and that he and Moselle were in the process of divorcing

— that explained a lot.

My next priority was to read the script, which was titled, not exactly thrillingly, *No Leave, No Love*. As I read on, I realized that the title was the best part and that I had never read such a load of junk in my life. I was disappointed and the next morning, armed with this dire script, went to see Johnny Hyde. Someone called Charles Martin had written this saga and he was also going to direct the film — his first ever. He had been introduced to MGM by his close friend Joan Crawford, who was then one of the brightest stars at MGM. She talked the studio into buying his script and engaging him to direct it.

The next item on the agenda was make-up. I was called early the next day to the studio and introduced to Jack Dawn, a famous make-up man, rather elderly, but whose opinions were highly respected. I was led into the make-up room and seated in what looked like a dentist's chair, which could be moved up or down as necessary. I was in the chair for what seemed like hours, with Jack Dawn working away on my face. What was he doing, I wondered, as he used a lot of brushes and pencils but no foundation, powder or lipstick — nothing resembling normal make-up. At last it was finished and I looked in the mirror. A Red Indian in full warpaint stared back at me! Jack Dawn had drawn a multicoloured map on my face in what looked like liquid greasepaint. A cream-coloured streak was painted down the bridge of my nose. There were two triangles in orange on each cheek and various other colours placed on the rest of my face. Interesting, I thought, but what was it all about? I was taken to meet the producer, whose name was Joe Pasternak, and the cameraman, Harold (Hal) Rosson, whose second claim to fame was that he had been married to Jean Harlow. I felt dreadful meeting them with my Technicolor face and hoped no one would laugh! The whole operation was a kind of code for them to decide how to photograph me, my good points and bad ones coloured to illustrate each one. I had thought my face was fairly in order, so the experience did not exactly inspire confidence. But I learned that this is what happened to all female newcomers under a long-term contract with MGM.

Joe Pasternak was an important producer at the studio. He had previously been partly responsible for Deanna Durbin's enormous success at another studio, Universal, and had produced all her early films there. It was he who, after watching my screen test made in England and showing it to MGM executives, immediately staked his claim to be producer of my first film in America. He was a short slim man with a soft voice and a rather pleasant smile. He was Hungarian and had fled to London when Hitler invaded, working as a bus-boy at a restaurant there before emigrating to America. Hal Rosson, the cameraman, was a man with a benign but alert expression and a beard; though small in stature, he gave the impression of a calm and strong personality, one who would stand for no temperamental or difficult star. I sat there with my Red Indian face whilst they discussed it. I did not say a word as I thought it would be too hilarious to see all my colours moving about. And I simply wanted to get away and take this face off and replace it with my own!

I was taken to visit Clark Gable, Greer Garson and Deborah Kerr on the set of the film they were making. This I did not think a good idea, rather like visiting backstage in the interval of a first night, but I was also thrilled at the thought of meeting them, especially as Greer Garson and Deborah Kerr were British. I first met Clark Gable, who was most disappointing, being much smaller than he appeared on film and not nearly so handsome. He was cordial enough, but his eyes kept straying to the set where the next scene was being prepared and he seemed rather tense and absent. I understood this; after all, he was in the middle of working. I left, after wishing the film well, and was then transferred to Greer Garson, who was sitting in her named chair and who glowered at me when I was introduced. She gave no smile nor any sign except that of annoyance at being interrupted in her thoughts, which did not seem to be happy ones. Then it was over to Deborah Kerr. This one I thought would be more human, being more or less my own age and not having been in Hollywood long. No such thing. She was worse than the other two put together. A frozen smile and a regal nod were all I received. I would have been furious if I had not been glad to leave and go home. Well, I thought, if this is an example of the way film stars behave, I do not want to meet any more.

The next stop was at the dress designer's, for measurements to be taken and clothes discussed. Irene, MGM's famous dress designer for many years, told me that my measurements were exactly the same as Lana Turner's, so I was her friend for life.

I finally met Van Johnson, my leading man, whom I liked straight away, mainly for his open and smiling face and his lovely sense of humour. He was about six feet two or three inches tall, with red-gold hair and greeny-blue eyes — really stunningly handsome, but did not seem to know it. He was also kind and considerate; he put me at ease by asking me about England and the theatre and showed concern that I was settling into what must be such a strange environment for me. I was relieved and knew that we would get on well and be happy working together.

I was then put through some lessons with Lilian Burns, the dialogue director for MGM. She had been instructed to Americanize my speech. She was tough as a regiment of old boots, violently anti-British and had a New York 'Bowery' accent. That is, almost incomprehensible. She began the first lesson by saying, 'Gotta lose the British accent, kid. Maybe you don't know dat de peeurest English is American talk, so leds go ta work, hey!' I thought privately that she could do with a few lessons herself and not just for her speech! She was tiny, dark and belligerent but was married to one of the most powerful film directors at MGM. I had no doubt that she had been engaged by MGM for this very reason. Her voice, which went with the accent, was shrill and persistent, allowing no competition. So I learned a soppy speech about a musician who had his violin stolen and was therefore heartbroken, and Lilian Burns coached me with my accent. Then Joe Pasternak was sent for to hear the miraculous transformation she had wrought. This was all a complete waste of time as I had already played an American girl in the show *Let's Face It* at the London Hippodrome and could drop into the accent whenever I wanted. I was then taken to meet Kay Thompson, the singing teacher, who was certainly the best thing to happen to me since I arrived. She was a tall, gangling blonde with an intelligent and witty personality. After I sang a couple of songs while she played the piano accompaniment, she sat back, gave me a grin and said, 'Gee, honey, you don't need to come to me for lessons, so forget it — just come and talk to me when you feel like it. If you are feeling down, then I'm here and glad to see you.' She was a great girl and we had some laughs together, which made everything seem easier. I had found a friend.

Strange things began to happen as I trotted dutifully between Lilian Burns and Kay for my lessons. One day as I persisted with my needless American-accent tutorial, Lilian Burns stopped me in full flow and walked over to the window, which was shuttered because of the sun. 'Well, gee, there's some son-of-a-bitch looking through the slats,' she announced crossly. I joined her at the window and saw the producer, Joe Pasternak, standing there with his smile much in

174

evidence. 'Just checking that you were OK,' he explained to me, 'and that you were being a good kid and working with Lilian!' I was alerted to something I did not quite like, but I hoped he was just being paternal.

I trotted off to Kay to sing a bit and have a chat. The telephone rang. Kay answered it. 'Hello, Joe,' she said brightly with a wink at me. Then 'OK yeah, sure she is, but Dorothy is very pretty too, Joe.' I had not yet met Pasternak's wife, but Kay informed me that she was heavily pregnant. What a louse. What a spot to be in before we had even started the film. I decided to be on my guard, without giving offence, if possible, but diplomacy was not one of my characteristics, to put it mildly. After this, whenever I went to the studio Pasternak seemed to be nearby, so I decided to stop visiting the studio unless I was called to wardrobe or make-up. I received many calls from various MGM would-be swains — not actors, but writers, assistant directors and other hangers-on. I used to get annoyed at the breezy way they would invite me to dinner or lunch with them 'tonight' or 'tomorrow'. I made excuses in a polite, English way, of course, which did not seem to work, so I decided to be more assertive. 'If you wish to have dinner with me you must make an appointment for at least two weeks in advance and not 'tonight' nor 'tomorrow',' I declared coldly and put the phone down. This worked, and I enjoyed it too.

During our first week in Hollywood, I met Louis B. Mayer and his 'court' when Mother and

I were summoned to the front office and into his sanctum. We had a very pleasant chat and the various producers and directors all seemed to be bursting with goodwill and earnest intentions that I should be happy at MGM. Soon after this, we received an invitation to attend a dinner and dance at LBM's palatial home in Bel Air. I was thrilled that we would be meeting all the major stars and other celebrities — we were just like a couple of country hicks.

Our excitement was somewhat tempered by an incident on the studio lot one day, when Mother came to pick me up after one of my lessons. We were walking towards the exit gates when I spied Frank Sinatra, standing forlornly on his own, as if he had lost his way. I had just alerted Mother with 'Oh look, there's Frank Sinatra!' when a figure approached us resolutely from another direction. I recognized him immediately as that fine actor Wallace Ford, who, though never a star, was respected highly by all who had witnessed his truly great performances. As he reached us he smiled his charming Irish smile then leaned towards us confidentially. 'Remember this, kids,' he said firmly, 'all the men are bums and all the dames are tarts!' Then he turned and strolled away. He must have known who we were, that we were 'tenderfeet' and thought he would tip us off. We had never met him before.

For the dinner and dance I acquired a beautiful dress from Saks in Beverly Hills, a real stunner, in white silk crêpe and shoes to match. Everyone that mattered in the movie business

176

was there and our host, Louis B. Mayer, greeted us warmly with a friendly smile. I was surprised at his easy charm and manner, and thought there must be something nice about this powerful giant after all, despite some of the horror stories that went around about his tyrannical style. But then, perhaps, with all these actors and artists and directors to control, that was necessary. A rather plump, jolly-looking woman came up to me and introduced herself. She was dressed in a plain flowered day dress which was past its prime. We had a long and fascinating talk — or rather, I listened while she talked! I saw Mother, a few feet away, giving me a reproving stare and went over to her. 'What's the matter?' I wanted to know.

'All these important people here, look, William Powell over there, and Norma Shearer, and you have to talk to the cook,' she growled.

'That was Elsa Maxwell,' I informed her.

'You see, that's what I mean,' she complained, never having heard of the world-famous society hostess, who had the entry to all the great houses in England and Europe and whose parties were legendary.

William Powell came over to me — Mother had found her own coterie and was not to be seen — and we got on tremendously; he had a great sense of humour and was curious about England and the war; also he wanted to know about London and the theatres. He was a staunch Anglophile, and it was a relief to discover that he was as attractive and amusing as he was in his films. We talked for so long that his wife, who was considerably younger than he, sashayed up, looking not too pleased, and darted me a 'keep-off' look. She retrieved him with expert speed! Gorgeous Loretta Young was there and many more of the famous beauties, but I noticed, as the party progressed, that many of them began to disintegrate slowly, that is, their make-up melted and their voices began to slur. I was disappointed and amazed to see all this loveliness disappearing, some voices becoming strident as their owners tore their rivals to pieces. I remembered Wallace Ford and his warning.

Then Louis B. Mayer asked me to dance. He was quite a good dancer, light on his feet as many rotund males are, and he was comfortably that. During the dance he looked straight into my eyes and announced, with a twinkle in his eyes, 'You're only dancing with me because I'm Louis B. Mayer.'

'I'm dancing with you because you asked me,' I replied with a grin and in any case it was true. He laughed at this and we had a pleasant trip round the floor for some time. He was not at all as one would have expected him to be — rather boyish in fact — but perhaps, I thought, these were just his party manners. He even escorted me to a chair and bowed. I liked him, to my surprise. It was time to leave, as the party was getting louder every minute, and some dresses were sliding off at the shoulders. We thanked Louis B. and departed to our steadfast Oldsmobile. It had been a good party but I wished there had been a few Brits there to talk to. It was reported to me the next day that Louis

B. had declared, 'The English girl was the best dressed there.' I was decidedly chuffed.

I had now been in Hollywood for six months and there was still no sign of the film starting. I would have been in quite a state if this had happened in England, but by now I had a few friends and was enjoying the gorgeous climate, the beaches and the sea; also the shopping — for clothes mainly, I was thrilled with the stylish dresses and beachwear. I was having a ball, in one sense. The only snag was that I had been put on a rigid diet and needed to lose 10 pounds; I then weighed eight stone six pounds and was five feet four inches in height — not exactly overweight by normal standards, but certainly by the standard required for the film cameras, which put at least 10 pounds on the artists. I wondered if Lana Turner was overweight, too, as I had her measurements. I was also prescribed pills by the doctor who had given me my medical check-up on arrival. These pills consisted of thyroid capsules, to speed up my metabolism, and pituitary capsules which did likewise. As I had never in my life taken any pills whatever, not even an aspirin, I kept forgetting to take one or the other, and when I did forget made up for it by taking double the amount next day. This was to have a disastrous effect some time later. All the beautiful food, therefore, I could not eat. It was cottage cheese and fruit; I could have steaks, which I do not particularly like anyway, and salad, salad, salad. I did not drink, so that was no problem, nor did I smoke, but how I longed for an American ice-cream soda and the tempting desserts. It also seemed to me rather stupid that the doctor had reported that I was under-nourished — the wartime diet was no fun at all — and gave me frequent injections of calcium, iron and liver, yet here I was on a diet! I used to ask Mother to buy a box of chocolates of my choice and then I would pick out one I fancied. 'Oh, Mother, eat that one please,' I would plead; then as she ate it, 'What's it like, how does it taste?'

After nearly eight months I received my first call to the studio to begin shooting at 7.30 a.m. As I was waiting for the camera to be set up, Van Johnson strolled over to me. 'You all right, kid?' he asked with his nice smile.

'Yes thanks, Van,' I managed to say.

'Don't worry, this picture is going to be a real stinker, so we may as well have a few laughs and forget it!'

'But this is my first film here,' I howled, 'and you are already established as number-one at the box office.'.

He just grinned. I was terribly nervous but braced up and tried to remember to speak in American and forget I was a Brit! And so it went on, with Charles Martin grinning his idiotic grin and the crew looking confused and frustrated. Martin was not, of course, exactly Kirkwood-friendly, not having forgotten how I had questioned his dire script. There was also another reason.

About three weeks before we started the film, Van and I, Martin and Mother had been invited to a swimming-pool party at Joe Pasternak's house in the afternoon. What a party it was — around an enormous swimming pool with a lavish buffet — with every MGM star plus a few others — Hedda Hopper, the formidable and powerful columnist, was one. When the time came to leave, Charles Martin offered to give me a lift home. Mother had made her own arrangements with one of her woman friends. The one redeeming feature of Martin was that he had a really good sense of humour, and I hoped that we could get on well together and make something of the film, which was so important to me and him as well, I thought. Suddenly he stopped the car outside a house. 'This is not my house,' I pointed out.

'No, it's mine,' he explained with a leer and with his face near to mine.

I was furious. 'Take me home at once,' I ordered unsmilingly. His face fell and he flushed alarmingly. What now? I thought, and braced myself to deliver a sharp kick. Thankfully that was not necessary as, with a grim expression (such a relief from his constant grin), he drove at full speed to my house. I opened the front door, and stepping with what I hoped was dignity, into my house, slammed it shut. What a nerve, I thought, simmering with anger. Naturally, I was prepared for some hostile treatment on the set — and I got it.

After a few days of shooting the film, another drama unfolded. I had a small dressing-room on the set, as did Van, and another large and glamorous one, which was also Judy Garland's when she was working on a film. I was just about to leave the set after the day's shooting when there was a discreet knock on the dressing-room door. Joe Pasternak stood there. 'Oh, hello, Joe,' I greeted him, wondering what on earth was wrong, as the producer of a film never appears unless there is trouble of some kind. He seemed quiet and thoughtful and said he would like to see me in my dressing room 'tomorrow after shooting stops'.

I did not see why he should not say whatever he had to say now in the working dressing room on the set. All my warning bells were on alert, remembering his stalking of me round the studio. I thought hard. 'I'm sorry, Joe, but I am fixed to see Johnny Hyde tomorrow evening.'

'Oh, Johnny Hyde,' he replied quietly. He left. The next day he rang Mother — I did not know about this — and asked her to come and see him at his office. Mother went, and when she returned home relayed what had happened. Joe Pasternak had said that I 'refused' to see him in my dressing room and added that it was very 'silly' of me; that he had wanted to discuss 'certain things' pertaining to the film. This cut no ice with me; I actually had a date, as I had told Pasternak, though it was not with Johnny Hyde; at the pool party, I had met a young man of my own age who had just returned from the war. His name was Tommy Breen and, although I did not know it then, he was the second son of Joe Breen, the head of Film Censorship in Hollywood, whom I met sometime later when Tommy took me to visit his family home in Malibu. Of course I should have telephoned

Johnny Hyde and put him in the picture, but as I was unused to deception I was not very good at it!

Off I went on my date with Tommy, his brother and his brother's girlfriend and we had a marvellous evening at an impressive restaurant and later visited a jazz club to hear Dizzy Gillespie — a terrific evening. I was not needed at the studio until the afternoon of the next day, but when I arrived there, I was given an urgent message saying that Joe Pasternak wished to see me at once. Whoops, I thought, trouble in store; I was right. Pasternak stood behind his desk looking dreadful, grey-faced, unshaven, without a tie, as if he had been awake all night. Straight away he launched into an angry monologue. 'You were not seeing Johnny Hyde, last night,' he stormed. 'You were with Tommy Breen; I rang Johnny and asked him if he had seen you lately and he told me he had not seen you since before the film started, when you complained about the script. You lied to me, why?' What could I say? Certainly not the truth, that I would rather face a gorilla than him in his office at any time. So I quietly said that I had promised to go out with Tommy Breen some time ago, and I was afraid that he — Pasternak — would not have approved of me going 'on the town' whilst making the film. This carried no weight at all and silence took over for what seemed an age. Finally Pasternak drew himself up to his full height of five foot seven inches and announced menacingly, 'Very well, I shall not let this make any difference to the making of the film. You may go.'

The last sentence chilled me, as I knew at once that this would not be the case. Now I had made enemies of the producer and the director, Charles Martin. What a sinister situation for me with the perishing film not a third of the way completed. So things began to happen. Two of my songs were cut, although this was no hardship as they did not come up to expectations, to put it kindly. They were surprisingly bad, given that they had been written by the songwriters who had composed 'The Trolley Song' for Judy Garland in *Meet Me in St Louis* and many more hit songs — mostly for her. The collection for *No Leave, No Love* was nowhere near this class, one of them being a monster of sickening sentimentality about a dog called 'Old Sad Eyes', which made me squirm and which I am certain would have inspired a similar reaction in any self-respecting dog! Charles Martin had his knife into me up to the hilt and, I noticed, I very rarely had a close-up. He reported to me with hilarity that the cameraman said to him just after we began the film, 'How do you expect me to photograph this British broad?' which did nothing for my confidence. However, Rosson, the cameraman, was a kind and gentle soul, it seemed to me, so I dismissed this vile comment as a Charles Martin original. I used to dread going to the studio every morning, but after a while I realized that the crew, the sound man called 'Chips', the assistant director, the lighting men and the assistant cameraman were on my side and had nothing but contempt for their director; but as professionals, they all continued their work doggedly and efficiently, but in silence. There were no jokes or happy conversations on this set, except from dear Van, who really kept me going with his stolid good humour and unruffled calm. He used to make me laugh with his simple jokes and funny stories. I was grateful to him.

Guy Lombardo and his orchestra were also in the film; he turned out to be a most pleasant man. Also Xavier Cugat and his South American orchestra, who were in the film, brought us a cheerful break on the set; they played between shots, and Van and I used to dance the rumba; or rather, Van danced the rumba and taught me to abandon my foxtrot for something different, which was great fun. Poor Hal Rosson was taken off the film, as it was considered by the hierarchy that he was not photographing me at all well. So we had another cameraman called Bob Surtees, who was much younger than Hal and more up-to-date with his lighting. I thought that my make-up was awful, too subdued and pale, so I did a 'Joan Crawford' and altered it myself in the dressing-room, just as she did. So, at last, I had a mouth and eyes that I recognized. Nothing was said about this, so it must have been an improvement.

Of course eventually there must be a crisis in such a situation, and it came soon enough. I had a scene with dear Guy Lombardo in which I had to say the word 'been'. I pronounced it just like that. Charles Martin stopped the camera and sound and piped up with a grin, 'It's pronounced 'bin' in America, not 'been'.' So we did the scene again. This time I again said 'been' as I could not register the difference in my head. We stopped again. This time I gritted my teeth and said 'bin' — I was certain that I did. But Martin stopped the shot and drawled, 'You said 'been' again' in a singsong voice. By now I was highly nervous and also furious. Guy Lombardo smiled at me and winked, never turning a hair. We did twenty-four takes on this perishing word, though by this time I did not know what I was saying. I was humiliated and nervous, but I said to myself, Don't crack, Kirkwood, and I did not, but after the last take I ran to my dressing-room on the set, shut the door and cried with rage and frustration.

I was reminded of those directors in my first English film when I was very young. There was no one I could complain to, certainly not the producer, Joe Pasternak, and, even if I could, complainers are not a very admirable lot. Better to put up with things and get on with it; everything passes, I thought. Guy Lombardo turned out to be a real friend. He and his wife took Mother and me to Hollywood races on one of the days I was not needed at the studio. We had a marvellous day with them and a superb lunch, although I had to stick to my cottage cheese and salad. When the film finished the whole crew came to me and hugged and kissed me; they were a lovely crowd and had been very kind to me. Apart from that, I simply walked out, ignoring Charles Martin, as did the whole crew. Many years later, when Van was visiting London, at the invitation of Thames TV for *This*

Is Your Life, he told me that when I had walked out of the studio on our last day of filming, 'We all wept', meaning himself and the crew. I was most touched.

I did not attend the première of the film, but Mother and I had gone quietly to a cinema where the film was being shown after the preview. I hardly recognized myself as I had been turned into a vapid *ingénue* with no chance to be myself. Nor had I been given any material to get my teeth into and prove that all the fuss made about me had been worthwhile.

I then had a letter from my brother who had just been 'demobbed' from the Merchant Navy as a wireless operator. He had had a terrific war, and was thankfully not injured. So I 'guaranteed' him, got him over to California and he came to stay with us. We had some wonderful days at the beach, swimming and sun-bathing and eating delicious American hamburgers, the like of which do not exist outside the States; it was the first time I had tasted them. The variety of food available was amazing — American, Swedish, English, Russian, Italian, Hungarian. Each restaurant was run by the natives of these countries, mostly by whole families who had emigrated, and the food was mostly superb. Of course, too, we visited Romanoff's, the legendary eaterie of the stars; and Kings restaurant for their famous cracked crab; and Jack's at the beach in Malibu for delicious seafood, lobsters and so on. I also went to Ciros restaurant, where I learned to dance the mambo, and visited the Mocambo, the most elite supper club in Los Angeles. I loved the music, with its vitality and joyful rhythm. What a joy it was after the nightmare of *No Leave, No Love*.

All the on-set dramas during the filming of *No Leave, No Love* were as nothing compared with the emotional turbulence that was in progress behind the scenes. At the age of twenty-nine, Van Johnson was Hollywood's most eligible bachelor. Women adored him, but the secret of his international success was the innocent boy-next-door charm that made him attractive to all age-groups, as well as across the sexual barriers. Also in the film was the American character actor Keenan Wynn, who was the same age as Van. As filming progressed, Keenan's wife, Evie, became obsessed by the notion that her husband had fallen in love with Van Johnson. Evie was a formidable character, and in the front office at MGM, her obsession created alarm and anxiety. Van was a hugely valuable asset to Metro, and was receiving 8,000 fan letters a week. Anything that threatened to cloud his popularity with the public was regarded as a serious risk to the studio. The outcome of this intense triangular drama was unexpected. Evie and Keenan Wynn were divorced, and in 1947, Evie became Mrs Van Johnson. They had a daughter, but their marriage eventually foundered.

By this time I had gone out with a few boyfriends, all good company and with the American sense of fun and humour, but I was not 'hooked' by any of them seriously. They were all beautifully behaved and well-mannered, which surprised me, as I had thought this was the prerogative of Englishmen, but most of them could have taught my countrymen a thing or two on that score. Some of them wanted to be serious, but I was not that way inclined after my experience with John, so I just enjoyed their company and the laughter and fun of this new world and no one was hurt. Mother had her own friends and many of them. She seemed to be at a party every night and was very much in demand, especially with those much younger than herself; but she never stayed out late and was always home when I came in.

Then came disaster. The studio dropped its option for the following year. Louis B. Mayer was away and knew nothing of this. After the shock subsided, I determined to go and see Benny Thau, Louis B. Mayer's second-in-command, and find out what all this was about. It struck me that the dropping of the option was premature, as I had many months to go before my year was up. What was it all about? My decision took some courage as the 'front office', where the hierarchy resided, was held in much awe. This was true even of the top stars, who were struck with fear when summoned to this dreaded court. For myself, I was rather nervous, but certainly not scared: the thought of leaving the studio was more of a relief than anything else.

Benny Thau turned out to be a charming man and almost embarrassed by the situation in which I was placed. I was able to state my case to him and left nothing out regarding my various

189

tribulations, including the director Charles Martin. I did not mention the Pasternak episode as he was also one of the hierarchy and in any case it was not important. Benny Thau listened sympathetically and then came up with a conciliatory suggestion. 'We do not want to let you go,' he said softly, 'but we would like you to stay with us for the next year at the same salary. I realize the problems you have had, for which you were not responsible, but you must realize that your earnings for next year would be extremely high and *No Leave, No Love* did not give you the chance to display your talents, so we are really in the dark until you have the chance to make another film for us.' I was not impressed.

I remembered a dinner at Claridge's, London, as the guest of Ben Goetz, the MGM representative in Britain. During the evening the head of Twentieth-Century Fox in Britain joined us. 'So, you beat us to the tape,' he smiled at Ben.

'Well now,' drawled Ben, 'you must not be greedy — after all you have Betty Grable and June Haver.'

'Yeah,' replied the Fox big-wig, 'But you've got Pat!' What a compliment, I was thrilled to bits, Mother glowed with pride. This all came back to me as I listened to Benny Thau. I decided what I must do. 'Thank you, Mr Thau,' I began.

'Oh! Please call me Ben,' he smiled.

I let that go past my ear and continued 'I do not wish to stay another year with MGM, thank you just the same.' I had one question for him

190

which was bothering me rather. 'Mr Thau, would you tell me please if I can expect to be paid my salary for the rest of this year?'

Benny laughed. 'Of course, Pat, don't worry about that, just go home and think things over and I hope that you will change your mind.'

So, I went home, but I did not change my mind. I felt as though I had been released from a prison sentence and greeted Mother with a happy hug. 'What are we going to do now?' she quavered.

I sat her down and told her. 'We are going to New York — back to the theatre.'

10

New York

Mother was tearful with relief when I told her of my decision. It was arranged that the William Morris office in Hollywood should alert their New York agency to appoint one of their representatives to meet us, find us a flat in New York and arrange for me to meet theatre producers and directors for discussions about getting me a show. At last the Hollywood office woke up and did something for me. We were full of the spirit of adventure and began to pack. We were in the midst of this when the telephone rang. It was Ben Lyon, who, at that time, was casting director for Darryl Zanuck at Twentieth-Century Fox, the studio that had offered me a similar contract to the one from MGM that I had chosen instead. Ben was excited. 'Pat you have to get over to Twentieth immediately — Darryl Zanuck wants to do a colour test of you.'

This stirred no great response in me, as all had been arranged at the New York end, and in any case I had had enough of Hollywood and films, if not forever then for some considerable time. I told Ben we were packing for New York and that everything had been arranged for meetings with theatre people.

Ben was apoplectic. 'No, no — you must

unpack; you know that Darryl Zanuck wanted you before; he is enthusiastic about making a colour test with you.'

'Sorry, Ben,' I replied, 'but it's too late. I am going back to the theatre, but thank you for calling me.' I felt sorry, in a way, that I had not signed with Twentieth-Century in the first place. I also would have liked to please Ben Lyon, who had always been a good friend of mine, as was his much loved wife, Bebe Daniels.

'Bebe and I send our love,' Ben said sadly. 'Let me know if there's anything I can do to help.'

We arrived in New York in stifling June heat, and the humidity was high. But we found our flat was just right for us as it was situated a stone's throw away from Central Park, but quiet. My first appointment was with Richard Rodgers of Rodgers and Hammerstein, an awesome icon of the theatre, who had written and produced *Oklahoma, Carousel* and a score of world successes with his partner. I had been assigned a New York representative of William Morris called Kenneth Later, who lived up to his name by being half-an-hour late for Richard Rodgers. The great man was unperturbed by this and retained his beautiful manners. He was a gently spoken, tall, slim man with an impressive calm about him. He did not smile a lot but when he did the sun came out. His office was large, quietly furnished and elegant. No Hollywood razzmatazz there. There were a number of other men present, part of his entourage, all as quiet and calm as he and seated round an enormous desk. Richard Rodgers asked me, 'Would you please sing something for us, Miss Kirkwood, anything you like.' I would have sung the 'Star Spangled Banner' for him, he was so kind and polite. Instead I sang 'How Are Things in Glocamorra' from *Finian's Rainbow*. The show had not yet opened but I knew the song well, as a short while before I left for New York, Yip Harburgh, who had written and composed it, had asked to see me with a view to playing the leading girl's part. I went to meet him with a representative of William Morris and sang for him while he accompanied me at the piano. He handed me the script to read at home and offered me the part on the spot. I read it but could not imagine how an Irish fairy story would be a success on Broadway at that time. But to make sure, I handed the script to Abe Lastfogel, the head of the William Morris Agency. Abe read it and turned it down flat. 'This will be a flop,' he said. 'Don't touch it.' How wrong he was. *Finian's Rainbow* was an enormous hit and ran and ran. Even so, I did not think I was right for the part anyway, that of a fey little Irish *ingénue*. I knew by then how important it was to be myself, doing what I could do best; I had on the other hand qualms about turning down a show with no work on the immediate horizon.

I chose 'Glocamorra' from *Finian's Rainbow* as it is a lovely song and the reaction of Richard Rodgers and that of his 'cabinet' was most flattering; then he asked me if I would sing another song. This time, I opted for a more robust and knock-'em-in-the-aisles number called 'I Got Rhythm'. I had barely finished this, before Richard Rodgers rose from his chair beaming and clapping saying, 'Well, gentlemen, I don't think we need to hear any more from Miss Kirkwood.' They all agreed and rose and clapped, smiling at me. It was a great moment and I could have laughed and cried at the same time. 'Now let us talk,' he continued. 'Please sit down, Miss Kirkwood. I am sorry that I do not have a show for you at this moment, not until later this year, but how would you like to play Annie in *Annie Get Your Gun* on the Chicago tour?' I was disappointed, for I did not want to do a tour; I wanted Broadway.

Then Ken Later spoke up. 'This girl does not want a tour,' he announced. 'This girl wants a Broadway show.' His manner was rough and I could have slapped him. Richard Rodgers looked disappointed now and said gently, 'Well, I cannot offer you anything else at this moment. Please think it over, my dear.' What I did not know, something that everyone in American theatre knew, was that the 'Chicago tour' meant playing the show in the most beautiful prestigious theatre and living in Chicago for however long the show ran. No touring about all over the place. Also *Annie Get Your Gun* was still running in New York and Chicago was the only other big city that would be showing it. Ken Later should have known this, and I should have grabbed it with both hands. It was a wonderful part, so right for me, and if I had made a success of it, Richard Rodgers would have put me in a Broadway show. Instead, Mary Martin, one of

Broadway's brightest stars, played Annie in Chicago.

I was then taken to meet George Kaufman, the playwright and producer, who was putting on a play called *Park Avenue*; he offered me the younger of two female leads, the other being for an older woman, who would play my mother. I was handed the script to see if I liked it and the part before I committed myself. Next came a meeting with a younger producer called Nat Carson, who had plans to make his Broadway debut with a new script called *The Sweet Bye and Bye*, with lyrics by Ogden Nash from the book by S.J. Perelman. I nearly fainted as I heard these illustrious names. S.J. Perelman, a legend on Broadway, and Ogden Nash, a wit that shone like a full moon, a genius of a poet. So hugging my two scripts I returned to the flat, feeling relieved and happy that I had received four offers altogether and now had to decide between two of them.

I settled down to read George Kaufman's play *Park Avenue*. I was half way through it when there was a telephone call from Abe Lastfogel, who sounded grave and quiet, not at all himself. 'What is the matter, Abe?' I wanted to know.

He paused, then informed me that he had to tell me something that in all his career he had not known happen before. He then went on to explain that the part of the mother was to be played by a British stage actress called Leonora Corbett — that she was George Kaufman's mistress and that she had 'hit the roof' when he told her that I was to play the part of her daughter. Ms Corbett made it quite clear that if George Kaufman insisted on me playing the part she would leave him. She also added, 'Me! Playing Pat Kirkwood's mother — what would London say?' Not much, was the answer to that; or probably, 'Leonora who?' as she had not been seen on stage or screen for a considerable time.

Now I was down to my last chance, *The Sweet Bye and Bye* script. I read it. It was wonderful, full of magic and the combined golden talents of Nash and Perelman. Of course, I realized that Nat Carson was a new producer, yet to be tested, but I could not see *The Sweet Bye and Bye* failing. I had the lead part and it was one of the best ever, I thought. I had yet to hear the music, but if it lived up to Ogden Nash's lyrics it would surely be great. It was a happy time for Mother and me! Except I still could not sleep. I was still taking my slimming tablets but had not been given anything to help me sleep. I now weighed 7 stone and was stimulated and over-energetic in the daytime, especially in the morning. Neither Mother nor I had considered consulting a doctor — the only one we knew was Dr Nelson in Hollywood who had first prescribed the pills.

Rehearsals began. I seemed to be in top form and was full of elation; I knew all my lines and those of everyone else — I was like an overwound clock. One morning the leading man and I were rehearsing a particularly important scene together, we were both completely absorbed in the play. The cast was silent and the rehearsal room still as we played this highly emotional scene. It was as if we were cut off from the rest of the world. When we finished there was a long pause. I came down to earth and asked my partner, 'Was it all right?'

He stared at me. 'You were wonderful,' he exclaimed with tears in his eyes. The director was dancing with delight. 'Great, great,' he exclaimed. 'Keep it just like that.' I found I was shaking a bit and felt very flushed. The director took my hand. 'Now, let's discuss the next scene,' I heard him say, but his voice seemed to come from a long way off.

Then I found that although his lips were moving, I could not hear what he was saying. I felt frightened. 'I'm sorry, I'm sorry, but I can't hear you. I just can't hear you.' He turned pale. 'I'll have to go home,' I managed to say. 'Can you get me to a taxi. I don't think I'm very well.' The cast all came round and tried to comfort me but it was no use, I could not hear them. The director saw me into a taxi, looking very concerned. I returned to the flat and at once asked Mother to find me a doctor. The doctor's name was Lowenstein, a psychiatrist. 'You're a German,' was my first greeting to him. 'I'm not staying here.' He gave me a kindly smile and said nothing, just took my hand gently and steered me into another room, where there was a narrow surgical bed and various pieces of medical equipment. Mother stayed in the surgery. He then gave me an injection and told me that I would experience some strange reactions, but that I must not be afraid as this would make me better. He sent for Mother to sit beside me.

Suddenly, I found myself in convulsions, my face twisting and stretching and my body writhing with contortions. 'Don't watch me, Mother!' I managed to say, as I twisted and turned in paroxysms, my face stretching into horrid shapes. I learned later that I had received a drug which brought on convulsions; I assume this was an effort to bring me back to normality through shock. It was hard work and seemed to go on forever. The convulsions were heavy and left me completely exhausted. This was ironic, as all I really needed was a good night's sleep, which I had not enjoyed for over three months, because of the slimming and pituitary tablets prescribed by my Beverly Hills doctor. It is sad to think that sleeping pills were unknown to Mother. If they had been prescribed by Dr Nelson and the slimming pills stopped, I would not have had to miss such golden opportunities in my career.

After the shock treatment I rested for a while; I heard Dr Lowenstein talking to someone on the telephone. Then he came in smiling and informed us that he had made arrangements for me to go to a very nice quiet hotel and have a good rest. I had no reaction to this, as I was still bemused, but Mother seemed to approve. Then he said he wished to speak to Mother alone and escorted her out of the room. My heart began to beat fast and I felt a conspiracy was afoot. What was this German doing? He had already tortured me; was I going to be captured and put in a Nazi camp?

Dr Lowenstein arrived in a large black car, driven by another man I had not seen before. We came to some traffic lights. It was dark now but light enough so that I could see there was a bridge across the road with a parapet. I opened the car door and ran across the traffic towards the bridge — the Germans were not going to get me, I would jump over the bridge. Like a flash Dr Lowenstein was after me and as I reached the parapet he pinned me with his arms so that I could not move. I was amazed at his strength, as he was not a young man, even grey-haired, but I was completely helpless and the doctor half lifted me into the car. We drove on, with the car door locked and the doctor holding both my wrists in a vice-like grip. He had saved my life.

We arrived at the hotel, which was some way out of New York, but I could not see much as it was dark and in any case I was not observing anything. We entered the vestibule, which was large and quiet and softly lit — it seemed comfortable and safe, with easy chairs and sofas and a deep carpet. I was suspicious. 'If this is a hotel, where is the reception desk,' I growled.

A large lady with a smiling face came towards us asking us to 'Come this way, please.' We were all shown to a pretty room with a narrow bed and windows looking out on to an enormous garden. Mother, Dr Lowenstein and the other man left and a nurse entered. I was put to bed. The nurse gave me an injection. I slept — at last. When I awoke it was early morning, and with the light my fears returned. I simply wished to die and would not eat. My weight went down to 5½ stone and I was in a state of semi-coma. The nurses were kindness itself, although I was refusing food, and took endless pains to, at least, make me drink a milky liquid through a teapot spout, which I did eventually, just to please them.

The head of Four Winds, the name of the clinic — I had realized it was not a hotel — was a man called Dr Lambert, older than the other doctors and very rarely seen, although he kept a close watch on the treatment of his patients and the whole place was well run. He was tall and grey-haired with a small moustache and a happy look about him. The chief doctor's name was Pfeiffer — another German! He was a gentle, caring person with a cheerful countenance and endless patience. He also was grey-haired and tall. The nurses were mature and dressed in ordinary clothes, no uniforms, and I began to know and to trust them. It was very quiet always; there were no 'scenes' of any kind, no disturbances. I learned later that the other patients were also suffering from mental and physical exhaustion. They were mostly of my own age. Dr Lambert told Mother that if I did not show improvement by Christmas, I was a lost cause and would not live. It was now November.

Then something unforgettable happened. I was brought up without religion, except that Brian and I were taught by Daddy to say our prayers every night. Apart from this, the only religious knowledge I possessed was from the scripture lessons at school. I had never been to church. One night at Four Winds, when I had almost been given up by the doctors, I had a clear vision of Jesus. I heard Him say, 'Take my hand.' I put out my hand and He took it. Then the entire room filled with flames and He said, 'Walk through the flames with me.' I was afraid but I did walk and then the flames disappeared. Then the room filled with water, and again I was afraid, but I took His hand and walked through the water. Strangely I was not disturbed by all this but was calm, as if it was an ordinary happening, one that had been expected. I never told my Mother nor anyone else — save my present husband Peter. I thought for a long time and came to the conclusion that God did not want me to die; that I had much to do and must work hard to get well again. I felt an enormous relief flow through my entire being, then I rang the emergency bell by the side of the bed. 'I'm hungry. Could I have something to eat?' The nurse who answered the bell was a favourite of mine with a smiling 'tea-cosy' look. With tears in her eyes she kissed my forehead and hurried away. I never looked back and felt my strength returning every day. It was the beginning of December. I was well enough now to be allowed up and I used to walk about with the nurses and visit the other patients, giving them the advice which Mother had given me a few months ago: 'Eat, rest, relax and get well!'

Mother and Aunt Freda, who had come to help, visited me with some interesting news; Walter Winchell, that brilliant and famous news broadcaster, had mentioned me 'kindly', which was not his usual way as he was noted for his acerbity and biting wit. He had said, 'The British star Pat Kirkwood is dangerously ill in hospital and is not expected to recover. Poor, unfortunate beautiful girl.' Unfortunately, he was not up-to-date as he broadcast this two or three days after my recovery had begun, frightening the life out of Mother and Aunt Freda who had just received the news that I was improving by leaps and bounds. I had met Walter Winchell in Hollywood at a party before the film began and thought him different from his radio persona; he was extremely courteous and good company and loved to rumba, being an expert in that energetic exercise. Altogether a good sort, I thought.

Mother told me of a strange experience she had in New York when I was very ill. One evening she left the flat to get some air and sat on a bench in Central Park feeling sad and weary. She looked up into the night sky and saw a large balloon, the size of the barrage balloons we were used to seeing in London during the war. It was travelling slowly across the sky, carrying a large illuminated banner below its belly which declared to the world 'PAT KIRKWOOD'. Mother was so dismayed she thought she was seeing things, completely missing the small print below my name, which said, 'In *No Leave, No Love* — Coming Shortly'. The next day she sent for Aunt Freda!

I was now able to relax and enjoy my freedom. I had my hair done and began to eat furiously everything placed before me. I went walking in the gardens and it was a wonderful experience to sniff the air again and see the pristine snow covering the trees and grass. I could not resist cupping the snow in my hands and burying my face in its cold, clean beauty. Doctors Lambert, Pfeiffer and Lowenstein came to see me with their smiling faces — dear Doctor Lambert with a large grin on his face. It was all magical to me, I felt thankful and humble to be well again. I shall never forget the kindness and care that I had received from the nurses and the doctors. I have felt so much gratitude toward them for the rest of my life.

Mother came to see me after having talked to Dr Lambert for some time, and she reported to me what he had said to her. 'As far as we are concerned your daughter is the most wholesome girl we have ever had here and she should never have been here in the first place. She can stay with us as long as she likes, without charge. I guarantee, Mrs Kirkwood, that she will never go through this ordeal again and will stay as she is now for the rest of her life.' He then asked Mother to explain what had happened in the last year and a half to bring me to such a state. After Mother had told him, he remarked, 'Poor darling, no wonder she had a nervous breakdown.' He was right, of course. If I could have slept, this crisis would never have happened. As I have said before, I had not slept properly for three months because of the thyroid and pituitary tablets which were given to me for slimming. This was my first and last nervous breakdown. All that was now behind me.

I later learned that Emile Littler had offered me the part of Annie in *Annie Get Your Gun* which he was producing in London at the

Coliseum. I did not know then that Mother had withheld this information from me for some time, as she did not then know when I would be sufficiently recovered. Strangely, the doctors had decided that I should be told. 'It is just what she needs,' said Dr Pfeiffer. But Mother was afraid that the news would upset me. Then Emile had sent more cables and even telephoned several times but to no avail. He had even had posters made featuring a drawing that looked unmistakably like me. *Annie Get Your Gun* opened in London two weeks after I left Four Winds.

I now wanted nothing more than to go back to London. We set to with packing but booking tickets was a problem. We had to go by ship on account of our huge pile of luggage and, in any case, the crossing would be a much needed holiday after our last eight months. Unfortunately everything was fully booked up and we did not know what on earth to do. I was told to go for a walk, as I was in the way — so I did. To my great surprise a chap driving a car whistled at me by the traffic lights, boosting my confidence. I felt reborn and walked through Central Park.

Someone, probably the William Morris office, had rung up Jack Buchanan, unforgettable for his countless musical comedy rôles in the West End in the mid-thirties. Apparently he was in New York after finishing a film and on his way home. After hearing of our dilemma he said he would try and get us a berth on the same ship, if possible, as time was getting short. We waited anxiously for a week then the news came that Jack had failed to book us on his ship but had found us three berths on *SS America* with two cabins, one for Freda and one for Mother and me. What joy! And how kind of Jack Buchanan to go to such trouble — particularly as we had never met.

Kenneth Later came to see us off, when we were waiting to board the ship, and how upset he was that we were leaving. 'It isn't too late,' he cried. 'Get the luggage off — you must stay. Everything will start to happen now — get the god-damned luggage off!' He was near to tears. We did not budge, but he was so sweet and concerned that we both hugged him before we boarded the ship. He had a good heart, dear Kenneth — but a rotten sense of time.

When we docked Aunt Pop was there to greet us, with her latest conquest in tow, a Lord somebody, who seemed bemused, but then, all her conquests were! At last we arrived in London and how I loved it, even more than I had before, and how thankful I was for everything. I had been away for over two years and was longing to start work again.

11

HRH — and All That

We moved into a large, dark, furnished flat in Burton Court, Chelsea, near the Chelsea Hospital, and settled in. George Black, sadly, had died just before I went to America. His successor, as the West End theatre's leading producer, was Val Parnell, who offered me *Starlight Roof* at the London Hippodrome, with Vic Oliver and a new face, Julie Andrews. The show also introduced another newcomer, namely Michael Bentine, who, although he was given only two minutes before the finale to establish himself, achieved an enormous success with his unique, oddball act based on a chair. He also had an eccentric personality both on and offstage — he never stopped talking. It was clear that he had a most unusual talent. He also had a fertile imagination — as I was to discover many years later when he published his autobiography. I read it out of curiosity and was shaken and surprised to read about myself thus: 'Pat Kirkwood was an outgoing uninhibited Lancashire lass' — no clogs and shawl I thought — 'and I met many people in her dressing room after the curtain, including Prince Philip.' The truth of the matter is that Michael was never ever in my dressing-room at all, apart from an occasional cup of tea in the interval along with other members of the cast, and certainly never with Prince Philip.

Starlight Roof was Val's first big show on his own and he was determined to make it another *Black Velvet*. It was his baby and he was full of enthusiasm. He intended the presentation and production to be as lavishly dressed and glamorous as George Black's enormously successful show had been — the first of its kind after the war and much needed after six weary years of rationing and austerity. His enthusiasm paid off. The clothes were sumptuous, if a little over the top, but, then, we were in a new era, post-war, and people were thirsty for glamour and spectacle. *Starlight Roof* had these in abundance.

On the first night Mother and Aunt Freda were sitting in the stalls, both highly nervous on my behalf as this was my first show after my illness. Strangely, I was completely calm and, for the first time ever, without first-night nerves — the show might have been running for years. Robert Nesbitt, who was directing, just as he had *Black Velvet*, was his usual kind and considerate self and wished me luck with a squeeze of the hand. Joan Davis, that brilliant, talented choreographer, who had also worked on *Black Velvet* and *Let's Face It*, gave me an affectionate hug, but could not speak. I felt that I had come home and did not mind that *Annie Get Your Gun* was a great success at the Coliseum with Dolores Gray, not me. *Starlight Roof* also turned out to be an enormous success and ran for fourteen months, twice daily with two matinées a week. All the performances were packed. Val Parnell was delighted and triumphant.

I found a new friend in the form of Fred Emney — that lovable, incorrigible and unbearably funny man. We seemed to share similar opinions about everything. He used to come all the way across the Hippodrome stage, as his dressing-room was on the opposite side, then up a steep flight of stairs. I always knew it was Fred from his heavy breathing — he was no lightweight — and his firm knock on the door. He used to tell me his troubles; one of them concerned his income tax, which, he said, 'worries me to death' and he didn't know how to pay. I took this seriously and was concerned for him until, a week or two later, I saw Fred standing outside the stage door, as he always did before a matinée — 'showing off' I told him — and smoking his usual cigar. I noticed a very smart new car in bright scarlet standing by the kerb opposite him. I had an awful thought, 'Is that yours, Fred?' I asked him.

'Yes, what do you think of her? Isn't she terrific?' I gave up worrying about Fred's income tax. One interval when we were having a cup of tea, he said thoughtfully, 'You know, Kirkwood' — he had begun to call me 'Kirkwood' just as Val did — 'I enjoy talking to you; it's like talking to another fella!'

Starlight Roof had the benefit of one of our foremost light-music composers, George Melachrino, but unfortunately the songs were not strong enough for a big West End revue, and the lyrics of some of them were quite a disaster, but I was not prepared to do battle over anything after my long absence from the stage. So I sang them, even though their impact was nil — no matter what I did to put them across. Also I had not yet got into my proper stride — I had no nerves and was being far too laid-back. Nerves are essential to a good performance, especially in a large theatre, as they give an edge and an 'attack' to one's performance; without them, one's personality fails to sparkle. I was not at my best. However, I was back in harness again and the show was a big success. Moreover, my finances improved after the large hole made in them by my hospitalization of eight months, so I was indeed thankful to be working again. It was a happy show and I made new friends.

I needed some new theatre photographs. My former photographer, Madame Vivienne, was a true genius as she knew how to light brunettes — a talent not possessed by other photographers in London, as they were all blonde mad — but, she had died whilst I was in America so I did not know where to go. Then I saw in a magazine some photographs by 'Baron' who had acquired the honour of being the royal photographer. I thought he must be a good one to have gained that position, so off I went for a sitting. Baron Nahum, to give him his full name, turned out to be a smallish man, dark-haired and with a kind, strong face. He was not exactly handsome but, with his sparkly eyes and warm smile, attractive. As the sitting progressed he chatted away and revealed a delightful sense of humour and a devastating wit — all of which made the portrait sitting, which I had always dreaded before, a pleasant experience and not a chore. We got on splendidly and at the end of the session he asked me if I would lunch with him the next day. I did and there began a most happy relationship — it was as if we had known each other for years. I had not experienced such companionship for some considerable time and my life became brighter for it.

This all happened while *Starlight Roof* was still running, and Baron was working hard, too. What with his many sittings, we could only see each other on Sundays. So we used to go out into the country, mostly to Cookham, for lunch and Baron used to play golf at the Temple course. He could only use his left arm, as his right shoulder and arm had been shattered when he was working at the front in Anzio, Italy, during the war. He taught himself to use his left arm and hand for his work and for his golf. He and his family came from Manchester, as had I; they were highly successful cotton merchants. His brother was a QC. Baron seemed to know everyone and was well liked by all, his natural charm being patent and rare. I was soon meeting people and visiting stately homes that I had never dreamed of seeing.

The first venture into this new world was the home of the Earl and Countess of Darnley, who were holding a children's party, and what a party it was. There seemed to be hundreds of little people eating jellies and throwing streamers, chatting at full strength and having a whale of a time. The Earl and Countess welcomed us warmly and, obviously, were very fond of Baron. In the grounds they had installed a children's train to which I was immediately drawn, having always loved trains of any size or shape. So I drove the train packed with toddlers, round and round the extensive tracks; the sun was shining and the children were blowing hooters and whistles with their paper hats askew. It was the greatest fun and a day I have never forgotten. That evening I blew through two shows like a breeze.

A few weeks later Baron whisked me off to Romsey to meet Earl Mountbatten and his wife Edwina. They were having a point-to-point race there and I found myself standing at the rails with the attractive Lady Mountbatten, who showed great interest in the theatre and wanted to know all about what I was doing in *Starlight Roof*, which songs I was singing, the clothes I was wearing. In fact she was so relaxed and 'real' that I forgot completely who she was and we chatted away comfortably, sharing a few laughs or, rather subdued giggles. Suddenly Lady Mountbatten looked startled. 'Are you not due at the theatre tonight?' she asked. I was petrified. I had completely forgotten the time; so had Baron, but then it was my show not his, so why should he remember? After a quick 'thank you and goodbye' to Lady M. I flew to where Baron was talking to the Earl. The latter took one look at my face, twigged what the crisis was, gave me a grin and shepherded me speedily to Baron's motor, a low-slung sports car. 'Good luck,' he

Portrait by Houston Rogers,
aged 16

In the garden at 'Fairlea'
our house in Didsbury,
Manchester, with my
inseparable friend

As Dandini in the
pantomime *Cinderella*
at the Prince's Theatre,
London, 1937

With Arthur Askey in the
film *Band Waggon*, 1940

With the great George Formby in the 1939 film
Come On George. Also in the film was Dirk Bogarde in his
first appearance as an 'extra'. The director of photography
was Ronald Neame, later one of Britain's most famous
film directors *(BFI Stills, Posters & Designs)*

A lot of fuss from Oxford
about my invasion of
their hallowed precincts
wearing a mortarboard!
(Hulton Getty Print)

With Van Johnson in the MGM film *No Leave, No Love*,
Hollywood 1946

A typical 'glamour' picture churned out by the studio
photographers

All dolled up for first night in the West End

Marriage to 'Sparky' in 1952. His death in 1954 was a major tragedy *(Gainsborough Studios)*

In the title role of Peter Pan. Mrs Darling was played by Evelyn Laye and 'Hook' by Sir Donald Wolfit at the Scala Theatre, London, 1953

With Mother after the first night of *Wonderful Town*, 1955

As the Edwardian male impersonator, Vesta Tilley, with Laurence Harvey in the part of Walter de Frece in the Eastman colour film *After The Ball*, 1957 *(BFI Stills, Posters and Designs)*

Portrait by Vivienne in 1957

With Evelyn Laye ('Boo' to her friends) with her husband
Frank Lawton and a friend at a birthday party
(Express Newspapers Limited)

At St Columba's Church,
London, on 14 May 1956.
Marriage to Hubert Gregg,
composer, playwright,
director, lyricist. He wrote
'Maybe It's because I'm a
Londoner', and became a
Freeman of the City of
London *(Star)*

Whilst playing the title role in Somerset Maugham's play *Lady Frederick*, 1971

Marriage to Peter in Gibraltar, 3 March 1981, in the garden at the Rock Hotel

At home in Yorkshire with my husband Peter and our West Highland terrier Jamie McGregor, aged 11 years *(Roger Scruton, Saga Magazine, May 1993)*

Photo-call at Wimbledon Theatre for 'Glamorous Nights of Music', 1993 *(Reproduced by kind permission of the Croydon Advertising Group)*

This Is Your Life, 1994. The moment of surprise by Michael Aspel at the Prince of Wales Theatre, London *(This Is Your Life, Thames Television, a Pearson Television Company)*

This Is Your Life. Greeting Van Johnson, last seen in Hollywood in 1946, who co-starred in the MGM film musical No Leave, No Love *(This Is Your Life, Thames Television, a Pearson Television Company)*

called as we shot away. It was after 5 p.m. and the curtain went up at 6.45 p.m.! Baron drove like a fiend, while I sat there dumb and numb. We had been driving for fifteen minutes when a cloudburst struck. The rain bounced off the road; the windscreen wipers gave up, and we could not see a thing; but Baron kept driving, how I cannot imagine, but he did. I could see by now that we were not going to be at the Hippodrome before the curtain went up.

When we reached Shepherd's Bush Baron stopped at a telephone box. I rang the theatre and told them I was caught in a cloudburst, where I was and that I would be a few minutes late — what a hope! I have never seen anyone drive like Baron did that day. When we arrived at the theatre I saw, as I jumped out, that his face was dripping with sweat, and no wonder. As I ran to the dressing room — the other side of the stage, of course — someone called, 'Don't worry; Vic [Oliver] is ad libbing!' I ran up the stairs to my dressing-room, threw open the door and there was dear Jeannie Carson, my understudy, already in my costume and Bessie my dresser, both as white as chalk. I felt horribly guilty. Jeannie was marvellous: without a word she slipped out of the dress and I slipped into it and Bessie zipped me up — no time for make-up. I entered on stage to hear Vic Oliver telling his ad-lib stories, which he stopped suddenly, 'Oh,' he chanted, 'now we shall begin!' Bless him, he was a tower of strength. It was the first and last time that I ever made a late entrance! Vic informed me afterwards that I was only two minutes late, thanks to Baron, Jeannie and Bessie. The show still jogged happily along with full houses.

Baron had an assignment to photograph General Franco in Spain, so off he went. He was absent for nearly a month and I missed him quite a bit. When he returned he started to make up the work he had missed, so was fully occupied and we did not see one another for some time, although we spoke on the telephone each day. I had gone back to my usual routine of playing two shows and matinées; then Mother would pick me up at the theatre; and home we'd go to supper and bed. This habit of working was formed when I was playing at the variety theatres at the age of fifteen. It suited me well and enabled me to give my best on stage. It also guarded my voice and general health. The theatre is a hard taskmaster.

Eventually Baron emerged from his cave and popped into the theatre for a few minutes in the interval to suggest that we have a 'night out' — dress up, have a nice dinner and, perhaps, a dance. This went down very well with me; the show had been running for nearly a year and I thought it would be a good thing to break the rules and relax. Baron also needed to refresh himself as he was tired and pale and stale — both of us were. So we made a date for the following Thursday; there was no matinée on Fridays and we perked up at the prospect of a 'night on the town' as Baron put it. The next Thursday I felt a thrill of anticipation and worked well through the two shows; then I dressed up for my night out with Baron. I had bought a gorgeous dress from Saks of Fifth Avenue, New York. It was a pale coral long dress with a straight high neck and cap sleeves, beautifully cut, the only decoration being one black velvet rose on the hip. I had a white ermine fitted jacket to wear over it, which looked just right, and my hair was pulled straight back and into a chignon low on my neck — I had long hair then. Bessie was delighted. She was always telling me I should 'go out more' and 'have some fun'. Mother, too, was pleased. She had paid one of her rare visits to the theatre and sat on the sofa in my dressing-room, beaming approval.

The curtain came down at 10.30 p.m. and we waited for the arrival of Baron. He had threatened to wear his dinner jacket which I had never seen him in before, and I wondered if it was going to be a triumph or a disaster. Time passed slowly. Bessie began to stalk up and down with a set face. It was now 10.45 p.m. Baron had mentioned to me that he was a member of something called the Thursday Club, of which Prince Philip was also a member, together with various theatre celebrities, authors and artists, all male — a 'stag club' in other words. The chaps used to compete with witticisms and hilarious anecdotes, as men will when they escape the tyranny of the 'skirt'! So they all gathered at Wheeler's, a world-famous fish and seafood restaurant in Old Compton Street, Soho, each Thursday. I remembered all this and that Baron must have been at the Thursday Club that lunchtime, today. Could he have got drunk? No, he was never a drinker; was he ill, with fish poisoning? No — at the great Wheelers? What a thought. Perhaps he could not squeeze into his dinner jacket; perhaps he had lost his black tie. Horrors, here was I dressed like a chicken for the oven. Be quiet, I told myself, and be patient. Mother had her sarcastic face on. Bessie was not pleased, even grim. The telephone rang. It was Baron. In a sepulchral whisper he announced, 'There will be three of us' then put the phone down.

'Who was that?' Mother snapped. 'Baron, I suppose — how nice of him to phone,' she said, with heavy sarcasm. I had a flash of intuition — he was bringing Prince Philip. I said nothing, and my mind went blank. Mother went to the bathroom her back registering severe disapproval. Seconds later there were footsteps on the stairs outside. Mother pulled the flush in the bathroom. Now this was not any old flush; it was quite the loudest in London; one could hear it in Leicester Square. At this precise moment Prince Philip's head came round the corner of the door, just as Mother emerged to the accompaniment of Niagara Falls. His knock had obviously been drowned out by the sound of cascading water. I was too stunned to remember my manners, also speechless, so the Prince entered followed by a sheepish Baron, not dressed in his dinner jacket etc. but his usual anonymous casual wear. I knew that Baron had sent 'him' in first because he knew he was disgustingly late and I would be furious. Then a man in naval uniform entered last. Everyone said, 'Good evening' and the commoners 'bobbed', all except Bessie, who, her face a bright pink, attempted a full curtsey, only to be stuck halfway, whereupon everyone, except Mother, helped her out of her misery. The man in uniform was introduced by Baron as Captain Roland 'Basher' Watkins, a good friend and wartime colleague of Prince Philip's in the British Pacific Fleet. The Prince, dressed in a suit, was serenely unruffled and smiling his charming smile. Everyone waited for something to happen. Baron broke our respectful silence; this, of course, should have been left to the Prince, but he did not have a chance against Baron's usual high spirits. 'Well, let's go, shall we? How about Les Ambassadeurs?' he suggested brightly. The welcome thought of something to eat floated inside my head, as I had not done so since lunchtime, and after two shows I was ready to repeat the experience.

So all the principals agreed and we left the dressing room at last. Mother had remained stoically calm ever since her dramatic entrance to the strains of Handel's *Water Music*, but, then, nothing ever impressed her. We arrived at Les Ambassadeurs after a drive in silence — at least on my part, in Baron's car. 'Basher' drove the Prince in his car. As we entered, Baron led the way, followed by me, then 'Basher' Watkins with the Prince bringing up the rear. Mr Williams, the 'maître d', who was a Hungarian and normally calm and gentle, suffered a face change as he saw Baron. 'Table for four, Williams,' ordered Baron. Mr Williams became apoplectic and very Hungarian.

'Mister Baron,' he almost shrieked, 'Why you do this to me always? We have no tables left, we are filled up. Do you know what time it is? We are finished, we are closed, they have just played the 'King'.' Suddenly Prince Philip's head came forward. 'Well, tell them to play it again,' he instructed. Williams, who had not spotted the Prince before this, as he had been checking his bookings on the desk, turned in a fury; then his mouth fell open, his flush faded and, he called tremulously, 'George, George, at once, here at once!' George was the head waiter, poor man. He appeared, like a jack-in-the box. Williams mopped his damp brow and the four of us were ushered into the restaurant to the only table left; two waiters prepared it in a flash, even before we reached it.

The place was packed tight to the walls, filled with actors and actresses — it seemed to be a veritable 'Who's Who' of the theatre. There also was I, dressed up to the nines, with three escorts and not one dinner jacket between them. Likewise, no one in the restaurant was in evening dress. I took a deep breath, walked to our table, which seemed to be miles away, with my three escorts following. Out of the corner of my eye I spotted Michael Wilding, Jean Simmons, Margaret Leighton and many more celebrities. The whole restaurant was silent, not a peep out of anyone. I just wanted to disappear into a hole in the ground, but remembered to keep my head up, my back straight and my face serene. We sat down. The Prince, Baron and 'Basher' sat opposite me, in a row like budgies, so I was sitting on my own facing them. 'Let's have a drink shall we?' piped up Baron. 'We don't want to bother with anything to eat, do we?' Then I made it quite clear that I would welcome some dinner. I sat and ate my meal whilst the three chaps watched with interest, which did not affect my appetite.

They all chatted away and seemed perfectly happy that we made an incongruous party and that all eyes were fixed on us. Ours was the only table with conversation going, it seemed. We made ready to leave. Prince Philip suddenly suggested that we go to the Milroy supper club upstairs, above Les A. This was an exclusive and highly fashionable club, patronized by the elite and the 'stinking rich' equally. I think it also served delicate snacks like caviar on toast or foie gras on pitta bread, but I cannot vouch for this. So, I trailed upstairs with the Prince and his entourage thinking that, perhaps, Baron and I could have the promised dance. Strangely there was hardly anyone there — and we were given a table immediately. Baron announced that Prince Philip did not wish us to call him, 'Your Highness,' but simply 'Himself' for the rest of the evening, which, I thought, would not be for long at this time of night — it was after one o'clock. 'Let's have some beer,' suggested 'Himself'. I was not enthusiastic, thinking that as I was experiencing a unique happening it should be suitably celebrated and certainly not with beer. 'I don't drink beer, thank you. I would like champagne,' I heard myself say, thinking at the same time, What a nerve!

'Himself' ordered a bottle of champagne for the four of us and we drank it with great pleasure, as it was the first and last drink of the evening. The small orchestra had arrived and began to play. 'Would you like to dance?' the Prince asked me. I did not refuse. As we walked on to the small dance floor, I saw with surprise that the band leader and musicians were the orchestra who played before me on stage for one of my songs in *Starlight Roof*. The leader, Santiago, played the maracas, a South American musical instrument shaped like two coconuts with a handle each and shaken by hand to the rhythm of the music.

The Prince and I began to dance a good old-fashioned foxtrot, ignoring all the South American nonsense. We danced in the old fashioned way, that is, at arm's length, as they do at functions and respectable balls. Personally I like this way as one can see one's partner's face, instead of having to look over his shoulder in the closer dancing style. There was no one else on the floor as we danced sedately past the orchestra. Santiago obviously saw me. He was astounded, but did not cease shaking his maracas and never missed a beat in spite of the fact that his eyes protruded like billiard balls and an amazed smile covered his face. 'Hubba hubba!' he exclaimed, which in English trans-lates as 'Well I'll be . . . ' We just sailed on. Then a clutch of people began to arrive at the club. They stood still and watched 'Himself' and me and then, to my dismay, the ladies in the group, with horrified expressions on their faces, turned to their male companions with a show of great agitation. Then the chaps turned to one another and indicated us dancing. They also looked agitated. What was this all about? I wondered. Then 'Himself' noticed the newcomers, more of whom were pouring in and all showing a similar reaction. I pointed this out to 'Himself', who glanced up briefly then began to mimic the shocked expressions on our new audience's faces. He was very funny indeed and we had a laugh or two. It was not possible for the new crowd to see his expressions as they were too far away, and in any case 'Himself' was careful to have his back to them when he did his impersonations. I was nervous. 'Should we sit down now?' I suggested. 'No,' he laughed, 'and that's an order!' I kept my face straight with an effort and we stayed on the floor for a further few minutes. I was, by this time, exhausted, as much by laughter as the foxtrot, in spite of the fact that Prince Philip was a really good dancer and great company.

What was all the fuss about? I wondered. Oh well, perhaps the visitors were surprised to see Prince Philip, I thought, then forgot about them. Baron told me later they were the 'courtiers' who like 'to play' at the Milroy from time to time. We were all ready to go now and wended our way out of the Milroy towards the cars. It had been a lovely, happy evening, as all of us possessed a similar sense of humour — in other words we had all got on together very well. As we were sorting ourselves out, with 'Basher' ready to drive Prince Philip and I already in Baron's car,

Baron cried out, 'Anyone fancy some scrambled eggs?' It was typical of Baron to suggest something like this just as we were all leaving. There was a chorus of 'oooh yes' from the rest of us — except me. So we drove to Baron's flat, which was not far away, and he began to cook our scrambled eggs on toast whilst the Prince, 'Basher' and I sat at the table watching him — it was a small kitchen-cum-breakfast room. As we were about to dive into our eggs two people arrived, a young couple. Baron explained that the young man was a Czechoslovakian and was apprenticed to him to learn photography. His girlfriend was pretty and dark with a genuine Cockney accent; she was very young and shy. Baron then introduced us, 'This is Captain Watkins, this is Miss Pat Kirkwood and this is Prince Philip.' At the sound of the Prince's name, the young girl stiffened like a stone statue, her smile disappeared and her eyes became wide and staring; she seemed to be in a trance. Her young man took her arm and guided her away, still in shock.

We finished our excellent scrambled eggs and then went home, 'Basher' driving the Prince to Buckingham Palace and Baron dropping me at my flat in St John's Wood that I shared with my mother. I crept into the flat thinking she would be asleep, but no. A tired voice said, 'Hello, is that you?'

'Oh, Mother, I have had a wonderful evening,' I replied.

'Tell me tomorrow. Do you know the time? Better get to bed; you have two shows to do.'

This brought me down to earth. I went to bed and slept like a dormouse.

The next morning, as I was going over the events of the previous evening in my head, I remembered how Prince Philip went very quiet from time to time; he seemed to be somewhere other than Les A or the Milroy. He had looked anxious and worried, and then, when he entered the conversation again it seemed to me that his gaiety was somewhat forced. I decided his thoughts had been at Balmoral with Princess Elizabeth and the prospective birth of the heir to the throne — a momentous and stressful time for fathers, too. The Prince had resembled a man who was struggling to enjoy himself, although his heart was not in it. And so ended this simple and delightful evening, though little did I know what repercussions it would bring. The first effect fell on poor Baron, who was sacked, or so he thought at the time; at least, he was not asked to take the first photographs of the brand new heir to the throne — Cecil Beaton took them — but, happily, he was forgiven and took the christening photographs later.

Prince Philip had a stern ticking-off from Earl Mountbatten. Captain 'Basher' Watkins and myself were allowed to go free. Some weeks later Bessie came into the dressing room one evening, chinking with laughter. 'What's the joke, Bessie?' I wanted to know. It seems she had been to the Dominion cinema to see a film. Two large ladies were sitting in front of her, and when the Gaumont British News appeared Prince Philip was seen at some ceremonial opening. 'Cor, it's

Him!' hissed one of the large ladies. 'Of course, you know, don't you, that he has a mistress already.'

'Go on,' said her companion with avid interest, 'Who?'

'Well,' proceeded the first, 'it's that actress, Pat — Pat something.'

'Roc?' suggested her listener.

'No, no, no,' replied the informant irritably.

'Burke?' suggested the friend.

'No, it's Pat Kirkwood,' she stated triumphantly. There was much chuntering after this announcement, and they never saw the rest of the GB News. Bessie and I had a good laugh at this, then proceeded to get ready for the show and forgot all about it.

The next revelation came out the following week. I met a very old acquaintance of mine whom I had not seen for years, a contemporary of the late George Black. He looked serious. I asked him if anything was wrong. 'Pat,' he said, 'I was in White's club the other day. A member I know came in and I heard him say to all and sundry, 'Well I do think that Prince Philip has gone too far.'

'Why? What do you mean?' said one of the members.

'He has just bought Pat Kirkwood a white Rolls-Royce!'

'Is it true, Pat?'

I was breathless, so could not do what I wanted to do, which was to burst into laughter. Also, we were in the middle of Regent Street. I found myself very angry suddenly and denied

224

this bizarre untruth so strongly that he could not possibly believe it; in fact I told him off for even asking me and not knowing better. It was so ridiculous that in the theatre Bessie and I, after a hysterical five minutes, forgot all about it, although I did have a twinge of alarm that it could have happened. Who had started such a rumour and, even more mysteriously, why? This was 1948 and yet, to this day — more than fifty years later — rumours of this sort, and worse, have been circulated about myself and the Prince that have absolutely no foundation. This has caused much embarrassment to the Prince, to myself, and to the Queen herself, I have no doubt, although I am sure that she has never given them any credence.

I express my astonishment in particular, that a 1996 biography of the Queen by Sarah Bradford should refer to these allegations in what was, I suppose, intended to be a serious and well-researched work. In it the author uses my name to vilify the Prince. I was particularly astounded at the suggestion that I had had a continuing relationship with Prince Philip, for I never saw him again, except once in the theatre audience; once after a Royal Command Performance, when I was presented to him; once after a tribute to Dame Irene Vanbrugh at the Drury Lane Theatre when, along with the rest of the cast, I was presented to him again; and once, about sixteen years ago, when my husband and I were part of a large number who shook hands with him at the London Guildhall during a function for the World Wildlife Fund, of which the Prince was Patron. He did not recognize me.

I also take this opportunity to set straight the record concerning Baron, now powerless to defend himself from the vile calumnies that have also appeared repeatedly in print. There has never been a scintilla of evidence to support any of these allegations as far as I am concerned. Indeed, when she read all this nonsense Captain Watkins's daughter, Dr Jennifer Kewley-Draskau, told the *Daily Express*, 'My father had a very strict regard for the sanctity of marriage and a deep regard for Princess Elizabeth. Certainly his admiration and friendship for Prince Philip would not have persisted if there was anything in this rumour.' This statement prompted the 'William Hickey' column of that newspaper to announce in a bold headline on Friday 26 January 1996, 'DUKE AND PAT CLEARED AT LAST'. So now we know! By way of a footnote I should add that in a paperback edition of the Bradford book, prompted by some pungent correspondence with the publishers, the offending references to me were expunged.

Drama lay ahead. Business suddenly dropped off during the summer of our second year with *Starlight Roof* and my agent, who also represented Vic Oliver, and Julie Andrews — who was then only thirteen years old and had caused a sensation in the show — persuaded us that the show was coming off and that we should sign up with Emile Littler for the pantomime *Humpty Dumpty*. We all signed. Val was hoping to break the record two-year run of *Black Velvet*, but *Starlight Roof* wound up after fourteen months.

I recall that some time later, after *Humpty Dumpty* had been running a few weeks at the London Casino, the stage director came to me before the matinée one day and whispered that Princess Elizabeth and the Duke of Edinburgh were in front of house, sitting in the stalls, but I must not tell anyone. When I went onstage I was searching the audience in between my lines and songs to see if this was really so, and it was. Because I was able to see the stalls a long way back, I could easily make out the royal couple in the centre, with Prince Philip in a gangway seat and Princess Elizabeth next to him. Towards the end of a pantomime it is traditional for the principal boy and the dame to have a comedy song sheet brought down at the back of the stage with the words of the song printed on it in large letters so the audience could sing along. Then the boy and the dame hold a competition to see which side of the audience can sing the loudest. The boy takes one side of the house and the dame the other, after tossing a large artificial coin. As it happened the royal couple were sitting on my side of the house, but I tried to forget they were there and carried on as usual, saying, 'Come along, my side — show them how to sing — loud and clear now!' Then I conducted my side. It was a silly old pantomime song of yore called, 'What I Want is a Proper Cuppa Coffee'. I sneaked a look at our honoured guests and, eureka, the Prince was singing away with all stops out. The Princess looked straight ahead,

227

keeping her face straight but with a slight smile coming through.

Julie Andrews and I became good friends during *Humpty Dumpty* and she was constantly in and out of my dressing room, investigating my make-up. 'What's this for?' she would ask. 'What's this?' She was a nice kid and I, having started young as 'The Schoolgirl Songstress', could identify with her, though I had not seen much of her during *Starlight Roof* as she was always whisked off home immediately after her song. I was a sort of adopted auntie to her.

After the pantomime finished Baron and I did not see each other often, mainly because I was getting tired of his laissez-faire attitude to time, the last straw being when we had booked to see the first night of Maurice Chevalier's one man show at the Hippodrome. I arrived at the theatre. Baron was not there yet, of course, so I waited for him in the foyer until the curtain was going up, then went to my seat alone. After nearly an hour Baron turned up, in his woolly sweater and corduroy trews — it was a very dressy first night — and grinned at me. He offered no apology, just the grin. I said nothing as I was used to this behaviour by now.

12

Danny Kaye

One day, at a press reception at the Savoy for Danny Kaye, Val Parnell introduced us. We could not shake hands as Danny had a glass of champagne in one hand and a pen in the other. Instead we shook our little fingers! Our eyes seemed to lock together. He was impressively gorgeous with his red gold hair, green eyes and tall, slim, figure. I remember saying, 'How do you do?' Danny said, 'You're pretty,' in a rather intense way, and that was the limit of our conversation. Shortly after, Val took me to lunch with Danny, his manager and his pianist. Danny was on good form — hilariously comical and great fun. Two nights later he opened at the Palladium and was an enormous success. He had a standing ovation which went on and on; the audience would not let him go. The press were ecstatic and no seats were available from then on.

Val and Helen, his wife, invited me to supper after the show at their flat; Helen, a dear, sweet woman and inveterate matchmaker, informed me, 'Danny is coming too!' I felt a small flip in my diaphragm. I was wary as it seemed all the females in London were after Danny. Wherever he went he was mobbed by hungry women, even a member of the royal family, Princess Marina, who entertained him in her home for tea and telephoned constantly. Danny related that he had called her 'honey' once and from then on she was hooked. Danny escaped with a grateful sigh — like most Americans he was profoundly impressed by titles. But not that impressed! I was determined not to join this particular hunting club, much as I was smitten. So I went to Val and Helen's supper with my armour on. No one else was there except Val, Helen and Danny. The evening was uneventful, save that Helen gave me a talking-to for being unkind to Danny — apparently he had a 'tremendous crush' on me. Helen was a romantic as well as a matchmaker, but I certainly had not been unkind to Danny; how could I be? So we ended up the evening with a first kiss in the hallway as I left by taxi and Danny stayed on — it was still early and he loved to talk.

As Danny was being fêted all over town, we did not see each other often. Then I started a film — Lewis Gilbert's *Once A Sinner*, in which I played my first serious dramatic role, as a woman driven to suicide — and Mother and I had to stay out of town where the studios were, so it was all difficult and fraught. We had phone calls and a few verbal fights, but sightings were rare and he was always accompanied by managers, agents, pianists and so on. His manager was formidable and guarded Danny like a Rottweiler — indeed Danny seemed to be scared of him, and in one of his telephone calls revealed that his manager had warned him, saying that he was getting too fond of me.

'Are you?' I asked. He assured me this was an understatement.

Ted Ray, who was also at the Palladium, asked what he thought of Danny and what was he like. He replied, 'I don't know, all he talks about is Pat Kirkwood.' I was delighted.

We did manage to have one date on our own, at the Nightingale Club in Berkeley Square, after his show. When I arrived Danny was sitting down, for once, and we sat and looked at each other for a while. Then we danced — not at arm's length — but were interrupted by some male twit who asked, 'Are you Danny Kaye?'

'Yes,' snapped Danny.

'And are you Pat Kirkwood?' he continued.

'Yes,' I sighed, wishing him at the North Pole. We carried on dancing, oblivious to the stares then sat down a while. We did not talk much. I do not remember what he said. We left soon after and took a taxi to my flat, which was in Burton Court. Mother was there, of course, probably in bed by then. We kissed beautifully, for a long time it seemed, on the landing outside, then Danny left and I floated into the flat.

'Is that you?' Mother called out.

'I think so,' I managed to say.

We had a few more meetings with the ogreish manager always present, and we still spoke on the telephone, but we never had another date alone. This was just as well, as I was informed by a friend that Danny was still married, though separated. So we never succeeded in getting together, but instead became good friends and stayed so for over twenty years. Whenever Danny arrived in England my agent, who also represented Danny over here, told me the first question he always asked was, 'How's Pat?' On one of his visits Danny asked me to be hostess for him at a tea party for the press at the Savoy, which I was pleased to do. I always saw him, briefly, when he came to England after long intervals; once he would not open the door to me before he asked 'Have you gone fat?'

'Of course not,' I laughed. We were free of our mutual crushes and enjoyed much gossip and laughter about our work and the people in the theatre profession. Altogether a happy and squeaky-clean relationship. Helen Parnell was disgusted: no match this time.

On Danny's last night at the Palladium he invited me to his end-of-run party on the stage after the show. *Starlight Roof* finished earlier, so I was able to slip over just in time to see the last half-hour of his performance from the wings. He had been onstage for 1½ hours and it was almost time for the curtain to come down, but the audience would not allow it and nor would Danny. He stopped once and asked them 'How will you get home?' (public transport was still not properly organized since the war and buses and trains finished early). The audience replied in a body shouting, 'We'll walk home.' The audience went mad. It was pandemonium. What had been so wonderful was how silent, almost reverent, they had been when he sang or talked to them. How they loved him. The curtain came down and I helped Danny to his dressing-room. He was all in. 'Go to the party, darling,' he gasped. 'I'll join you all in a few minutes.'

The Palladium stage was awash with guests, mostly VIPs and theatre stars. A fabulous feast was spread on trestle tables onstage and bottles of champagne stood like an army of soldiers waiting for a command. They did not have long to wait. Val and Helen came over to me and introduced me to various people: Sharman Douglas and her brother, whose father was Lewis W. Douglas, the American Ambassador to the UK: the Marquis of Milford-Haven; David Metcalfe, the son of 'Fruity' Metcalfe, the Duke of Windsor's great friend for many years. Milford-Haven was a most charming and amusing man and we were on the same wavelength at once, talking like mad. David Metcalfe was a long, lean chap with a stammer, which did not interfere with his complete confidence and unique personality; he was not handsome at all but had an endearing little boy's face and manner, together with an aura of innocence which was most appealing. He never stopped talking, putting over his personality firmly and amusingly. I was beginning to enjoy myself when Danny entered, as fresh as a daisy, but immediately surrounded by admirers who formed a thorn hedge round him and were obviously there to stay. As we began to move off, Danny saw me and came over. We had a hug and a kiss and went our different ways, Danny saying quietly, 'I shall miss you'. When I turned the radio on the next morning I heard him singing, 'I never knew I could miss anybody, honey, like I'm missing you.' It was recorded at Heathrow and I knew it was for me.

When we left the Palladium party the night before, David Milford-Haven hailed a taxi and he and I went to the Milroy to have some supper. We did not dance, just talked, and then he saw me home. As he stood on the steps of the block of flats, he asked me if I would like to have dinner with him one night. Yes, I would, so he took my telephone number — writing it on his shirt cuff, which I found hilarious — and left. I liked him. He was nice.

The other David had somehow disappeared, and I wondered if he had got himself home all right. He had. In a few days he popped back with a vengeance and I was swept out to lunch, tea, dinner, the Café de Paris and the Four Hundred Club, without time to draw breath. He rang me almost every day, and I was breathless, mostly with laughter, as he really was a natural comedian. He didn't try to be funny, but he was so completely himself that he did not realize how unusual and unconventional his behaviour was; especially when he was angry with something, for his stammer became highly charged and clear. He was always hard-up, he said, so how he could afford to squire me round all these establishments I cannot imagine, but he was great fun and I grew very fond of him — though he was seven years younger than I. He was a sort of baby brother to me, and I enjoyed his company enormously. We went to the Dorchester one afternoon for tea and when he was given the bill he rose to his six foot four inches, towering above the waiter and pronounced that this was 'a

234

d-d-d-disgrace', that he 'w-w-w-would not p-p-pay' and that the 'D-D-D-Dorchester had s-s-s-seen the l-l-l-last of him'. All this at full volume and accompanied by two long waving arms. The tea lounge was full and the customers seemed delighted, seeming to treat David's fury as a novel form of cabaret. No one laughed, as David was so obviously in earnest and, as usual, had not noticed any other people in the place besides ourselves. We just walked out.

Suddenly David Milford-Haven turned up again with a telephone call. This was some time after he had asked me to come to dinner with him 'some day', so I had written him off really and, in any case, I was taken up ferociously by the other David. David M-H explained that he had sent his shirt to the laundry with my telephone number still on the cuff and had had quite a struggle to find it again. He was rather absent-minded. So we went out to dinner at Larues, a very popular and celebrated restaurant. We had a quiet, chatty and pleasant evening and it struck me that he needed looking after; he was such a gentle and rather vague chap — very different from David M. As we were leaving the restaurant I noticed that he had a large hole in his sock, which endeared him to me. I told David M about our date and he was apoplectic about it, saying some catty things about his namesake and making sure that I did not have time to repeat my 'disloyalty'! All this gadding-about was new to me and although I enjoyed it for a while I was glad to resume the more disciplined life of the theatre.

13

Noel Coward

Something miraculous happened. I met the man I was eventually to marry, despite being determined never to make the same mistake after my first disastrous experience. I had met him some years before, in 1942, when John and I lived in the Selsdon Park Hotel near Croydon. John used to play golf with him often and told me what a marvellous man he was, how kind and what a nice sense of humour he had. I, however, had taken a dislike to this paragon and said to John, 'I don't know how you can bear to play golf with such a conceited arrogant man. Who does he think he is?' Now, six years later, there he was sitting in the stalls with a dark-haired, tanned lady. He told me some considerable time later that when I saw him I gave him a look which said, in effect, 'Why are you sitting there?' This shocked me, as I would never have dreamed of making faces onstage, no matter who was in the audience. But apparently I did. The next day he rang me at the theatre and asked me if I would have dinner with him. I was going to say, 'Thanks, but no thanks.' Then I suddenly changed my mind and thought, Yes, I will have dinner with him, just to find out why other people liked him so much and also to bring him down a peg or two.

After the show he picked me up at the stage door in a battered old baby Austin and we went to dinner. I must admit he was very good-looking, tall and slim with a small well-set head, with dark hair and a slightly tanned complexion, from all the golf he played. More importantly I discovered a gentle, humorous and sensitive human being who listened well and did not talk about himself all the time, but when he did, was interesting and modest. He also had a lovely melting smile and good teeth. I was amazed and impressed. We went out together a few times and I began to look forward to these occasions more and more. One evening I came out of the stage door to see, not the old baby Austin, but an enormous and elegant car with a wine-coloured silk roof. 'What is this?' I wanted to know. 'Is it yours?' thinking he had borrowed it. It was. It was a Porsche, a German car, but it was spelt with an 'H' not a 'P'. Why was that? He explained that during the war Hitler had all the Porsches reinitialled, and used some of them for his propaganda circuses. He told me it was his mistress. I asked him why he had used the Austin on two or three occasions instead of the Porsche (Horsche). He said that he was testing me to see if I would deign to travel in a knocked-out old Austin.

He had been a ship-owner but had retired early after Marshal Tito of Yugoslavia had confiscated all his ships. He had gained — and then lost — a fortune and was still only forty-four. He had been born and brought up in the Ukraine, where his father was the Greek

Vice-Consul in Berdyansk. When he was eleven and a cadet in the Tsar's army, he was taken from his family and thrown into a Bolshevik jail with the resident rats for company. The story of his escape and how he reached his family after many miles on foot came to light over the years we were together and then only spasmodically, as he did not want to talk about it. It would have made a fine book, however, especially as he found his family only just in time to catch the last boat out of Russia before a long trek through Europe and eventually to Britain. His mother, travelling with her two sons and two daughters, had sewn her jewellery into a toy teddy-bear and managed to keep it from harm; she was a heroic and admirable Yorkshirewoman.

My hero's name was Spiro de Spero Gabriele but I called him 'Sparky'. After we had known each other for six months he asked me to marry him. I pointed out that I was still legally married to John, even though we had been separated for five years. I was not aware that a new law had come in to the effect that after that length of separation a divorce was granted automatically. I knew nothing of the law or of lawyers, never having needed to know. We had an extremely long engagement, four years in fact! John had heard about Sparky and me and announced to a theatre colleague, 'She will die my wife.' This was during the pantomime *Humpty Dumpty* at London Casino, in which I played Little Tommy Tucker with Julie Andrews in the title role. Carole Lynne, the principal girl, was most sympathetic and supportive as she knew what was happening — I did not tell her but she knew.

Sparky decided that enough was enough and at the end of the pantomime whisked me off to Cannes for a holiday. I was so thrilled with the French Riviera, which I had never seen before, only having left England once when I went to the United States. It was early spring and the sunshine and beauty was a godsend for me. We went everywhere. I recall visiting a casino one night to have dinner and dance, whilst a glorious firework display outside on the terrace lit up the sky with colour. We were happy — the fireworks expressed exactly how we felt. Edwina Mountbatten was also there and as we danced she gave me a roguish grin and asked, 'Did you manage to arrive at the Hippodrome in time for the show, or did you get into trouble?'

'I got into trouble,' I replied.

'I thought you would,' she laughed. She was a delightful person.

When we returned to London I had the offer of two shows: one was written by Eric Maschwitz and called *Belinda Fair*; I went to hear the music and it was superb. The other show was called *Hat in the Air* and the idea was that Bobby Howes and I would star together in it. My agent and Jack Waller, who planned to present it, were most enthusiastic about Bobby and I being together again, as we had been such a good team in two shows before, *Lady Behave* (1942) and *Let's Face It* (1943). The latter was at the London Hippodrome, an American import with a Cole Porter score in which I introduced the song 'Just One of Those Things' to London and it was a great success. When I read the script of *Hat in the Air* I did not find it inspiring. Bernard Delfont, who finally presented the show in the West End, was also keen that Bobby and I should work together again. In spite of my doubts I accepted.

Rehearsals for *Hat in the Air* — as it was called initially — began. The songs were good, with excellent lyrics and melodious music. Bobby was unhappy, being his usual perfectionist self, as he thought the script was dire. He was right. We seemed to be on tour forever; almost every night a new bit of script was handed to us which got worse and worse.

Finally we readied ourselves for the opening night at the Saville Theatre, London. We had acquired a new title, *Roundabout*, which included a magnificent circus scene with a great dancer, Marilyn Hightower. None of us had remembered the well-established theatre suspicion that a circus scene in any show spelt total disaster. At this time, in the West End, there existed a 'claque' or gang who had taken to booing and cat-calling during musical shows, causing great distress to the artists. The management had warned us they were in front. 'Just press on,' they said. As the curtain went up on the first night, we were all determined that this was going to be a success in spite of the poor script, or, rather because of all the work we had put into it. There was a great feeling of hope and joy and the atmosphere was electric, which communicated itself to the audience and — Hallelujah! — they were with us all the way, the first half going tremendously well. During the interval the 'claque' in the gallery sent a note to the stage manager saying, 'We are enjoying the show but could Bobby Howes speak up.' Bobby of all people — who always had a clear strong voice. Bobby was furious. Up went the curtain again and the fabulous circus scene began, with Marilyn Hightower dancing beautifully amid the bright colours shimmering in the lights of the circus ring. It was really splendid and received an ovation. All was well again. A new song for me came just before the finale. Would I manage to remember all those lyrics after so little rehearsal? I did, the laughs came just where they should and, at the end, the applause was tremendous, to my heartfelt relief. I moved to the side of the stage, where Bessie was watching. I knew she had been nervous for me, but now her face was alight. I tried to get past her to the quick-change room for the finale, but she stood firm, with happy tears running down her plump, pink face. 'You've done it,' she cried and pushed me back onstage — and when Bessie pushed there was no argument! I had not noticed that the applause was still going, because I was so relieved that it was over, but now I realized that I had stopped the show solid and the encores and bravos were for me. What a joy. Then a quick change and we were onstage for the finale, all of us dancing round the circus ring in pairs. The audience went wild; we were all laughing or crying with relief and happiness that we had won through. It was a glorious moment.

Bobby stepped forward and the audience

quietened to hear his speech. Then disaster struck. 'We are glad you enjoyed the show, Ladies and Gentlemen,' Bobby began. 'Of course, we don't take any notice of you lot up there,' he said, waving his arms contemptuously at the gallery. 'It's the people down here that matter,' he said, indicating the stalls. 'They're the important ones.' All hell broke loose; the claque in the gallery sounded like a herd of stampeding wild animals ready for the kill. Then the stalls took up the challenge; someone threw his coat at another chap and the whole of the stalls began a tirade of insults and threats to the gallery. It was bedlam. Then Bobby began to shout back at the gallery. I wanted to pull him back so that the curtain could fall, but he was too far beyond the curtain-fall line and if the curtain had been brought down behind him he would have been completely isolated. Also he could have fallen into the orchestra pit. He was in a dangerous position. Another problem was that Bobby was in no mood to be pulled back; his Irish dander was up and he gave as good as he got. The company was devastated, however, as they saw our show, finally a success after so many problems, simply melt away like a beautiful ice-cream palace. Then Bobby shouted to the gallery, 'And it's my birthday.' It was all so sad — our dear Bobby, so talented, so witty, so lovable, standing there committing professional suicide. The announcement drew renewed hoots and sardonic laughter from the detestable gang and then luckily, he stepped back a little, just enough to allow the curtain to come down at last. A great star had been dimmed. It was a tragedy.

The press, next day, hardly mentioned the show, concentrating instead on the fracas; no one had ever seen anything like it in the theatre, and hopefully never would again. Why did Bobby do it when the show had been such a success? Mother had been sitting behind Sally Ann Howes, Bobby's beautiful young daughter, who, during the horror, had been clutching her evening bag, desperately murmuring, 'Daddy don't; Daddy don't,' in her agony, half rising in her seat.

The greatest danger faced by a star is to become too sure of one's public and too certain that stardom will last forever. The 'number one' spotlight will shine down forever, whilst one stands centre stage accepting the constant ovations with a dignified nod of the head. The succinct 'Don't give up the day job' is sound advice for actors, but it means much more than it says. It means keep your feet on the ground, or, at least, one foot — and also make sure the exit door opens. *Roundabout* ran for just three weeks. A terribly sad experience for all concerned.

Sparky and I decided to see a show to cheer us up and we chose *Maid to Measure*, which had just opened to good reviews. I wanted to see Jessie Matthews, whom I had admired for so long but never seen on stage. In the interval the front-of-house manager came to where we were sitting; he seemed agitated and we learned that Mother had rung the theatre and asked him to deliver a message to me that I must come home at once as something had happened. I was imagining all sorts of things. We found a taxi and arrived home in an anxious state. Mother, however, greeted us with a smiling face, almost laughing. There had been a telephone call which she had answered and a voice at the end of the line said, 'I would like to speak to Miss Kirkwood.' Mother asked for his name and the voice replied, 'Noël Coward.'

Mother replied, 'Don't be ridiculous,' and put the phone down!

The caller rang again, this time chuckling loudly: 'This really is Noël Coward speaking,' he insisted, then went on to say that he was writing a new show and would like me to be in it; would Mother and I meet him at his home in Gerald Road to hear the score? I was stunned: it seemed too good to be true after being in the *Roundabout* doldrums.

We arrived at Noël's home and were shown into a large drawing-room with a platform at one end on which stood a grand piano. Noël was standing in the centre of the room facing the door through which we entered. He did not come forward but stood, unsmiling, and looked at me seriously. 'Get that hair cut, you look like the MGM lion,' were Noël's first words to me. Then he stepped forward, pushed all the hair off my face and, grabbing it at the back, remarked 'There's nothing wrong with that face — show it!'

'Yes, Sir,' I replied, though I was laughing my head off, as his expression belied the sternness of his words. He then leapt up on to the stage and announced that he would play the score — the music and songs — of his show *Ace of Clubs*. Oh dear, a black card, I thought: I had become quite superstitious after *Roundabout* with its circus scene. Noël played the songs pointing out which would be mine and which Graham Payn's and Sylvia Cecil's. Graham and I would be co-starring. I worked with Sylvia years before in the summer show at Barrfields Pavilion at Largs on the west coast of Scotland, and had been much in awe of her as a sixteen- or seventeen-year-old. She had a formidable reputation as a diva *par excellence* as well as being a most handsome woman with Titian hair and a creamy skin. All looked very hopeful as we settled down to hear the score played by the Master himself.

To my surprise some of the songs did not seem up to Noël's standard. I was disappointed with my own songs. The first one, 'My Kind of Man', seemed well below par. However, there was a sweet and romantic duet with Graham called 'This Could be True'. My next song was called 'Josephine', a skit on Napoleon and his mistress, but the lyrics did not contain the master's usual wit. In the second half I would be singing 'Why Does Love Get in the Way?', a sad little complaint which did not carry much weight. Finally, there was one called 'Chase Me, Charlie', a delightfully bouncy song about an alley cat. It was charming and ingenuous but not a 'show-stopper' nor strong enough for the end of the show. What was I to say? I was disappointed and amazed that Noël had not seen the weakness of the songs he had given the character Pinkie Leroy, the name of my part. Pinkie Leroy was a singer in a third-rate night club and, surely, one or two more robust songs would have been suitable for the character and setting of the club.

I rang my agent and told him I had been offered the female lead part in Noël Coward's new musical play *Ace of Clubs*. He advised me not to take it. 'It will be a flop,' he prophesied. 'It's already been turned down by Val Parnell and Emile Littler.' What to do?

I rang Val and asked what he thought. 'Don't do it,' he said. 'It will flop.' Oh dear! I did so want to work in a Noël Coward show.

Noël had told me had written it for me and I had replied 'You're fibbing' and he had laughed. I could not think of anything more wonderful, but could I stand another flop so soon? I rang my agent again. 'I am accepting *Ace of Clubs*. If it is a flop, I would rather be in a flop by Noël Coward than a success by anyone else!' Little was I to know that these words would be recorded in Noël's diaries and be recounted in a revue, *Noël/Cole — Let's Do it*, at Chichester Festival Theatre over forty years later.

Rehearsals went like a dream. What a joy it was to work with Noël, the first time I had ever had a director in his class, and the best of it all was that he always allowed me to produce my songs on my own before he gave final approval. This was how I had always worked in variety when doing a single act, and I appreciated the freedom it gave me to give the songs my own interpretation. To my delight, he always gave his approval, sitting in the stalls and saying, 'Keep it like that, Patreeecia' — his nickname for me. He especially liked my rendition of 'Chase Me, Charlie' and when I had finished, he leapt onstage and said excitedly, 'That is exactly right. Now, do not make any alterations until you have asked me, but in the meantime it stays at it is.' It was such a wonderful experience to work with one who knew exactly what the theatre was all about and how everything should be done. However, there was a side to Noël that was quite awesome. For any artist who did not meet his standards of dedication to their work, who was late for rehearsals or showed signs of arrogance or argued with his decisions, he revealed a soul-searing rage. Poor Sylvia came in for this experience. As I was sitting further back than Noël in the stalls, alone, Sylvia approached Noël and said something to him, which I could not hear, but Noël exploded and I thought it best to escape quietly, not wishing to see her humiliation — she was transfixed with horror. What on earth had she done to deserve this? Later, I learned from the pianist, who had been in the wings, that Sylvia had asked to be given equal star billing with myself and Graham. What he said to her was enough to make her retire for ever. Our pianist, Robb Stewart, himself a talented composer, who often worked with Noël on shows, comforted Sylvia as she left in tears. He was a kind and compassionate person and to cheer her up he said, 'Don't worry, dear, it doesn't mean a thing. Just let it go in one ear and out the other.' It was the lunch hour and what they did not know was that Noël was walking behind them and heard every word. Fortunately, this made Noël laugh to himself, as what he had been trying to do was 'to wake Sylvia up' to the part she was playing, as he thought she was being too lady-like; her part was that of a tough sleazy night-club owner past her best. Noël later related all this to me with a chuckle, saying, 'So all my efforts to sting Sylvia into giving a performance were thrown away!' I learned that Noel's rages, when directed at an artist, were meant to help their performance and, indeed, the play, but I sincerely hoped that I would never be on the receiving end of one of them. The billing stayed put.

The curtain went up on the dress rehearsal. It all seemed to go splendidly and rattled along with tremendous pace and enthusiasm. In one number I was dressed in Empire fashion as Josephine, but before I made my entrance the very young June Whitfield, who was playing one of my handmaidens, had one line to speak the moment before I made my entrance. The line was, 'Hist, she approaches,' spoken by June in a shrill Cockney accent. This one line got the biggest laugh in the show, and on the first night I had to wait before I could start my song. From then on, I waited for June's laugh to die down before leaving the wings. Even in those days June's timing was immaculate.

When the curtain came down, Noël was white-faced and obviously displeased about something or someone but it was not the artists, who had all been dismissed, except for Graham and I who were cooling off, sitting onstage at one of the 'night-club' tables. Suddenly our musical director, Mantovani, appeared onstage from the orchestra pit. Noël turned on him furiously: 'That was not my music,' he hissed. 'That was piddling on flannel.' This was just the beginning! Mantovani's face was a tragic mask. Graham and I wanted to creep offstage but we dared not move; we were trapped and forced to witness Mantovani's humiliation. It was dreadfully sad, I thought. Perhaps Noël's mother had said something derogatory about the music; she had not come onstage to be introduced to anyone. Whatever it was, Noël was furious and so was Mantovani. It was a pity as the show had gone so well. Graham and I, at last, managed to creep away.

I had never before had the experience of a musical play like *Ace of Clubs*, with many acting scenes. The only lines I had spoken had been in pantomime and musical shows, where they acted simply as a bridge between songs. I was concerned because I seemed to be standing for a long time doing nothing. One day, at rehearsals, I interrupted the verbal flow, excusing myself of course, and into the darkness of the auditorium spoke thus: 'Noël, do you realize I have nothing to do here for ages except just stand still?' Noël's reply floated back. 'Don't worry, darling, we are having a little white wheelbarrow made that you can wheel up and down, up and down!' — putting me firmly in my place. I was learning one of the principles of acting, to be able to listen without thinking of one's next line. It was important to be able to say and do nothing at all, but be still and realize that repose is a powerful quality that can focus the audience's attention on the actor using it, just by the fact of doing nothing while everyone else is acting their heads off. Some artists are gifted with this quality. Evelyn Laye had always possessed it. Patricia Hodge is another with a natural repose. If one does not possess this ability it is most difficult to learn, but not impossible. It seemed to me that if one could learn to listen then one would automatically acquire repose. One can't listen and walk about or fidget at the same time. Noël's wisdom taught me this crucial lesson.

Another amusing incident occurred when Graham and I were rehearsing our song 'This Could be True'. We had not been expecting to rehearse the number on this particular day and I was wearing a straight skirt so that, when we came to our waltz, I was unable to lift my legs more than two inches from the floor. The result was disaster. When we had stopped there was an ominous silence from the stalls. 'Er, Noël,' I began cautiously, 'I'm sorry, but I am wearing the wrong skirt. You see, I didn't know I was going to dance today.'

A voice drifted out of the blackness: 'Neither did I — and I was right!'

We opened at the Palace, Manchester. From the beginning the show went wonderfully, and the audience loved it. Graham stopped the show with 'I Like America'; then Sylvia did the same

250

with 'Evening in Summer'. The comedy number, 'Three Juvenile Delinquents', also went over well. The audience was hostile towards me, which I had felt from curtain up, and not one of my songs, not even 'Chase Me, Charlie' received anything like the applause of the others. What was it all about? I wondered. Then I remembered that this had happened to me on other occasions in Manchester. I had been under the illusion that one's home town — and Manchester was mine — would welcome in triumph someone from their own place. Not so, as I had learned before. The North has a long-standing and invincible dislike of the South, especially London, so that if a native Northerner escapes to work there and, even worse, makes a success and stays there, they are automatically branded as traitors.

The curtain came down to an ovation, and the show was a great success. Noël literally bounced into my dressing-room, beaming and happy. I was not so happy. 'Oh Noël,' I wailed, 'I was the only one who didn't stop the show; they didn't like me!'

'Oh yes, you had to fight them every inch of the way,' he agreed. 'But rise above it!' We all trooped out to a celebration supper given by Tom Arnold, our management, who having more faith than the others, had mounted the production. After a splendid supper at the Midland Hotel, he made a victory speech. 'Well, we seem to have a hit on our hands,' he grinned happily and went on to congratulate us. But I was not happy and when Mother and I retired to our suite, I burst into tears and cried inconsolably. Mother tried to cheer me up, but it was no use and finally she went to bed and I tossed and turned until nearly dawn.

I was woken by Mother shaking me; it was nine o'clock in the morning. She had all the newspapers under her arm. 'Get up, get up, and read these reviews. They're wonderful, especially for you.' They were beyond my dreams and managed to console me for the less-than-warm reception I had had the night before. That night the show went splendidly again and this time the audience was all for me — and my songs. No one stopped the show though! There was a permanent notice on the reception desk at the Midland Hotel saying, 'Sorry, no tickets for *Ace of Clubs*!' We were sold out throughout our three weeks there. One incident stays in my memory. It was after the first night when Noël, Graham, Sylvia and I entered the dining-room at the hotel. It was packed and everyone there rose to their feet and applauded. It was most moving and thrilling.

We left Manchester to open at the Royal Court Theatre, Liverpool, and again the audience was in raptures; the reviews were enthusiastic and we all felt quite blasé about it! The next hurdle was Birmingham, which was our last week on tour, and here we met a brick wall. The audience was hostile and the reviews less than ecstatic. What a shock after our triumphs in Manchester and Liverpool. It was a bad omen, as Birmingham was close to London; perhaps our previous success had been too much and Birmingham decided to give us a lesson. But the week passed, as all weeks do, and at last we were London-bound.

We opened at the Cambridge Theatre, not one famed for its popularity, but we were all in good spirits and full of hope. All went well, though the audience was slightly cooler than Manchester. Frank Sinatra and Ava Gardner were in front which was quite a thrill. The interval came, and suddenly there was chaos in the auditorium. Sinatra and Gardner had been on their way to the bar when a press photographer, perhaps more than one by the noise, had tried to photograph them with flash cameras. Sinatra had punched him in the face, grabbed his camera and smashed it. Good old pandemonium once more reigned. The stalls did not like this one bit, especially Sinatra's choice of language, which rang through the theatre. The photographer was removed and Sinatra and Gardner left, by request. The curtain went up on a slightly miffed audience but they soon settled and the second half went well, my 'Chase Me, Charlie' having a great reception, as did all the other numbers; the whole company was working tremendously well. The curtain came down to a storm of applause, and there were cries of 'Author', 'Author'. Noël stepped on stage and then the gallery let him have it: boos, whistles, hisses, the lot, chaos. Noël stood there, white-faced, unable to speak for the dreadful noise, but stood his ground and did not move — just waited. It seemed like forever, but eventually the tumult died down out of exhaustion and the realization that Noël was not going to give way. He was like a statue. Then he beckoned me forward, then Sylvia Cecil, as if nothing at all had happened and made the speech he would have made anyway. The curtain fell to more boos and whistles. The press next day, of course, concentrated on the Sinatra incident and the heckling of the galleryites, almost ignoring the show. Backstage all was silent, but we gathered ourselves together to attend the first-night party at the Dorchester, which Tom Arnold was hosting. Instead of being the triumphant first night we had all expected, it was more like a wake. Everyone in the theatre seemed to be at this enormous party, and Noël's face was a study of misery. After our enormous success on tour and the fabulous notices we had had — one of which said *Ace of Clubs* was the greatest musical since *Oklahoma* — it was a dreadful shock to be heckled, especially as it was directed most venomously towards Noël.

The show staggered on for six months or so. One night was brightened by the presence of Marlene Dietrich, Michael Wilding and Clifton Webb in the audience. Noël brought them all to my dressing-room and I was thrilled, not having met Dietrich before. Michael said he had loved the show; Clifton smiled charmingly, but Dietrich said not a word, never taking her eyes off the dressing-table mirror while tugging and straightening the jacket of her suit and checking her make-up.

The next day Noël called a rehearsal and gave us all a telling-off. We had experienced these before, but I had always been excluded from criticism — nice for me but also worrying as I

254

began to feel like a teacher's favourite and would be heartily disliked soon. This time, however I was given a dressing-down as well, Noël saying that I was 'over the top' and 'overdid' everything. I collapsed like a deflated balloon and some struggled to hide their grins. By now I had discovered the reason for the unfriendliness of some of the cast towards me — the happy relationship that Noël and I shared, which caused some jealousy. How stupid; it did not harm anyone; it was simply that I liked Noël and he liked me and we shared a similar sense of humour. I had never encountered this sort of attitude before, as musicals are generally full of happy people who work too hard to develop neuroses.

A notice went up on Christmas Eve informing us that the show was closing — what a present!

Happier memories of the show, of course, I had in abundance. Val and Helen Parnell brought Jack Benny round to see me back-stage after one performance. He was so relaxed and pleasant and told so many hilarious stories that we were all in fits of laughter. He was so at home he might have been living in my dressing-room for years. Time went quickly and Helen kept urging Val to come home and have his supper. 'Daddy,' — as she always called him — 'it's late and you've had nothing to eat.' 'Daddy' stayed put and Jack Benny continued his brilliant and intriguing stories. Finally we all left the theatre at half-past one in the morning.

Getting to know Noël Coward was an exhilarating experience. The first thing that struck me was the vitality that surged from him effortlessly; then the voice, rather low-pitched and extremely attractive — a young voice, almost boyish, as indeed was his personality, especially if he was caught off-guard, alone. Then, his eyes appeared large, almost childlike, and very blue; but this only happened if he was surprised suddenly. It was a revelation and in complete contrast to his typically sophisticated, slightly cynical expression, which, I believe, was a protection against the world and his own vulnerability. Yes, he was a terror when his own standards were not reached, but that was because he was a dedicated perfectionist; such people will always suffer; but he was also compassionate and sensitive to other people's troubles.

Noël, on occasion, could be very cruel, too. I once had a set-to with him over my dresses. He said, 'Your clothes have been a byword of horror for years.'

I looked down at Noël from the stage and said coolly, 'Speaking of clothes, have you not heard that striped shirts are out of fashion? All you need is a straw hat and a banjo.'

Next day I was in my dressing-room when there was a gentle knock on the door and a familiar voice murmured, 'Patreeecia.' I was inclined to say, 'Go away,' but instead I said, 'Come in.'

It was Noël, of course, beaming innocently, with two enormous bunches of violets in his hand. Over the top of them he grinned and said, 'I meant every word.' I melted and we were OK again. I was sad and shocked that Noël, of all people, whom I adored, should attack me this way. How surprised he would have been when, some years later, the Victoria & Albert Museum were asking me for my stage clothes from the forties. Alas, I had already given them to Bingley Little Theatre in Yorkshire.

I also remember one evening, when Noël and some members of the cast were invited to a party by the parents of an aspiring young actress, hoping, perhaps, to advance their daughter's career on the stage. During the evening she was encouraged by some of the younger members of the cast to do her impersonations. Noël was not amused. At the conclusion, his hostess asked him if he would play something for them. He sat down at the piano and sang extremely loudly, 'Don't put your daughter on the stage, Mrs Worthington!' This was many years ago, and today the lady in question has had many successes, is wonderfully well known — and very well liked — especially by me. If she should read this and remember the incident, I hope she will think kindly of me for not mentioning her name.

I have kept two souvenirs from *Ace of Clubs*, which I treasure. One of them was handed to me by Coley (Cole Lesley) one day as I entered the stage door. It was a colourful painting, about eight by six inches, of Napoleon without a hat, in a black frame. On the picture, written boldly in what looked like black paint, were the words, 'To Baby from Boney'. I knew, or thought I did, who had sent this to me, as I was singing the song 'Josephine' in the show. 'Was it Noël who sent

me this?' I asked Coley. He just 'twinkled' at me
— Coley would never have winked — and
walked into the theatre. The other souvenir was
not something to see but something to
remember. It was one evening after the show in
Manchester and Noël, Graham, Coley and I
were having our supper at the Midland. We were
all chatting away when Noël suddenly looked
very serious, so we all stopped talking. Turning
to me, Noël said, 'Patreeecia, whenever you walk
onstage you light up the theatre; I consider you
an important personality and you will be
working for me for the next ten years.' I was so
touched I had to leave the dining-room; but I
remembered to write down everything Noël said
to me so I could keep it always and not forget a
word. What an infinite variety of thoughts lay in
that slim head.

An amusing example of how his mind worked
was in his game of Russian Roulette — as I came
to think of it — with 'Sparky'. When I told Noël
about Sparky's unusual background — how he
had been born in Ukraine; been a cadet in the
Tsar's army until the Bolshevik Revolution,
when he was thrown into jail; had subsequently
made his escape and finally arrived in Britain
after many hardships — I could see from the
expression on Noel's face that he was suspicious
of all this, thinking that Sparky had made it up
and that he was a *poseur*. One evening after the
show, Noël arrived in my dressing-room with a
beautiful woman whom he introduced as Mrs
Wilson, the wife of a very successful producer in
New York. She was a true blue 100 per cent

Russian princess, and I hazarded a guess that Noël was putting Sparky to the test to see if he really had been born and bred in Russia. The princess was introduced to Sparky and she immediately started to speak to him rapidly in her native tongue. Sparky, of course, responded immediately with equal fluency in the same language and the two of them rattled on for some time. Noël's face was full of shocked surprise. Yah-boo! I thought, as Noël quickly reminded the Russian princess that they had a supper date with her husband. As they reached the door the princess looked back sadly at Sparky and said, 'There aren't many of us left, are there?' Noël was impressed but deflated — which was good for him. To know Noël was to love him, but one had to know him first. He used his many talents to the full; his work was his life, and we should all be thankful for his utter dedication to the theatre. He will never be replaced.

14

Sparky

I decided I should do a long variety tour, as I had not done one for some time and I wanted and needed the stimulus and challenge of touring with my single act. I needed to rediscover that sense of 'attack' with a variety audience in the large theatres such as the Birmingham Hippodrome, Liverpool Empire and Glasgow Empire. I needed to shake off the glamour of the West End and get down to brass tacks again. This was my own ground and I was never happier than when I was alone onstage singing — the larger the theatre the better. Space and light and warmth and those wonderful people out there in the dark. I was booked to play the Coventry Hippodrome, but failed to appear on the opening night. I was given permission for this absence in order to fulfil an appointment with Her Majesty the Queen at the London Palladium for a command performance.

Then it was back to London and a show called *Fancy Free* with Tommy Trinder at the Prince of Wales. I had previously been booked to play in cabaret at the Colony restaurant and the Astor Club. I rang my agent to ask if he could postpone the cabaret dates, as I had to do fourteen performances of *Fancy Free* a week and could not possibly do an hour's cabaret at the

Colony and half an hour at the Astor Club after the evening show. The cabaret could not be postponed, it seemed, so during the opening week of *Fancy Free* at Birmingham I was rehearsing new numbers for the cabaret as well as the show.

We opened at the Prince of Wales, but something was wrong. Tommy was in trouble. First, he was highly nervous and tightened up — unusual for him — and second, the audience failed to respond to his jokes. This was serious. The rest of the show went with a swing, but I was not comfortable with my choice of songs which I had not had much time to perfect given my hectic schedule. But the audience was kind and seemed to like them and my act went well.

Fancy Free was a revue and we had an excellent dancing duo from Canada who went down a storm. We reached the finale. Tommy stepped forward to make a speech, which had not been called for, and I wished he had not done it. Two or three in the gallery were noisy. 'Not as easy as Brighton, Tommy,' one of them yelled. Tommy had to step back and eat humble pie, which was not his favourite dish. So ended the first night. We plodded on, but things did not improve. Tommy was angry at not getting the laughs, so he turned nasty with the cast, including me. After each performance he would insist on making a long speech, which became longer every night. He turned round to the rest of the cast once and waved his arms, saying to the audience, 'We don't need this lot do we? They might as well go home.' So I walked offstage. To my surprise and delight all but three of the cast followed me, including our dancing ladies, making a noisy exit down the scenery steps. I was given a wigging — nicely — from the manager for leaving the stage, but I could see he approved of what I had done, even though I had contravened stage etiquette. I also knew, however, that Trinder was not entitled to insult his colleagues and his co-star, which was me, as he had done. These interminable speeches bored the audience, there were no laughs and the girl dancers complained to me that they were missing their transport home after the show. So I did not regret what I had done, only that I had not done it sooner. Tommy was becoming unbearable to work with, rude and insulting and altogether nasty. This was a new experience for me and not one I wished to repeat.

The climax came one evening when a member of the cast suggested that I told a mildly funny story to Tommy when we had our duet in the first act. 'Might cheer him up,' suggested my chum. So I did. It was a silly little story but rather cute and jolly. The worst thing happened; I had a big laugh from the audience. Tommy did not laugh — he was apoplectic with rage and scowled at me for the rest of our duo spot. It was early in the show, so I thought he might simmer down later. The result was that when we came to the finale, instead of plunging into his speech marathon, he announced to the audience, 'Well, we have a new comic in the show.' He pulled me forward. 'So you want to be funny, eh? Go on, be funny.' He then left the stage, went down the side steps and sat in the stalls with his arms folded — there was plenty of room for him anyway, as there was practically no one in them.

I did not know what to do. I smiled at the house and walked forward a little. What could I do? Tell a funny story? No, no, not that. Do my 'Charlie Chaplin' walk? No, worse. A blinding flash of inspiration came to me in the form of a speech that dear Bobby Howes used to make on first nights. I took a deep breath. 'Ladies and Gentlemen, if you have enjoyed our show half as much as we have enjoyed playing it to you, then we have had a lovely evening together. Thank you for coming in — thank you for staying in. Goodnight and God bless.' Applause, then — quickly — 'curtain' I called to the stage staff in the wings. Down it came, leaving Tommy still sitting in the stalls with his arms folded and unable to get back onstage. Bobby Howes had come to my rescue.

Val Parnell was not very happy with *Fancy Free* either, saying 'I don't understand why *Fancy Free* is not doing well. If you and Trinder can't get 'em in, who can?' He paused. 'I don't know what they want any more — I don't know what they want.' He was very depressed. So we had a cup of tea. Then Val advised me, 'Go back to America, Kirkwood, on the first plane or ship — there is nothing here.' I reminded Val that I had come back from the United States only three years ago. I had never seen Val so down. Normally he was a cheery, bluff sort of person. There was nothing to say that would get him out of his depression, so I left, to finish my cabaret at the Astor, followed by the Colony at 3 a.m., and then went home.

One evening, when I was about to make my entrance in the second show at the theatre, I felt dizzy and slowly collapsed on the floor of the dressing-room. I was out for the count. Bessie immediately alerted the stage director and an announcement was given out on the intercom. The theatre doctor came and gave his opinion that he had never known anyone so low in blood sugar and ordered me home at once. I was home for four weeks suffering with 'severe nervous exhaustion'. It was interesting to note that my part in the show was taken not by one leading lady but by three — one of whom also collapsed and ended up in hospital. Sparky came to see me every day and held my hands in his; it was wonderful to see him.

He took me to Montreux, Switzerland, for a break to meet his great aunt, the dowager Baroness Falz-Fein, related to the Curzon family. She must have been in her late eighties, but she was so charming and her eyes so twinkly she could have been much younger. She had something I had always imagined as being the height of luxury, but never seen — a mink bedspread. An icon burned at the head of her bed. She took us to lunch at Vevy and we sat under the trees; it was a beautiful day. She was far from rich, but her apartment was full of treasures, one of which, a Fabergé dish, she gave to me. Her married home had been the Villa Calma, along the edge of the water at Lac Leman, and had now been taken over by a trust.

Her husband had died, or been shot, I gathered, during the Russian Revolution. I was taken to a moving and beautiful Greek Orthodox church service and I lit a candle.

When we returned, Mother had calmed down and no longer attacked Sparky, which was a relief. I was accustomed to these tirades as, whenever I was asked to lunch by a man more than once, Mother started her usual routine: 'He's after your money, he's after your money' — although I pointed out that I did not have any money except what I earned. Over the years all this had the effect of making me wonder if I was so unattractive that the only reason a chap asked me out was indeed my money. Although I was now thirty years old I was still extremely naïve, but not as much as I was at twenty-three, when I did not know that a baby was alive inside its mother — I thought it only began to live when the doctor smacked its bottom!

I had been so close to Mother when I started to work; indeed on tour I knew no one else for years. When I married John, Mother went home to Daddy. Then, when we separated, she came back. We never went out anywhere and never had a holiday, but I was quite content with my work and going home to the flat afterwards. All this made it difficult to communicate with people as I had become extremely shy. Mother had her own friends, whom she used to see whilst I was at the theatre, but we never had anyone visiting the flat. Also, Mother's side of the family, when she rarely took me to see them between shows, talked about people I did not know and I felt left out — I sat there like a dummy. They seemed to think I had become a strange new person since I appeared in *Black Velvet*. Aunt Pop, who had always been a jolly soul and used to laugh and chat with me, hardly gave me a glance, never even asked me about the shows I was in and hardly ever came to see them. Even my mother, too, seemed to lose interest in the theatre, and after the first nights never came again. I longed for someone close to me to be 'in front', to tell me if my performance was OK and my make-up not too much or too little. Mother seemed to have given up on the theatre entirely and me with it. The only people I knew were those I worked with, and as I was mainly onstage in the parts I played, some of them marathons, I never had the chance to make real friends. However, work was all, and as I had always been a bit of a loner by nature, especially after Brian was born, I was not really unhappy. But I did miss that mythical 'someone in front'. I was not aware of being lonely at this time, but on reflection now, I realize that I was. That was in the early forties, but now I had Sparky I was not lonely any more.

One morning, whilst Mother and I were having breakfast, there came a knock on the door. It was John, whom I had not seen since 1943. 'What are you here for?' said Mother.

'To tell you that you can have your divorce,' answered John. I could hardly believe it, but John had not finished yet. 'It will cost you some money,' he added with a cold smile.

'How much?' asked Mother.

'Two hundred and fifty pounds,' he said — it

had always been 'two hundred and fifty pounds' whenever he asked me for money. 'In cash,' he added. 'You can take it to my solicitor's in Soho.' As I climbed the wooden stairs to the solicitor's in a tacky part of Soho, I thought, What a way to end a marriage. I had no solicitor of my own. I thought that John would do whatever had to be done in return for what he demanded, and I had no knowledge whatever of the divorce laws.

A few weeks later I received in the post a large white paper edged with thick black ink one and a half inches wide. I thought someone had died, but no. It was a certificate of divorce, which declared me to be the guilty party for my 'desertion'! I was numb with shock and then anger. It was John who had deserted me after he went into the army and never contacted me either by letter or telephone. Nor did he ever suggest our getting together again. I did not even know where he had been posted until someone told me. It is true that he paid some brief visits, when he asked for a cheque for 'income tax' — 'two hundred and fifty pounds', of course. Each time he was out of the flat within a few minutes. We had been separated for nine years now and could have had a simple and honest divorce for that reason alone, which he must have known about. I had also learned of his many adulteries, but had no proof, as I was working in London and he was in the Orkneys. So there I was, with a black smear on me forever as 'the guilty party', a falsehood that has haunted me ever since. Mother was dreadfully upset. We cried together. When I told Sparky he was torn between wanting to rip John apart and feeling joyful that we were now free to marry after four years of waiting. Sparky told me later that John had been to see him to try and persuade him not to marry me.

We put the nastiness behind us and announced our engagement. We were married on 22 February 1952, the day after my thirty-first birthday. Sparky was determined to have a lavish reception and we did, at the Dorchester, attended by many of my friends from the theatre and Sparky's golfing chums; he was a great golfer, almost an addict, and played nearly every day in all weathers. We went to Bournemouth for our honeymoon, as Sparky said there was a good golf course there! I was quite happy with this arrangement — Sparky had already taken me to Montreux, Cannes, St Moritz and Paris, twice, once with Mother.

Sparky and I moved into our new house. It was my first home; at last I could sit in a chair that was mine. I was in heaven and Sparky was most happy, too, as the corridor which ran the length of the flat was just right for him to practise his putting! Suddenly I realized I had never cooked anything in my life as, first, on the variety circuits Mother and I had lived in digs. Then, in London, Mother had done the cooking whilst I worked. I had never had any instruction or guidance from her regarding cooking or sewing or all the other responsibilities of most wives — though one day I did cook bacon and eggs for Sparky without burning anything, much to my surprise! I had received a large, heavy

Good Housekeeping book from my dear friend Maggie Cummins, Peggy's mother, and decided to study the secrets of this cooking business.

Mother was now settled happily in a flat not far away which she called her 'cage in the sky'. She had her own coterie of friends as usual but we saw her nearly every day, so all was now ironed out. Thankfully, she at last became fond of Sparky and we were all very happy. However, I was anxious to work again, as I had been away too long — eight months — a dangerous thing to do.

15

Television

A new world opened up to me. Television was in the ascendant and my first appearance in this new medium was a twenty-minute spot on my own in a programme called *Starlight*. I took to television like a duck to water and was asked to do another. I loved the atmosphere of Alexandra Palace, then the television centre. There was a tremendous air of excitement and discovery in the studio and all who worked there were dedicated and talented, always striving for perfection and new ideas; I was fortunate to be part of this new world.

When I finished this second *Starlight*, I rushed to get changed and go home but as I was about to leave there was a knock at the door. There stood a slight figure with black hair and beard to match and large, serious and intense dark eyes. 'My name is Michael Mills,' he began. 'Will you be my 'Marie Lloyd'?' He was a television producer of note, I knew, but what did he mean? Marie Lloyd had been deceased for many years. It turned out that he was about to direct and produce a massive play with music on the life story of Marie Lloyd, the greatest music-hall star of all time. She had been lauded by Sir Max Beerbohm and, indeed, every serious critic of the day had heaped praise on her. Much more than a

270

singer of comedy songs, she was a fine artiste who was loved and revered by the public, high and low — rather in the same way as Gracie Fields, a legend in her own time.

Would I play Marie Lloyd? What a question! I was thrilled and excited at the thought. There were to be eight weeks of rehearsal and research, an enormous cast and the show would run for two hours on the 'box' — live, of course, then, and all the better for it. I was to play her from the age of twelve until she died at fifty-two.

This was the biggest, most complicated programme BBC television had ever attempted up till then. The production was at Lime Grove Studios, Shepherd's Bush, the old Gainsborough studio — a British film studio pre-war, later taken over by the BBC. In fact we had to use two studios, as the production was so immense — one for the 'straight' scenes (that is, the story line), and one for the musical numbers. I noted with alarm that the studios were a long way apart. To reach the music studio after a drama scene I had to run out of the studio with the floor manager grasping my hand, down a long corridor, across the floor of the music studio and up some steps to get onstage for the numbers. The orchestra conducted by dear Eric Robinson, was in yet another studio, out of sight somewhere — crowned with earphones so they could hear me for the numbers. I could not see the orchestra at all — I just relied on Eric, which was the best thing any artist could do at any time. He was a rock and I adored him; he always stayed calm and never wavered. We were still in rehearsal at a church hall in Shepherd's Bush, but we had examined the set-up in the two studios and I began to have serious qualms as to how this complicated show would ever go on. But Michael Mills was cool and determined and always reassured me — he had to when I discovered there were over fifty quick changes! I was in every scene save two, and all the costumes were Victorian, which did not make things any easier. Much of the time in-between rehearsals was spent in doing research at the V & A Museum and meeting Marie Lloyd's family, her daughter, her sister and her brother Sid, who were the most wonderful characters — full of vitality.

We came to the day of transmission. Dotted about the studio floor — the acting one — were changing rooms, cupboards really, complete with make-up and costumes. Sharing the space were cameras, large cables and lighting equipment — it is a wonder we all lived through it. But, somehow, we plunged into it with a mad, inspired enthusiasm and we did it, thanks to a marvellous and talented cast, including that unique personality Peter Bull. We were ably assisted by a superb and efficient make-up and wardrobe department. A dotty dedication was shown by all concerned with the production, especially our lifebelt, father and tower of strength Michael Mills, who was surely one of the most brilliant and talented producers the BBC ever had.

The wardrobe ladies dressed me in the quick changes whilst I ran. One of the costumes was not fastened down the back in time for me to face the cameras, but as I played to them facing front all was well and I was wearing knee-length Victorian bloomers and a long-sleeved high-necked vest of the same period. Underneath the costume, propriety was not breached. The make-up girl had quite a difficult time, as she had to age me from twelve years to fifty-two, which was the dying scene — all this done on the move. But everyone concerned kept their heads and they might have been doing these almost impossible changes for years.

The last scene showed Marie Lloyd onstage, singing her famous song 'I'm One of the Ruins that Cromwell Knocked about a Bit.' She was very ill and staggered about the stage to the delight of the audience, who assumed she was acting drunk to suit the song. The more she fell about the more they laughed and cheered. Finally she collapsed to deafening applause and laughter. Suddenly a most touching thing happened. One of our technicians, who was standing at the side of the stage, thought the show was over and that I had collapsed, exhausted. He dashed across the stage, not realizing the cameras were still running, and tried to lift me up. 'Don't worry,' he said, 'It's all over now,' but it wasn't, as I was supposed to struggle up and take my last bow, clutching the curtain, then stumble backwards fast, hit the back of the stage and slither to the floor dead. I hissed at the kind technician, 'Go away! We're still on the air.' He left at the double but strangely enough, it was a marvellous touch, for it looked as if it was all in the script. The make-up girl had done her work well, I looked ghastly, at death's door and ninety-five! The performance ended with an errand boy on a bicycle calling at Marie's home with a bouquet of flowers. 'For Miss Marie Lloyd,' he announced, and the maid who answered the door tearfully murmured, 'B-but she's d-dead.' The errand boy did not take this in — he'd done his job — and cycled away whistling, 'My Old Man Said Follow the Van,' Marie's most loved and famous song. He faded out of sight, the orchestra swelled up and, at full power, played the rest of the song. What a finish! A touch of genius and so very heart-breaking, as the music played over the credits until the end.

There was silence in the studio. Then everyone — the crew, the actors, the make-up and wardrobe staff — burst into spontaneous applause, the studio ringing with this joyous sound. Some of the crew were up in the roof with the lights and cheering. Some people were in tears. Even Peter Bull, usually a stoic, came over to me with tears running down his cheeks. He could not speak, but offered me a mint from the tin he always carried, marked 'Curiously Strong'. I shall never ever forget that scene as long as I live, nor the glorious camaraderie of everyone connected with *Our Marie* — a 'live show' if ever there was one. We repeated the performance four days later and again, by public demand, one year after.

The script was written by Alfred Shaughnessy — and what a great script it was, taken from the book *Our Marie* by Naomi Jacobs. I was invited by the mayor of Shoreditch, where Marie Lloyd was born, to be presented with a large silver box engraved with the words, 'To Pat Kirkwood, in appreciation of her television performance in *Our Marie*. Presented by His Worship the Mayor on behalf of the people of Shoreditch' and dated 26 February 1953. I treasure it still. It is my Oscar.

Michael Bond kindly agreed to allow me to quote an extract from his recent book *Bears and Forbears*, in which he recalls his experiences as a BBC cameraman in Studio G:

> The most successful and still the most talked about episode was 'The Story of Marie Lloyd'. Pat Kirkwood, who played the lead, had so many costume changes they completely filled three six-foot rails. There was no room for a quick-change tent, so she spent half the time dashing wildly about the studio changing clothes in order to be ready for her entrance in the next scene. At the end of it all she received that very rare accolade, a totally spontaneous ovation from everyone in the studio — cameramen, sound crew, scene hands, electricians, make-up girls, dressers and the rest of the cast.

After that it seemed that I was never off the box. The next project to come up was *The Great Little Tilley*, the life story of another great star called Vesta Tilley, who was a male impersonator of renown and who had become a star at the age of five. It was produced by Brian Tesler and was also live, of course, running about the same length as *Our Marie*, but less difficult to mount because we did not have the death scene to bother about, nor the fussy Victorian dresses and underwear. The programme was another marathon. I wondered if I would receive my round of applause from the crew and actors, as I had in 'Marie' — I did! So I went home with a very large head and a very large grin.

It was about this time that Cecil McGivern, the head of light entertainment, suggested I sign an exclusive contract with the BBC, relinquishing all other engagements in theatre, films, everything. 'If you accept this offer you will become the greatest star since Gracie Fields.' I was staggered. He went on, 'You are too much occupied in keeping slim' — I wasn't — 'and looking good' — I wasn't. 'The fact is,' he continued, 'you have a 'fat' personality and you should use it; don't concern yourself with appearance. What do you say?' As I had but a few moments before coming off the studio floor after the 'Tilley' show and was not yet down to earth I thought I should wait a bit. I thanked him for his offer and asked for some time to think it over. I decided against it, eventually, as I did not wish to give up the theatre, my first love, for this new one, although I was most happy with the medium. Also I thought it was possible to be seen on television too much.

I remember, whilst rehearsing for *Peter Pan*, slipping away to have some lunch at Bertorelli's opposite the Scala Theatre. I sat at a table in the window, which faced another table opposite. Every time I took a bite of food I faced a family of four, all staring, four pairs of eyes watching. Eventually I had to move to another table. Bobby Howes always stopped people, who came up to him in the middle of his meal after the show and asked for his autograph, with a decisive, unsmiling, 'No! I'm eating my supper.' Likewise, after a strenuous performance, outside the stage door, when someone asked for his autograph, he would ask, 'Have you seen the show?' and if they had not he would not give it — but he would for those who held programmes. Katharine Hepburn and some others would never sign autographs on principle, not least because some actors' signatures have been forged for nefarious purposes or swapped for others considered more valuable.

After the success of the Marie Lloyd programme I began to think how I could find a part as good as that one. Like a flash I had an inspiration: Eliza Dolittle in *Pygmalion*, which could be transformed into a stage musical, of course. To whom could I take this idea? I made my suggestion about *Pygmalion* to Jack Hylton. He blew up, and I thought he would have a stroke. 'A musical of *Pygmalion*!' he bellowed. 'Are you mad? You can't make a musical of Bernard Shaw. Forget it, nobody would put it on.' I was crushed and went home instead of taking my idea immediately to Emile Littler — a mistake.

About this time the BBC broadcast a

277

television command performance in the presence of Her Majesty the Queen and Prince Philip and I was asked to appear. This was the first time television had its own Command Performance and I do not recall another ever being held on any channel since. It was held at Lime Grove, Shepherd's Bush, where both the 'Marie Lloyd' and 'Vesta Tilley' programmes had been made and it was one of the last shows to be made live, as tapes and recordings came soon after. After the performance we all stood in line to be presented to Her Majesty and the Prince; Terry Thomas was on my right and Al Read on my left. The Queen walked slowly along the line, stopping at each one of us for a few words. When she came to me she asked if I found a great difference between appearing on television compared to the theatre and we had quite a long discussion. I had not seen Her Majesty so close since I was presented to King George VI, Queen Elizabeth and the two Princesses at Windsor Castle in the forties when the Queen was a young girl. Now I saw she had grown into a pretty adult, which the media's cameras always seemed to miss. She had the most enviable complexion and a beautiful smile which reached her eyes and made them sparkle. She was rather shy then, which added to her charm.

Then Prince Philip came along and when he reached me said, 'I haven't seen you since that evening at Les A. Oh! I did enjoy it.' I was shattered and could see Terry Thomas's ears twitching. After all the stupid rumours of the previous four years, Prince Philip had put his foot in it — again! Anyway, I smiled and said nothing as there was nothing to say really. But I comforted myself with the thought that his words were quite ingenuous and no one hearing them could possibly doubt their innocence unless they had maggots in the head.

I had a disappointment coming though. The BBC decided to hold an awards ceremony for the best performance of the year — 1953. I was told that my 'Marie Lloyd' performance had gained the votes of a massive majority of viewers. I was beside myself with joy and looked forward to receiving my medal or whatever the award was, but a hurdle appeared: there was no BBC category for light entertainment. How anyone could categorize the 'Marie Lloyd' story as 'light entertainment' and not 'drama' was incredible, as the songs were incidental to the story, which was sad and tragic, the acting twice as important as the few songs I sang. So I did not receive an award after all, even though I was firmly top of the poll. The following year some good came out of it as the BBC brought in a light entertainment award for the first time.

Marie Lloyd was not my first dramatic role. In 1949, I had played the lead in the film, *Once a Sinner*, directed by Lewis Gilbert, the best director I ever had as he left me as I am and did not confuse me with over-direction. The film was not bad and gained me an excellent half-page review from Leonard Mosley. Many years later I was delighted to see Lewis Gilbert when he appeared on the screen in my *This is Your Life* on Thames TV, when he spoke very kindly of me.

In December 1953 I opened in *Peter Pan* at the Scala. I was feeling nervous as it was the first straight work I had ever done in the theatre, but I was delighted that Evelyn Laye was playing Mrs Darling and Donald Wolfit was playing Hook. I also had a taste of the North and South divide before I had opened, when a photograph of me as Peter Pan appeared in the *Daily Sketch* above a caption which read, 'A Lancashire Peter Pan?' This surprised me, as I had always assumed the prejudice came from the North and not the South. I loved the part and had my hair cut like a boy's — quite a sacrifice but worth it, I thought.

The first night was a great success. What a joy it was to work with Evelyn and Donald Wolfit, who suggested that instead of the wooden swords normally used in the fight scene between Peter and Hook we should have real ones. 'What do you feel about that?' asked Donald.

'Terrific,' I replied with a happy grin. We took fencing lessons and got on with it. The swords were rapiers, which gave me pause for thought, but we fought the good fight, with no holds barred, and no damages, miraculously. How we enjoyed it. I became Donald's slave for life. What a great chap he was, as well as a fine actor, and so modest with it. I really enjoyed playing Peter Pan and was extremely relieved that in my first straight part, which so many fine actresses had performed, I had not made a clanger.

The first night, especially, had been exciting. I received an ovation and rushed to my dressing-room where Mother, Sparky and my lovely Grandma were waiting. Who should also be present but the drama critic of the *Daily Telegraph*, the long-standing and highly respected W A Darlington. How he had appeared so quickly was a miracle; he must have come through the pass-door even before the audience had left. He was beaming and congratulated me on my performance. 'Thank you — but I wasn't fey, was I?' I asked. It was almost a law that Peter should be a little 'strange', but I played him like a young boy — a bit like Richmal Crompton's William. Mr Darlington laughed. 'No, you were not fey,' he replied, 'but you were the happiest little Peter Pan I ever saw.' I was most touched, he was such a nice person — silver-haired but young at heart. Then came a knock on the door and a rude shock; it was a critic, as he called himself, from the *Daily Sketch*. He also seemed half drunk. I asked him in, introduced him to all present and asked him if he would like a drink. Yes, he would. Then he asked me, with a leer, what my tights were made of. Lisle, I told him, thinking it was a strange question. He was most unpleasant, but left as soon as he had finished his drink. I had excellent reviews except from the *Daily Sketch* — again — who made a virulent personal attack upon me. Sparky was so infuriated that he wrote a strong letter to the editor demanding an apology. The critic, Maurice Wiltshire, was sacked and never heard of again. During the run at the Scala, I was thrilled when Dame Sybil Thorndike and her grandchildren came backstage to meet me. I had never met her before and thought it was really splendid of her to trouble to come and see me. She was so complimentary — that famous voice filling the dressing-room — and I had the impression of someone honest, strong, fearless and kind to a degree. Another happy experience not to be forgotten.

Shortly after I had opened in *Peter Pan*, Daddy arrived for Christmas; also Aunt Pop and Uncle Clifford — always called Uncle Joe by the family. I was busy in the kitchen when Uncle came in to say that Daddy was not well and had a high temperature. I had not realized this as he was always pale and after welcoming him I had scooted into the kitchen to prepare dinner. It was a shock to learn that he was ill. We put him to bed and sent for a doctor, who diagnosed bronchitis. How on earth he had made the journey only Daddy knew, but he was never a complainer no matter how ill, which was rarely. The next day, Christmas Eve, Sparky and I had to go to a television show as guests. We came home as early as we could to see Mother sitting by Daddy's bedside holding his hand whilst they watched television. I felt a lump in my throat. Daddy kept saying that he wanted to go to Mother's flat, but he could not be moved. He seemed to get better and happier but on 28 December, after we had seen Daddy comfortable, Sparky and I were having a quiet talk in our bedroom about his condition when, suddenly, we heard a loud rasping wheeze from his room. I went into his room anxiously. 'Are you all right, Daddy?'

The wheezing had stopped. He said quite strongly, 'Yes, yes,' as if he just wanted to sleep and be left in peace. Then, after I had returned to our room, Sparky whispered, 'Listen' — I had been talking, but stopped to hear a terrifying noise coming from Daddy, as if he was fighting for breath. We leapt up and went to his room to find him sitting on the edge of the bed and rasping, 'I'm going, I'm going.' A chill struck me. Sparky lifted his thin and frail body off the bed, whilst I quickly brought a chair. We set him in the hall where there was more air and telephoned the doctor. He was at a ball at the Dorchester, I was told. I rang the hotel but they could not find him; they said he was not there. Daddy's head was on his chest and his face was grey. 'He's dying, he's dying,' I whispered tearfully to Sparky. I don't know how I knew; I had not seen anyone die before; I just knew. I ran to the telephone to tell Mother to come at once. Then I put my arms round him saying, 'Hang on, Daddy, hang on. Mother is coming.' Sparky opened the front door of the flat. We waited for what seemed forever as Father's breathing became more and more difficult.

He struggled to say something. 'Where's your Mother?' were the last words he spoke and his head fell forward on to my arm.

Mother, at last, arrived, looked at my father, stroked his head. 'Poor darling, you couldn't fight any more,' were her words.

The press had got hold of the news and a placard went up at one of the vendors in Baker Street, saying, 'Star bereaved.' Mother told me,

283

as I did not go out of the flat. I had a performance that night and went to the theatre, but I asked the stage director to please put a message on the tannoy to the cast, not to talk to me. 'If no one talks to me, I'll be all right,' I explained. He looked at me strangely, but made the announcement and later it occurred to me that he had probably not seen a newspaper and did not know what had happened; he must have thought that I was potty or had the flu! The cast were all wonderful and did not speak to me, as I had asked, until the end of the show when Norah Gorsen, who played Wendy, asked me how I was feeling and gave me her sympathy. She was a sweet girl and rightly cast in the part; I could not imagine a better Wendy.

I got through the show all right, although there are many lines in *Peter Pan* pertaining to death — notably, 'To die must be an awfully big adventure' — which needed a deep breath and a bit of concentration. After the curtain fell, I climbed the stairs to my dressing-room to see a vision before me, standing outside the door. It was Evelyn Laye with a bottle of champagne and a large glass. 'Come on, drink this,' she said firmly.

'Oh, I don't want any, thank you, Boo.'

'Yes, you do, get in,' and she shut the door. This was my first experience of her infinite capacity for compassion and concern. She was known to everyone in the theatre as Boo. When I first called her Evelyn, during rehearsals, she informed me that I must call her Boo as everyone did. I had to say to her that I thought it did not suit her at all and 'Evelyn' was more suitable for her position and that 'Boo' was a silly name anyway! She replied that if anyone called her Evelyn it meant they did not like her! So it was 'Boo' from then on. She made a perfect Mrs Darling, bringing her own ease and grace to the part.

On the home front, Sparky had suffered from high blood pressure for years before we met, although I was not aware of this until after we were married. He loved cream cakes and anything sweet so I had put him on a diet of no fat, or very little, and certainly no sweets. If any chocolates came into the flat I locked them up. He was so fit, and looked it, playing his beloved golf most days, sometimes twice a day, and he never seemed tired. He did, however, smoke like a chimney, except that he only took short puffs and never inhaled; I sometimes wondered why he bothered as this was not smoking at all! His teeth were always white and so were his eyes, nor did he have that smoker's 'pong' about him or his clothes. There was a problem, however, for whenever Sparky went out for his 'constitutional' he also had an object in view. He came home one afternoon with a smear of cream in the corner of his mouth. He confessed that he had found a marvellous patisserie in Park Lane, which specialized in fabulous creamy cakes. This had been going on for some time, it seems. What to do? I put him on his oath not to walk down Park Lane anymore and walk in the park instead. I would have gone with him to make sure, but he always took his walk when I was out or had a matinée. Anyway I trusted him, and I don't think he wavered. He used to call the patisserie 'the Black Hole'!

After *Peter Pan* finished its run at the Scala we took it on tour all over the country, beginning with a week in a theatre at East Ham. It was a firm tradition that whoever played *Peter Pan* must follow the London run with a three-month tour. Sparky had not been too well, so we went to see a heart specialist at Lister House, who took chest X-rays. Mother and I did not take this too seriously as Sparky was a dedicated hypochondriac, who, on the onset of a cold would announce, 'This is the finish of me — I'm handing in my chips.' He was quite serious, always. If he had a pain in his back, it was the beginning of osteoarthritis at least. The specialist seemed unconcerned about the X-ray, and when Sparky asked if he could still play golf replied, 'Oh, certainly — twice a day if you wish.' Sparky brightened and Mother and I and 'himself' went home laughing together, but Sparky nevertheless declared that he was going to sleep in the deep armchair in the bedroom and would not go to bed until he was practically asleep. When I asked him why, he replied that his heart beat too loudly in bed and kept him awake. After the specialist, who was one of the top men in his field, had been so dismissive of Sparky's complaints, Mother and I decided that it was just one of his idiosyncrasies. Mother gave her opinion that all he was suffering from was intense hypochondria. A week later I had a bad dream, that Sparky was drowning in a sea of mud and calling me to help him. I woke up to find him standing by the bed, calling for me to wake up. He was in a terrible state and very pale. I rang the doctor at once, who did not seem very impressed and advised me to give him two aspirins. Sparky settled down thereafter and slept straight away with my arms round him.

Peter Pan opened at East Ham and Boo and I were to go by tube. It was a bitterly cold day. Arctic in fact, but Sparky insisted on seeing me off, although I tried to persuade him to stay in the warm flat, where Mother was. The tube station, Baker Street, was only yards away, however, so he came with me, stopping to get his precious cigarettes. There was a long flight of steps down to the trains and he decided to stay at the top and not come down. As I reached the platform I looked back at him and waved. I was struck at once by how unwell he looked and I hesitated, feeling a shaft of fear through me. Boo grabbed me and said to hurry as we were late. When we reached the theatre Boo, who always travelled with a kettle and various other comforts, brought out a bottle of rum, boiled the kettle and poured out a hot rum drink. I still felt a restive anxiety, but we finished the play — luckily there was only the evening show that day, no matinée.

The week dragged by and the bitter weather continued. Came Wednesday and we had to do a matinée and evening show. In the first performance, during the flying scene, whilst I was in the air, I had a most strange feeling. I felt as if something or someone was pulling me back.

I shook my head briskly and the feeling went. Boo and I were sharing a dressing-room that week and when I told her of the pulling sensation I had experienced she massaged my neck and head expertly and informed me that I was suffering from stress. She was such a wise person and so very understanding. I felt better. When I arrived home, as usual, I had some supper and then the three of us sat and talked for a while until Sparky went down in the lift to get some cigarettes from the machine. When he came back he seemed tired, so Mother and I ceased our chatter on the sofa. Sparky was standing by the fireplace and said, 'Well, girls . . . ' His eyes rolled to the back of his head and he began to fall, very slowly, on to the floor, turning as he did, and finished stretched out. I had risen from the sofa to give him a kiss but never reached him before he began to fall. Mother and I stood as if in a trance. Suddenly I remembered that in the case of a faint or stroke the thing to do was to throw cold water over the head and I ran to the kitchen, filled a jug and threw it over Sparky's head and face. Sparky did not move. Mother said there was a doctor on the ground floor somewhere. It was now 12.45 a.m. I ran down the ground floor corridor, it was a long one with potted palms on either side and various flat doors. Which was the doctor's? I rang the nearest one on the left. No answer. Then I saw, opposite an arch, two steps leading down to a flat on the left. I rang the bell and in a trice a man in pyjamas appeared. 'Please, come at once. It's my husband, number 133.' I left our door open and sat on the floor by Sparky waiting for the doctor; it seemed forever. Finally he appeared, fully dressed, in a suit and tie. I had expected him to come in his pyjamas as this was obviously an emergency. 'Is it a stroke?' I asked. He did not reply, but examined Sparky quickly and then told us, 'He is dead — coronary. He was dead when his eyes rolled back, before he fell. Nothing could have been done to save him.' I knelt on the floor and put my arms round Sparky; I did not care what the doctor or anyone else thought. The doctor left.

It was 29 January, a month and a day after Daddy's death. We put Sparky on the sofa and I folded his arms across his chest, put a napkin under his chin and tied it on top of his head so that his mouth would not fall open. I had read somewhere that this was the right thing to do. I don't remember much more except that my own doctor, whom Mother had rung and who had been attending me since I was eighteen, gave me an injection. I went to bed and slept.

When I awoke in the morning the first thing I noticed was the utter silence; there was no sound at all. Then I remembered that Sparky had gone; he had gone; where was he? He would not be happy without me; where was he? Suddenly I heard terrible moans and groans coming from me, as though from some wounded animal deep inside me, nothing to do with me at all and beyond my control. The sounds shook my entire body; I could not stop them. Mother and Millie, our daily, came to me. Then I was violently sick. I got up and dressed. Aunt Freda arrived, then the undertaker. I insisted that Sparky should stay in the flat, not at the undertaker's as Daddy had done. So he lay in state in a coffin in his room, with a candle burning by his side, until the funeral. Later in the morning Boo and her husband Frank Lawton arrived and, typical of Boo, she had brought a coat of mine and a few other things that I had left at the theatre. When she and Frank entered, Boo, completely ignoring Mother and Aunt Freda, came to me as I was sitting in an armchair. She went down on her knees with her lovely face close to mine. Then she spoke words of great comfort to me, telling me of her faith in the afterlife and how I must not grieve. Sparky had not died but was only passing over, that he would return and be with me always; although I would not be able to see him, he would be here. Then she left, leaving her loving presence behind her.

Sparky's good friends arrived to see him, especially his regular golfing companions, who were much affected. Sparky looked wonderful, his tan still intact, as if he was about to speak at any moment. My own doctor, who had come to see him, even leaned forward close to his face. I asked him why and he replied that he looked so well he wondered if he was still breathing. The newspaper placard in Baker Street had carried the message 'Star bereaved again,' Millie told me. Sparky had been fifty years old on Christmas Day, just before our second wedding anniversary on 22 February — but at least we had had six happy years together.

There was one lighter moment among all this

misery — there usually is. When the coffin was being carried into the church the golf ball and putter I had put in for Sparky rattled loudly, Helen Parnell told me, and scared the wits out of the bearers. How Sparky would have laughed.

16

Las Vegas

The happiest incident I remember from *Peter Pan* at the Scala, London, was watching Boo Laye from the wings playing a trick on Donald Wolfit. She dressed up as an extra pirate with all the proper gear — boots, cutlass, pirate hat, black moustache and trousers — and went on at the end of the line of pirates during their song and walkabout. Donald was singing the pirate song and the chorus all ambled round him doing a pirate dance and singing along. He gave a bewildered look at the last one, sensing there was an extra. He couldn't figure it out and the rest of the cast, offstage, watched with hilarity, as the prank was out of the bag by then. Boo, without a tremor or a mistake, still ambled round him, singing robustly in a deep bass voice with the top of her boots flapping like a round of applause. Suddenly Donald twigged that pirate number twelve was no less than Mrs Darling, and he was hard put not to crack up and split his sides, but he didn't. It was a gorgeous and successful prank and when he came offstage he gave Boo a hearty smack on her pirate trousers.

During the London run Boo came to me with some dress designs and a problem. She had been offered a leading role in a new West End show, but not the star part. She was not sure whether she should take it or not. The dress designs were superb and elegant and the show was to open at the London Hippodrome. The plot Boo outlined to me seemed to me to be greatly superior to most British musicals at that time. I encouraged her to take it, pointing out that no doubt during rehearsals her part would be considerably enlarged. This is exactly what happened, and *Wedding in Paris* was a gigantic success, with Boo leading the way and dominating the entire show — a great come-back for her.

After East Ham, Mother, Boo and I travelled by train to Cardiff to begin the tour, which, for me, was to last for three months. I was glad that Boo was with us, although she was not doing the whole tour. Boo ordered me to sleep on my back with my hands on my diaphragm as that would send me off to 'Noddy Land' adding that this was what the Chinese did. Captain Hook was played by Stanley Holloway in place of Donald. He was rather withdrawn, I found, different from the robust and outgoing Donald. Indeed I do not remember him speaking to me at all during the entire tour, except on stage, but I learned that he was suffering from an eye problem. Also, I supposed, Hook was a new dimension for him. He and his wife were staying at the same hotel, but I never would have known it if I had not seen them.

During the week at Cardiff, Michael Mills came to see me and informed me that the BBC had offered me my own live show, to run for one hour every two weeks for as long as it was successful. At the same time, Val Parnell rang and set before me an offer to go to Las Vegas. I told him that Mother and I planned to go to Italy for a holiday after all the misery of the last few months. Val's reply was, 'Kirkwood, I want you to go to Las Vegas with my London Palladium show.'

I replied, rather haughtily, 'Thank you, but no. I'm going to Italy on holiday.'

'But it's just what you need after all your troubles — to get away to the sun.' Val was losing his Irish temper.

'I can do that in Italy,' I reminded him.

'Not you, Kirkwood — you'd be bored to death with nothing to do,' was his typical response.

Las Vegas it was. First, however, I had to do my one-woman show for BBC Television, the first woman's weekly series in Britain. There were four programmes, and in my judgement were rather like the curate's egg, good in parts — but awful in others. Michael seemed to have lost his genius for exciting ideas, but, then, I was not so bright myself at that time. On the first of the series we were fortunate to have David Hughes, greatly talented and with a glorious voice, and Terry Thomas. This should have been a marvellous set-up, but we had to do a mawkish little song about my getting married and singing about 'The Rest of My Married Life'. This was all I needed and I could not finish the song at rehearsals, shamefully breaking down before continuing. Then there was a song called 'Little Things Mean a Lot', which required me to caress my wedding ring in close-up. Michael seemed to have based the programme on my bereavement, which was not very jolly either for the viewers or myself and in achingly bad taste, embarrassing for all concerned. The whole series was a frightful mess. The viewers thought so too, for my mail was far from ecstatic. I did not know who the writers were, as I was concentrating on wading through it all. However, after the first three shows, just before I was bound to leave for Las Vegas, the BBC considerately released me. So Mother and I found ourselves bound for New York on the Cunard liner, R.M.S. *Queen Elizabeth*. For the last of the series Petula Clark took over my part and — delightful idea — it was arranged that 'Pet' should call me on the ship to see how I was. We spoke for nearly five minutes, and the viewers must have been surprised and intrigued at such a novelty.

In New York we stayed at a hotel for one night. As we were unpacking, Jerry White, the American producer of many New York hits, rang me and asked me to come and see the show *The Pajama Game*. So I went. He said that he would like me to play the lead when the show came to London, but I did not think the part was right for me (that of a wet and dreary *ingénue*), so I had to refuse the offer. The show's biggest success was a comparatively small but terrific part for a dancer, whose one song, 'Steam Heat', stole the show — rightly so as the dancer was sensational. Her name was Shirley MacLaine, who shot to stardom straight after and stayed there.

Next day we flew to Las Vegas, a dreadful

journey of ten hours, with no food, no tea, no stewards in a small cramped plane packed full of cast members. Thankfully, they included Richard Hearne, with whom I had played two panto-mimes, one at the Coliseum and one at the Casino. What a relief it was to see him. He was his usual ebullient, witty self and it made the journey bearable. Dickie and I were co-starring in the Vegas production, called, not very inspiringly, *The London Palladium Show*.

I loved, just loved, Las Vegas and the sun — I was never out of the pool — and we were a most happy company as well, which made it all perfect. We became friends with an agent and his wife, who were great fun. I laughed a lot — especially when the husband said one day, 'You know, kid, you are not at all sexy onstage. You look like a young choirboy singing up there!' This reminded me of an incident some years before, when I was opening in a club in Dudley for Whitbread's whilst appearing there at the Hippodrome. A manager of the firm, who was looking after Mother and me, remarked, 'You know, you have no sex appeal. From the stage you give the impression of the kind of girl a man would like to take home to meet his mother.' The press and some theatre managements had been determined to change me into a 'sex symbol', which I was not, so I welcomed these opinions.

Our opening night at Las Vegas came. This was my first stage appearance in America, but I was not nervous because I felt it was no use getting into a tizz about whether the audience would like me or not, which was what I normally did. I could only give them my choice and hope that they would like it too. So I opened with a song called 'Ring out the Bells', which was actually written originally for the Crazy Gang on the coronation of King George VI. Val, as usual during rehearsals, interfered with my choice, shouting from the stalls, 'You can't sing that, Kirkwood — it's far too English.' I did, of course, and the audience loved it. Val had been so worried about what I was going to sing — he always did, which was so very annoying — that he called in Johnny Ray's manager to listen whilst I was rehearsing and give his opinion on the songs I had chosen. I was pleased to hear from the pianist that Val had asked the manager if he thought the choice of songs was suitable and the manager had replied, 'Hell yes, but she could sing the telephone directory and be great.'

I knew I had a good programme, with a blend of American and English songs, and I turned out to be right. The show was a tremendous success and we had a standing ovation at the end. What was even better was that the show became fully booked for our entire run and became the sensation of Sunset Strip, leaving all the other shows, with some very big stars, at the starting post. The Las Vegans were a lovely audience and I am glad to say that I had a great personal success. When I went to see another show on the Strip, which started later than ours, the compere, who also starred in it with his band, announced, 'We have with us tonight the wonderful Pat Kirkwood — take a bow, Pat.' I was thrilled: it was so unexpected and the audience clapped and cheered. Mother, who had taken to waiting outside for the show to finish, reported that two couples had come out of the audience and one of the wives had loudly and firmly declared, 'Well, that girl!' — that was me — 'Jane Powell — Ha! Frank Sinatra — Ha! She could lose them all.' A good review straight from the audience is precious indeed and was the only favourable one Mother ever reported to me.

The weeks flew by. Danny Kaye and his accompanist Sammy Praegar paid a surprise visit; they both sat on the lawn in sun chairs with their feet up and two newspapers hiding their faces. Our manager came to us in our apartment and told us there was somebody who wanted to see me by the pool. 'Who?' I asked.

'I don't know who they are,' he fibbed. I was intrigued as I did not know anyone there except the agent and his wife, who had now departed, and my colleagues. So I walked quickly out to the pool saw the two newspapers held like screens over the two faces and two pairs of legs in shorts. I knew straight away that it was Danny and Sammy. What a welcome we had. They came to see the show. I was quite nervous with Danny in front, but then I always am when great artists, or even ordinary ones, are in attendance. I have always asked our front-of-house manager not to tell me if anyone famous was in from our profession. After the show Danny asked me if I had been nervous, to which I had replied, 'Of course not!'

I did two interviews on television and then it was time to go back to London. We had continued to have full houses and marvellous receptions — the whole event had been a great success and I could not but feel a little sad at leaving. When we reached New York I had a telephone call from my loyal friend Bryan Michie — I shall never forget him for sitting in the Cumberland Hotel all night all those years ago waiting for the audition with George and Edward Black (see page 105). Bryan informed me that Jack Hylton was bringing the hit show, *Wonderful Town*, then still running in New York, to London and that the authors, Jerome Chodorov and Joseph Fields, had complete control over casting.

The authors had heard about my success in Las Vegas and would like me 'to be kind enough' to give them an audition for the part being played in New York by Rosalind Russell. As Bryan had just arrived in New York he brought the script with him, stating that the sooner I fixed up the audition the better, as the authors wanted the leading part to be settled. I only had that evening to run quickly over my part, and the audition was fixed for the next morning at a theatre. It was a wonderful part — the character's name was Ruth Sherwood — but oh dear, what a marathon: never offstage except for the interval; impossibly quick changes of complete costumes; and an adagio dance, which would mean being flung about all over the stage. I did not see the show, as it was better not to see another person in the part I might be playing — that might be intimidating and also influence one's own performance. The next morning

Bryan, Mother and I arrived at the theatre to audition only to find the two authors already waiting for us.

We were introduced by Bryan Michie and I liked them both at once; they were natural and welcoming, and helped to calm my inward nerves. Jerome Chodorov was a broad, stocky chap with black curly hair and a ruddy benign face — he was a Russian. Joseph Fields was slim, elegant and suave. We went inside the theatre and I climbed the steps on to the stage, clutching my script. To my surprise Jerome Chodorov followed me. He was to read the other parts in the scenes I was to speak. In one he had to take the part of my sister and it was quite hilarious to hear this booming voice giving out the lines of the pretty and feminine Eileen. Luckily I had no trouble with the American accent, but Jerome Chodorov's accent was American-Russian. We finished the dialogue. Bryan, Mother and Joseph Fields were sitting in the stalls. 'Great, kid,' boomed Jerome Chodorov. 'Just great.'

Joseph Fields called from the stalls, 'Now, Miss Kirkwood, would you kindly sing for us — anything you wish.' I looked around, there was no piano. I pointed this out, but Fields called out, 'Well, honey, just sing without one.'

Panic clutched me — what should I sing? My mind was a blank.

Chodorov whispered to me, 'Ruth Sherwood would have done it.' That brought my mind back and a song flashed into my memory. It was called 'I Feel a Song Coming On', which I had sung many times on television, so I waded in and gave it my very best and loudest voice. Jerome Chodorov stood beside me all the time.

The three in the stalls applauded and to my surprise Joseph Fields stood up and in an amazed voice said, 'My sister wrote that.' I gasped; someone was looking after me, I thought. 'How did you pick that song?' he continued. 'Did you know that Dorothy Fields wrote it?' I laughed and told him that I did not know why I chose it; perhaps his sister did! And, yes, I did remember now that Dorothy Fields, a famous songwriter, had indeed written it, but as I had not expected to sing at all, the choice had simply been a happy inspiration.

It was a happy morning indeed. 'Well, you sing a helluva lot better than Rosalind Russell,' laughed Joseph Fields. I got the part and Mother, Bryan and I sailed away on a large white cloud. I learned later that Rosalind Russell had an apartment made for her in the theatre so she could sleep immediately the curtain fell and she also had vitamin yeast injections every day to keep going. I trembled inside. The show was to open in February and it was now only September, so I had plenty of time to get to grips with the part. One problem was that I had been offered a pantomime at Manchester Palace, playing principal boy, which I had accepted but not signed the contract. I quickly had to let them know that I was not available and phoned my agent. He was glad to know there was a change of plan, as *Wonderful Town* was an important show. Rehearsals were to begin in London.

We opened at the Manchester Opera House to

a rather confused audience on the first night — it was a very American show — but had excellent reviews the next day. The response was similar to *Ace of Clubs*, but we played there for eight weeks and had full houses throughout. The show ran into Christmas and Jack Hylton decided to play the show twice daily during that week. I nearly passed out when I heard this, because the part of Ruth was extremely hard work. Out of the 2½-hour show I was onstage for 2¼ hours, excluding the lightning-quick changes in a cubicle in the wings. Bessie and I worked together in silence, grappling with complete changes of costume, all in a matter of seconds. We never missed a change once. I quaked with the fear that I would not be able to keep it up for two shows a day, every day. But I did, by going to the hotel straight after the show, and to bed after a sandwich and a hot milk, then next day sleeping until it was time for the matinée. One more decision by Jack Hylton was to record all the songs for the show on stage on the Friday morning, in addition to the two shows. I must have been extremely fit, I thought to myself, to sing all morning for the recording and then do two performances. As is traditional in the theatre, we had Christmas Day to ourselves — the only day in the year that actors have off apart from Sundays.

Wonderful Town, taken from the highly successful book and play written by Ruth McKenney, was one of the most interesting shows I did. I had quite a few problems to face: I had never coped with a New York accent

302

before; never played a comedy part; nor a plain, but intelligent and erudite woman whom men avoided like the plague. To play a plain woman one has to think plain, rather than wear glasses and scrape your hair back. Rosalind Russell was certainly not plain, indeed she was beautiful, and played the part just as she was. I proved my point when I refused to play the part with glasses on and my hair scraped back.

The Leonard Bernstein score was tremendous and far superior to any musical show before, in that the music was almost classical and highly sophisticated, as were the lyrics by Betty Comden and Adolph Green, a top-class team. *Wonderful Town* became a sort of cult show. It was way above the heads of most of the British public and way ahead of its time — long before Bernstein's *West Side Story* came on the scene — and established a new and vital breed of musical.

At the Prince's Theatre in London, we had an unforgettable first night, the audience stopping the show frequently with waves of applause. The new, younger element, loved its wit, vitality and brilliant music. Shani Wallis, who played my sister Eileen, and I had a strenuous finale song, 'The Wrong Note Rag', in which we had to climb up and down a long flight of stairs at rifle pace with the whole company onstage singing along. It was a hilarious, crazy number and at the finish the audience went wild and we had to do it all over again. We had a tremendous reception and I lost count of the curtain calls. Then I had to make a speech, which I loathe doing, but this time was different. I rattled on quite easily, but before I finished the audience gave another ovation and then the final curtain fell. It was a triumphant night.

Leonard Bernstein, who had conducted at our dress rehearsal, which thrilled us all to bits, came to a supper party given by Jack Hylton and sat next to me, much to my delight. It was my birthday too and I had a beautiful cake to cut — a very special first night. Then to cap it all, Leonard Bernstein asked me to go to the Stork Club, named after the famous New York club, and I did not refuse. We talked quite easily together and although I was a bit overawed he soon put me at ease, as he had a great sense of humour which I appreciated after all the excitement at the theatre. He brought me down to earth. One of the nice things about him was that he did not talk about himself all the time, but was interested in what I had to say as well. Suddenly I realized it was very late and that I had a matinée tomorrow. So, feeling like Cinderella, I asked him if he could get me a taxi as it was now nearly 3 a.m. and I was wilting. 'Oh, don't go,' he pleaded. 'Stay a while.' I reminded him that I had a matinée tomorrow. 'I admire the discipline,' he replied, 'but regret the circumstances.'

I arrived home then realized that after this wonderful evening there would be no Sparky there, ushering me in with a charming smile to tell it all to. I entered the flat to see Mother, Aunt Pop and Uncle Joe waiting for me, because they had thoughtfully realized that I would miss

Sparky being there. It was a most considerate and kind thing to do and I was overcome, especially as it was so very late and they must have waited a long time. The reviews the next day were mainly excellent, save for a few traditionalists who probably could not understand the music or the comedy and who disliked anything American on principle.

It was a happy company and Shani Wallis and I became like the sisters we were on stage. She was a delightful girl, honest and free of all malice or envy, as well as being highly talented. She made an impressive success as Eileen in the show. We were also blessed with an exceptionally strong and talented stage director, Gerry Phillips, who was a tower of strength to me when I had to make a dash across the backstage for one of my many quick changes. He simply grabbed my hand and we ran and leaped over the various hazards backstage where the next scene's set was waiting. One night, though, something went wrong. In one scene Shani and I, having moved to a dreadful basement flat, were unpacking two large suitcases to take out our next scene's pyjamas when I found my suitcase was locked, which caused quite a pause in the dialogue. What to do? Only one thing: I took the suitcase to the side of the stage and handed it to Gerry. He had the keys all ready, as he had seen what had happened, unlocked the perishing thing and then I walked back to the bed, crashed it down and opened it. The audience loved all this and gave a round of applause with some laughter. Shani was also laughing with them — she was a good giggler when anything went wrong and never panicked.

After we had been running for some time Jack Hylton gave me a lecture. 'You must go out a bit,' he said, and I realized that I had not been anywhere since the opening night. He continued, 'You never go anywhere except home and the theatre, and it is not good. You should have some fun.' I nearly laughed. In the first place I did not know anyone to go out with and, even if I had, I would not wish to waste my energy on anything so unimportant: 'the show's the thing' to quote an old maxim of the theatre. I know he meant it kindly but it was not on.

Despite this, during the next evening's interval, our competent and likeable stage director, Peter Bentley, a former Navy commander, invited me to his club the following evening. The club — the Buxton — was full to bursting with actors and singers, some of whom I knew by sight. There was nowhere to sit, though Mother and Peter had managed to fade away somewhere. No one had their stage make-up on except me. Suddenly I saw an orange box at the side of the bar and I sat on it and waited for Peter to return. I couldn't see Mother anywhere. To the left of me was a small archway, which I could see led to a large room with tables and chairs all filled. All at once a head appeared round the archway. It said, 'You don't know me, do you?'

I replied, 'Yes I do; you're Hubert Gregg.'

It said, 'What are you doing sitting on an orange box?'

'Because I like it,' I replied — I was still talking to just a head, albeit a handsome one.

'I've seen the show,' continued the head, 'twice.'

'You deserve the George Medal,' I quipped.

The owner of the head emerged, came up to me, took my hand and raised me up, saying, 'You can't sit here, come with me,' and led the way into the large room still holding my hand and forging his way through the crowd with his broad shoulders. He found two places at a table then went to find Mother and settled her as well. 'Had anything to eat?' he asked. No, I had not, so we were fitted up with some ham sandwiches. I was very impressed. Of course I had heard of him. His first marriage had been to my dear chum Zoë Gail and I had seen him on the box and in films a few times, but I had never met him before. We talked quite a long time and he was charming and witty, making me laugh, which had not happened for some time. He had an air of confidence and optimism which was very attractive. It was getting late though, so I thanked him, and Mother and I left, Hubert following to see us to our car, which was parked outside the Prince's stage door only yards away and, strangely, next to Hubert's car. I was about to go to our car when, to my surprise, I heard myself say, 'Well, who's driving who home?' Hubert leapt into his car — a Lagonda no less — turned it round and announced 'I am driving you home'. Mother was not best pleased but said nothing.

When he dropped me at my flat in Hyde Park

Square he asked if I would like to go out with him some time. 'Yes, I would, but only on a Sunday,' I said cautiously. We made a date for the following one and Hubert drove away. I entered my flat and did a pirouette all to myself, saying out loud, 'He's nice!' Then I had the bowl of soup that Millie always left for me and went to bed happily.

The following Sunday Hubert arrived and asked me where I would like to go. 'Cookham,' I replied, which is in Berkshire. Hubert was shattered as it was quite a way off, but he did not say anything. I think he was stunned. But it was where I used to go with Baron, where he played golf. It is a most beautiful place, in the heart of the country, with a marvellous old inn, the Bell and Dragon, which served excellent food. I was longing for some fresh air and selfish enough not to feel guilty about it. We had a perfect day and walked and talked and laughed in the sunshine. We had a late lunch after a long walk. It began to get dark but we decided to have a stroll in the church grounds. Hubert was beginning to be rather affectionate, so I asked him to give me a piggy-back as I was afraid of rats. This he did until we were out of the long grass and greenery and in the open space before the church. He put me down, we looked at each other and then kissed for the first time. The whole church lit up with floodlights simultaneously. How we laughed, as someone had obviously heard us talking in the grounds and thought we were up to no good. I liked to think that 'someone' was approving our kiss, and that it was a good omen.

We drove home, stopping for a few more kisses, which got better every time. We also stopped at a roadside café for Hubert to have a coffee, as he was feeling tired by this time, no wonder. When we reached Hyde Park Square Hubert said, 'Let's go out after the show one night. You wear a long thing' — gesturing to describe an evening dress — 'and I'll wear a dinner jacket. We'll go to the Four Hundred and have a dance — what do you say?' It sounded wonderful. I had not been out for a long time, but I was wary of the lovely idea because of the show. But then I remembered JH saying I needed to get out more . . . I will, and pooh to the show!

We went to the Four Hundred, had supper and danced. Hubert was an excellent mover and we fitted very well together, just as one person. Then Hubert put his cheek against mine and danced close, which I was not ready for. 'Why are you dancing like an American?' I asked frostily. He laughed, a small, surprised laugh, but we had no more cheek-to-cheek palaver. He told me, a long time after, that he had determined to marry me then and there. Hubert rang me every day and we saw each other on Sundays. The week seemed long to me, and it made me realize how lonely I had become. Hubert brought me back to life and made me laugh again.

I was beginning to feel tired though this was nothing to do with being in love — which I was. Hubert had behaved impeccably and had respected my devotion to the discipline that my part in the show demanded. He suggested that I should have a rest — a holiday — so I determined to ask JH for one. I asked him, via our manager, if he would come and see me in my dressing-room before the show. When he arrived I told him I had been feeling over-tired for some time — the show had now been running for eight months — and would he please allow me to have a two-week holiday. To my utter surprise he just said 'yes' quite firmly. Then, just as he reached the door to leave, he turned round and said, 'Oh, by the way, don't tell any of the cast.'

Hubert and I were delighted at the verdict and he booked us in to a hotel on a small island, the Ile de Porquerolles, one of three islands off the coast near Toulon. Porquerolles was similar to Sark in the Channel Isles in that no motor vehicles were allowed and it was also home to a 'Dame' — a French one — who lived in the manor house. It sounded heavenly; Hubert had been there twice before and had loved it.

On the Saturday before we were due to leave, having done the matinée, I was about to redo my make-up for the second show, but found I could not lift my hairbrush. I knew that I was in for a bout of complete exhaustion just as in *Fancy Free*, when I was playing two cabarets and fourteen shows a week. 'Bessie,' I cried, 'I can't go on, I can't do the show!' Bessie left in a flash, very flushed and anxious, and came back with Peter Bentley, who took my pulse and said I must go home at once. I could barely walk, but Bessie and Peter helped me out of the dressing-room and down the stairs to the car where Mother, having been alerted by Bessie, was already waiting. What rotten luck, I thought, on the last show before my holiday. We arrived at Hyde Park Square and Mother supported me with her arm round my waist, then she rolled me into bed. Mother stayed with me that night and next morning and called our doctor, who advised me to stay in bed for at least a week. 'I can't do that,' I replied. 'I am catching a plane on Monday to go on a holiday for two weeks.'

'You must forget all that,' he said sternly.

I gathered what strength I had and replied, 'Doctor, I am going to catch that plane if I have to crawl there.'

It was some time before I could begin to enjoy the holiday as I was still in a state of exhaustion, but Hubert was so caring and patient that I was on my feet a week later. Then I had a nasty shock: my agent in London called to say that JH had put the notice up for *Wonderful Town*. Then I realized the reason he had asked me not to mention my holiday to the rest of the cast. He had planned to put the blame on me for closing, because I had, apparently, 'walked out of the show'. Clearly the production had been dying on its feet anyway, as we had had to accept cuts in our payments. I was much distressed, especially as 'someone' had informed the press that 'Pat Kirkwood, who collapsed at the Prince's Theatre on Saturday, arrived in Paris on Monday.'

I was certainly in no shape yet to undertake the return journey, a long and tiring one involving a ferry-boat to Marseilles, a train journey to Paris and then a flight to Heathrow. I was furious at JH for his treachery. I was upset to think that people had been led to believe I had walked out of the show — something I would never do — and resented the stain put upon my professional reputation. I told my agent that I was not coming back as the journey was beyond me at the time. I also sent a telegram to the cast, saying how much I wished I could be with them, which I did. Then I forgot all the skullduggery and started to enjoy the rest of my holiday.

On 7 November 1955 I was honoured to appear before the Queen and Prince Philip at a royal command performance at the Victoria Palace, and there met Lena Horne. We two, along with Ruby Murray, shared a dressing-room, as is usual with a large cast on such occasions. I found Lena Horne to be a modest and delightful person and also great fun. She had a childlike quality, which belied her sophisticated stage personality. This is often true of theatre stars; it seems that they have two personae, one onstage, one offstage, which is a sensible way of keeping the feet on the ground and a clear head. They also develop the ability to switch off from the unreality of the theatre and on to the real world, which is essential if a balanced life is to be achieved.

17

Chrysanthemum

Hubert and I were married at St Columba's Church, London, on 14 May 1956. I had wanted a simple wedding. The only guests were Aunt Pop, Uncle Clifford ('Joe'), my Mother and Hubert's brother Frank, and there was no choir, no organist, no pomp and circumstance. So it was, until we stepped outside the church where a barrage of press photographers was waiting.

I was aware that Hubert and I would have problems, the first being that he was on the 'straight' side of the theatre — acting, writing, directing — whilst I was on the musical side. I also knew that the main danger to marriages within our profession was the separations necessitated by working apart. Determined, as we both were, to stay close, we were also fortunate to receive offers which made this possible, and in the first years of our marriage we had a television series, a radio series and a film in which we could work together. We were thus able to share whatever problems we had and the joy of understanding each other's ups and downs. We were ideally happy, like a couple of kids, and as we both had a similar sense of humour, laughter was always with us.

In our first film together — *Stars in Your Eyes* — Hubert wrote the songs and co-directed. In the television series he wrote some of the songs and also had a single spot in which he sang and played the piano. He wrote the radio series *My Patricia* and many of the songs. He always wrote both the lyrics and the music of all his compositions which is rare. Irving Berlin and Cole Porter did the same, as did Noël Coward, of course, but very few others that I recall.

John (now Sir John) Woolf, his brother Jimmy, and Peter Rogers, all formidably successful film producers, were keen to make a film of *The Great Little Tilley* television show I had done for the BBC and wanted Hubert to write the screen play. I had tried to keep in mind what Robertson Hare had said to me at a dance at the Green Room Club the night Hubert became president. I had never met 'Bunny' Hare before, but as we danced he said in that memorable voice, 'Keep him writing, keep him writing!' We had only lately been married and I remembered giving exactly the same advice to Hubert on the first night we met.

In the meantime Henry Sherek, a well-known independent theatre manager, asked me if I would come to his office. He wanted me to play Eliza Dolittle in Shaw's *Pygmalion* for the BBC. Would I not! Could I do it? No answer. On the first day of rehearsals I entered the rehearsal room to see the rest of the cast, with the exception of Keith Michell, in a group at the top of the room. I walked up to them to say 'Good morning', but they did not stop their conversation, talking about 'Dear John' — Gielgud, of course — the topic that seemed to be forever at the forefront of their minds and conversation. Then they gave a start as if I had said a rude word, quickly murmured 'Morning' and returned to 'Dear John'. So I sat down in a chair a few feet away. Keith Michell arrived with our director Peter Potter. Michell seemed friendlier than his colleagues in skirts. They were all women, except for a nice sympathetic young actor who was playing Freddie Eynsford-Hill, who came and spoke to me. He obviously disliked the rudeness he had witnessed.

I spoke to the director about working with him in the evenings on my own. I said I needed some extra help with the last scenes, which I was finding difficult. He seemed less than enthusiastic but did not dismiss the idea. Rehearsals began with waves of hostility coming from the 'Dear John' group, but I gritted my teeth and concentrated hard. Keith Michell was distant, but he too had a marathon part and I understood. We came, a few days later, to the formidable last scenes. The director had not mentioned the subject of my evening rehearsals again, so I ploughed on.

Whilst Keith Michell and I were rehearsing the last scenes I noticed him looking over my shoulder to where the 'group' was sitting. He started to laugh. I whipped round quickly just in time to see one of them pulling faces at him. She was a well-known character actress called Avice Landone and was certainly old enough to know better. I ignored all this, although I was surprised that Michell, who was a fine actor, would behave so badly. I do not recall receiving any guidance whatever from the director, but I discovered that he was working with Michell in the evenings.

The BBC wished me to do a boost 'shot' interview on television with Henry Sherek in order to promote *Pygmalion*. He began by asking me, 'Where were you born?'

'Manchester,' I replied.

'Eeeh By Gum!' he came out with, struggling with an exaggerated northern accent that was especially poorly done, for he came from central Europe, Czechoslovakia, I think.

I rallied from this insult and came out with, 'And where were you born?' with a sweet smile.

This shook him. 'Oh, er, er, oh, oh, all over the place' was his limp answer. So, I won that round.

Sherek then began to shower compliments on Keith Michell. 'Keith Michell,' he bumbled to the camera, 'is going to be the biggest star in the world. You must watch him in *Pygmalion* and you will see a great performance. Don't miss it!' Suddenly I twigged the whole set-up. Sherek had only asked me to play Eliza because my name then, after so many appearances on television, would be a draw; his ulterior motive was to give Keith Michell, who had not yet made any impact on the box, the chance of becoming the 'greatest star in the world'. This accounted for the lack of direction given and the barely veiled nastiness of the female cast. It was all revealed. I was, I am ashamed to say, a mite angry at this, but it was the best thing that could have happened to rid me of my nerves and doubts as to whether I could bring it off. It was 'all stations go' after that and I was ready to fight like hell. Hubert was a great help to me at this time, hearing my lines and giving me the confidence to face rehearsals.

Came the night of the performance. I was calm and sure — no nerves — and reminded myself how I loved playing on television and all I had achieved in this medium. When we came to the dreadful final scenes there was a great shock in store for me. Michell had altered his reading of the lines, giving a completely different performance from the one we'd so painstakingly rehearsed. I hung on to my lines with the courage of despair and was glad to reach my dressing-room. I thought that all was lost. Then there was a small knock on the door. There stood Gladys Boot, who played Higgins's mother in the play. She was so encouraging and sincere, obviously aware of what had happened and on my side. What a lovely person. I shall never forget her.

Another appalling set-back occurred during the live performance, when I came to the memorable 'Not bloody likely' line at the end of the tea-party scene. I gave it all I had but someone had turned the sound down on that famous phrase which had shaken a generation many years ago. I knew at once that the word which I had spoken very distinctly — knowing that it was the most shocking line in the play — had been smothered by the lack of sound and ruined the end of the scene. How this came about remained a mystery, but every actor immediately knows by instinct when the sound goes down.

One review of the play said that I had fluffed the line. Untrue. How, or by whom, this wicked trick was accomplished I never found out, not even enquiring after the performance because the deed was done and could not be undone. Who would admit to it anyway? I went home in a deep depression, but next day found that I had received the most warming reviews and the majority of the critics wrote seriously considered and constructive pieces. W. A. Darlington of the *Telegraph* wrote the wisest one, approving my performance in the first act and saying, 'In the tea-party scene she could hardly have been bettered, but it was in the last scenes that her lack of dramatic experience let her down. In the closing act she seemed to be reciting her lines rather than thinking them. (I was hanging on to my lines like glue wondering what Michell was going to do next) 'Also Keith Michell tended to fall away towards the end.'

The *Scotsman* went over the top and pronounced, 'Pat Kirkwood's performance in *Pygmalion* was the ideal Eliza that Shaw created and intended — how he would have approved.' I blushed to read it. But the last word came from the *Evening Standard* with the headline, 'Pat Kirkwood Tops the TV Poll' and reported, 'Pat Kirkwood was the most popular star of last week's TV programmes say *Evening Standard* readers. She polled twice as many votes as the runner-up Petula Clark.'

Hubert and I had the film of *Vesta Tilley* to think about. I was surprised that the producers had chosen this story rather than the more dramatic and human one of Marie Lloyd, which I much preferred. The trouble with the 'Vesta Tilley' story was that there was none! She became a star when she was five and stayed in that position all her life; married Sir Walter de Freece; was never ill and, so far as anyone knew, had no troubles whatsoever. Poor Hubert was desperate to find a storyline that had some dramatic conflict. Having played the part on television I found it difficult to get under the skin of the character. I met her elderly dresser, but there was no family, as was the case with the Marie Lloyd part. The dresser seemed not to know the real Vesta Tilley, but revealed that towards her end she had suffered from mental instability, a kind of egomania, and had attacked her dresser, trying to strangle her. This was no help to the film story, which was supposed to end on her triumphant retirement, and obviously we could not use the episode in any case, although it was the only dramatic one.

I decided that the star had not been in contact with the outside world at all and had lived a life that revolved entirely round work. I did my best to try and find some human quality in the character, but ended up disliking her. This was in striking contrast to my feelings for Marie Lloyd, whom I came to love during my investigation into her life. Also Vesta Tilley's success was partly due to the fact that her persona of a woman dressed as a man was titillating to some people. It was the first time that a woman had appeared onstage dressed immaculately as a man. Of course she had been a perfectionist, dedicated to

319

her craft, but I much preferred the healthier talent of Marie Lloyd, whose personality was warm and open — enormously loveable.

Hubert finally found a dramatic scene from Vesta Tilley's life, discovering that she had once been taken to hospital suffering from a rhubarb allergy. So a whole scene was inserted in the film with Vesta looking pale and wan in bed and Sir Walter de Freece visiting her with flowers and lots of sympathy. Laurence Harvey, who played de Freece and co-starred in the film, was almost in hysterics when the time came to do the shooting. So was I; it was difficult to keep our faces straight, let alone concerned and serious. The film, I thought, is going to be a 'stinker', and so it would have been without some of the songs and a truly moving scene, thanks to Hubert, when Vesta Tilley retired. We were both glad when the film was finished.

With delight I played Brighton Hippodrome as Jack in the pantomime *Jack and the Beanstalk*. I was back to my old routine, working with my happy and normal musical chums. The clothes were, as usual, simply perfect, and the ones I wore in the finale were especially gorgeous. A completely silver fitted suit encased my entire body from head to toe. All that could be seen was my face enclosed in a close-fitting hood, as though I had been painted silver. It was fabulous, like a suit of armour.

We gave a party one Sunday evening and John Clements, Kay Hammond, Gilbert Harding and my colleagues in the pantomime came. It was the greatest fun. The hotel staff were wonderful and

320

laid on a splendid buffet in the upstairs bar, after which we went to another room and played 'the game', a popular theatrical form of charades. What a party! I was sorry when the run of the show was over and we went back to London.

A friend of Hubert's alerted us to a show just opened outside London on a 'try-out' and told us we should go and see it, as the two leading parts were ideal for us. So we raced up to London and saw the show. It was called *Chrysanthemum* and the friend had been spot-on: the roles were perfect for both of us and the music and lyrics a joy, witty, melodic, romantic and original — especially the comedy numbers. It was set in 1912, the ragtime era. We met Robb Stewart, the composer, whom I already knew, as he had been the rehearsal pianist for *Ace of Clubs* and had also worked with Noël Coward on many musicals. He was enormously talented, but modest and rather shy. He should have been more confident and sure of his many gifts.

Neville Phillips was responsible for the book and was completely different from Robb, being suave, sophisticated and sure of himself, with bags of charm. Our agent reported there was a new management from abroad looking for a show to present in London. The script and musical numbers were sent to us and we met the 'new management' — a genial, quiet man called Sandor Gorlinsky and his pretty wife. He had been Maria Callas's manager for some time before she died. As he had not been in Britain for many years he had not heard of either of us, so he asked us to learn the songs and sing them for him — in other words a perishing audition. Peter Saunders, the highly successful producer of *The Mousetrap*, a great friend of Hubert's for many years, kindly offered his own flat for the audition. So we learned the songs and presented ourselves on the appointed date. Sandor Gorlinsky had a dreadful cold and could hardly speak, which I did not think was a good start, but we sang the entire score, Gorlinsky being given a large whisky by Peter before we began. When we finished, Gorlinsky said quietly but firmly, 'Yes, let's do it!' Dear Robb's face almost melted and his eyes rolled up as he gazed at Neville. He could not believe it.

Strangely, my heart sank. Oh dear, another musical marathon, I thought. I wanted to stay in our house with Hubert and realized, with a shock, that I wanted a child. One of the main reasons for changing my mind was that Hubert would have the chance to shine and that his talent ought to be recognized. The other reason was that we could stay together and not be separated by our work.

On the subject of children Hubert was adamant. He did not want them at all — not even one — ever. I had broached the subject before, but his reaction was firm and serious. He said, 'No, not you. Any woman can have children, but they can't do what you can do. So stay with your work; that is what you are meant to do.' In fact, we were happy as we were and one cannot have everything. It was not selfishness on his part, he simply thought my work should come first and, in a way, he was right. The list of childless female stars is formidable. Dame Anna Neagle, Dame Edith Evans, Evelyn Laye, Jessie Matthews, Frances Day, Elaine Page and many others. The theatre demands all the energy and dedication one can muster. It is also a precarious profession financially and in every other way — though, in my opinion, the only one.

I was amazed at my negative reaction to *Chrysanthemum*, although I had experienced a similar one before at the finale of a royal command performance, when we all stood in line onstage. The applause was deafening and Her Majesty rose to acknowledge the artists and the audience. Suddenly I thought, What am I doing here? I don't want to be here at all. I want to leave the business. It was an extraordinary feeling and I never told anyone about it; likewise, I never told even Hubert about my odd response when Gorlinsky said he would do the show with us. I should have been delighted, and a little while later I was. Hubert's face was alight. We opened in Manchester to a splendid reception; it seemed I had been forgiven for going to London and the audience was loudly approving, especially for the two duets Hubert and I had together. The tour continued for a long time, thirteen weeks in all.

We came to the opening night at the Prince of Wales Theatre and were accorded a rapturous reception at the finale. We were delirious with joy and relief — the whole cast was — and Hubert had made a personal success. He had come through the challenge with flying colours and the audience loved him. We stopped the show with our second duet, 'Love is a Game', and had to do it again as they would not let us go. The press was mostly wonderful and we had some great reviews. Our director, Eleanor Fazan, and our brilliant choreographer, Alfred Rodrigues, deservedly received much praise, and Hubert had a rave write-up in the *Sunday Express*. He bounced into the bedroom with the newspaper in his hand and his face abeam. 'I hope you don't mind, darling, but I've pinched the write-up in the *Express*.' Of course I didn't — it was my reason for doing the show — so I laughed and assured him that I was as overjoyed as he and we had a big hug and a dance. The bookings were tremendous; we were packed out; happy with the show, living in our dream house; our pet Alsatian Charlie Brown . . . We had everything, we thought, and so we did. One critic had gone somewhat over the top and written, 'Everyone connected with the show should go down on their knees to Pat Kirkwood.' This was absurd as the whole cast was terrific but Rod made us laugh when, on the second night, he walked towards me on hands and knees, grinning hugely. Eleanor did not find this amusing — and with reason.

One evening in January there was a thick 'pea-souper' of freezing fog, which must have come down during the show otherwise the theatre would have been empty. When we left the stage door after the show, we looked out into nothing but a thick yellow silent curtain. 'We can't go home in this. Let's stay the night in town,' I protested. Hubert would have none of it and wanted to drive the eighteen miles home. I was appalled, keeping in mind that after a strenuous show one must keep warm and get home as soon as possible. Hubert, who was a 'home-body', was adamant — he would have walked home — and I gave in against my better judgement. I was too tired to argue. He suggested I put my head out of the window and keep my eye on the kerb, all eighteen miles of it, which I could barely see, and we didn't get home until three the next morning. Inevitably as I prepared to go on the next day I felt extremely ill. I could neither breathe nor speak and felt as if I was dying, I was so weak. I managed to croak painfully, 'Get the doctor, I'm dying.' An hour later he arrived and what scared me was that he took one look at me and went a ghastly white, his hand shaking as he took out a syringe and injected me — with what I had no idea. Then he left. Gradually I felt better but I was off for a whole week.

Ingrid Bergman cancelled her booking to see the show with some friends and, worse still, so did David Merrick, an important American producer, who had also intended to see the show with the idea of bringing it to New York. What a disaster! I was still very shaky, especially my legs, but my voice was back and so was I. Before the week was out I was completely recovered, but Hubert had gone under with flu during the time I was ill, no doubt as a result of the fog. For two nights, then, neither of us had been onstage

— what chaos and what rotten luck. The bookings were down considerably and for the first time we had not met our break figure by a large margin and had to leave the Prince of Wales and transfer to the Apollo.

The first hazard which greeted us was the small size of the Apollo stage, which meant that our scenery did not fit. The second blow was that we had no time for a lighting rehearsal at our dress rehearsal, as the stage crew were fighting with the scenery, so we opened without one. Our wonderful stage director, Gerry Phillips, tucked himself into the prompt corner and telephoned all the lighting cues to the electricians during the first night and never missed a cue throughout the entire performance. After the first few scenes there was a dreadful wait on the darkened stage as the stage hands struggled to fit the too large scenery into place. Hubert and I and all of us were pacing about like frustrated tigers, seeing our show go down the drain after a splendid opening to a marvellous audience, including the press who had all turned up to give us another chance. The audience was patient but their enthusiasm began to fade after more delays. It was chaos, but somehow after the first act calm was restored but, for the cast, hope was not. In spite of this the press remained loyal and gave us some kind reviews once more.

Despite the critics' generosity we knew the show was fated, and Sandor Gorlinsky was in no position to nurse it, as a more experienced and wealthy management might have done. Hubert and I had received no salary for eight weeks, understandably — the bookings were still suffering from the effects of our absence. We knew that the curtain was about to fall on the show, and it did, after a run of four months. This was a personal tragedy for us: where would we find a show so right for us and a marvellous cast who had worked hard and devotedly. The *Stage* newspaper — the actor's bible — published a large headline asking, 'What happened to *Chrysanthemum*?' Hubert wrote a diplomatic reply whilst I remained shattered.

We were brightened by an offer from the BBC to make a half-hour series called *From Me to You*, which after a sticky beginning became a comforting success.

After this I was given a contract with ATV, the company headed by Lew Grade, later Sir Lew, and, later still, Baron Grade of Elstree. I was to do a solo series called *Pat Kirkwood Sings*, six half-hour shows featuring the work of various composers, a different one each week. This was an idea of mine. I managed to engage a firstclass pianist, Donald Phillips, who had accompanied me at the London Palladium. We rehearsed the whole six programmes: Cole Porter, Jerome Kern, Irving Berlin, Rodgers and Hammerstein, George Gershwin and the last one, called 'British composers', which included Ivor Novello and Hubert Gregg. We worked from 10 a.m. until 2 p.m., had a sandwich and then resumed until 5 p.m. It was a joy to sing these wonderful songs, my voice was in good form and Donald was enthusiastic about the programmes — we both were. I could not wait to begin the series, which was scheduled to begin in ten days' time.

I rang ATV to say we were ready and could I speak to the producer of *Pat Kirkwood Sings*? There was a long pause after which the operator said there was no such programme on the schedule. I was stunned. What to do? No use ringing my agent, I thought; better to ring one of the executives and ask for an explanation. I was informed that there had been a 'mix-up' and could I wait three months for the series? Why had I not been informed of this before? At the back of my mind flashed something I had heard years ago, that a contract became invalid after a three month delay. I replied, 'No, I cannot wait for three months.' This had no effect. So, there it was: a signed contract for six half-hour programmes, apparently cancelled without any reason being given. I had no solicitor, had never had one; nor had Hubert, who was in the flat with me having finished a radio programme of his own. He too was shattered and could not advise me; he was, in any case, reluctant to interfere in my career. How I wish he had, especially on this occasion. I could not ask him as I was fearful that he might put his own career in jeopardy. In desperation I rang Equity, the actors' union, and reported what had happened. Equity rang ATV then rang me back. 'Are you prepared to go to court?' I was asked.

Then I made one of the greatest mistakes of my life. 'Certainly,' I replied — one word causing us so much misery for such a long time. I quickly realized that I had been too hasty and became scared of what I had done.

Came another call from Equity. 'Would you settle out of court?' My instinct was to say no and go ahead — I had a cast-iron case — but if I did, would I ever work again? And would Hubert? Despite the legalistic power of Equity, the reality in those days was that an actress who offended a management would be hard put to get another engagement, even in the West End; those in charge of television also controlled the theatres. I agreed to settle out of court and then received a call from my agent, who said he had been in touch with ATV. They had suggested that I do two single singing spots on two different shows, but without payment! By this time I was so terrified by the enormity of what I had done that, though disgusted with the suggestion and longing to refuse it out of hand, I realized that if I turned them down both our careers might suffer. Regretfully I agreed to the monstrous proposal, hoping it would eliminate any harm done to us by my rash call to Equity. I did the two singing spots but had an uneasy feeling of hostility towards me, even from the audience — that might have been my imagination, but I don't think so.

The sixties were looming and as early as 1958/9, our generation of stars sensed they were being slowly smothered before being thrown out of the window. The warning of the imminent fall was all too evident. Established names found themselves out of work. One I remember in particular, the great actor Kenneth More, a great friend of Hubert, having to fight for survival. He was eventually rewarded with a CBE in 1970, but by then the massacre was almost over.

In the meantime 'a reliable source', as the tabloids say, informed me that I had been banned from the West End. True or not, it was two years before we reappeared there. We waited in vain for the phone to ring until, in 1961, we were rescued by being asked to play in *Pools Paradise*, a new farce written by successful comedy playwright Philip King, who had many long runs to his credit. *Sailor Beware* was one which ran and ran. We were delighted at the prospect of working together again. Hubert had continued to write and direct his own plays, as well as others, and received many accolades from actors who appreciated his direction. One actress of note told me that she had learned more from Hubert than from anyone in her career. The theatre was in a state of confusion and plays dropped like flies all over the West End. It was the 'new wave' which washed our generation on to the beach, to make way for plays like *Look Back in Anger* by John Osborne, an apt expression of our lot's mood — washed out, yet still in our prime.

However we had Philip King's farce to concentrate on. It was directed by Henry Kendall, a formidable comedy actor and man of the theatre, who was also a director and writer. He had a sharp and glossy wit that made rehearsals a pleasure and we all held him in great affection and respect for his knowledge and flair as a director. He had a heart condition which he ignored, sipping his gins and tonics, which he was not supposed to do. We did a short tour before opening at the Phoenix Theatre, London. The reviews were mostly malevolent, some dismissive. *Pools Paradise* was the first flop Philip King had ever experienced. It seemed there was a 'new wave' of critics, too, which had no time for farce, Philip's speciality, the young finding it difficult to understand the crazy humour and the speed of the comedy situations. Farce is an art form that simply fell out of favour, until Joe Orton revived it. It was not basic enough for the new generation, I suppose, though they understood 'Fings Ain't What they Used to be', and appreciated the funny bits. *Pools Paradise* died of mortal wounds, although the audience loved it, being, I would guess, mostly of an older generation. Practically overnight our wartime generation's music, clothes, plays, standards and beliefs were destroyed, along with our language. It was not really what we expected after six years of war, won for the safety and security of the next generation in the bright new world. Instead of a pat on the head for all the suffering and misery we had endured, we received a concerted clout.

There was a break in the clouds, however. Four glossy mop-topped, happy and well-scrubbed youngsters suddenly appeared on the horizon, singing their own songs. The Beatles lifted our spirits with their youth and vitality, and we all loved them. 'From Me to You' was the first song from this unique foursome Hubert and I heard on the car radio whilst driving to Portugal for a short holiday. We were absolutely charmed.

18

Portugal

The year prior to *Chrysanthemum* — 1957 — we had taken a holiday in Portugal and discovered a small 'paradise on earth' in the Algarve, then not yet discovered commercially. We fell in love with it and with the Portuguese, who had a glorious sense of fun. They were the only Europeans, in my experience, with whom one could share the British sense of humour. Our haven was *Nossa Senhora da Luz* — 'Our Lady of Light' — but more commonly known as Praia da Luz. It was certainly well named, for we had never seen such a limpid, clear light as that which shone on the secluded half-circular beach and bay. We were enchanted. Only two other English people lived in the village, both male. One an artist, the other a writer. The two were extremely intelligent and talented with an irresistible wit and *joie de vivre.* We made friends with them. There were no houses in Praia da Luz other than small fishermen's cottages and one or two large homes belonging to families from Lisbon who came for a few weeks in the summer. No one else knew of this idyllic place. We returned home refreshed and ready for work, a commodity which did not seem to be thick on the ground. I at least had the pantomime *Jack and the Beanstalk* at Brighton. Then there was a ghastly silence again, so we had a conference and decided to emigrate to Portugal instead of waiting for the phone to ring.

Just before this momentous decision I had come up with a plot for a play — this was normally Hubert's province. We rang an established playwright and took him out to an expensive lunch which we could ill afford. The playwright liked the idea and said he would go to work on it right away and ring us when he had finished it. He did write it, did not ring us and gave the play to Jack Hulbert and Cicely Courtneidge and we never saw him again. This very same playwright, Ronald Millar, wrote some of Lady Thatcher's speeches and was given a knighthood! This proverbial last straw confirmed our decision to leave for Portugal. It was 1961. I would like to stress that at no time did we request nor receive any tax advantage for emigrating to Portugal, our plan being to have our home and base in Portugal and travel to England when we had an offer of work.

After I finished the pantomime we packed immediately, and left the Thames at Tower Bridge on a cargo ship — the *Zealand* — with the car below deck. The voyage took three days. At Lisbon we were greeted by the tourist board in force — they must have seen the press I suppose — and were given a tremendous welcome. We were booked into a superb hotel before being taken out to dinner at a large restaurant to see and hear *Fado*, the traditional songs of Portugal, to the music of guitars and mandolins played by students from Evora.

We arrived at Praia da Luz to a great welcome from our artist friends, Gerry and Tony, with whom we had arranged to stay at their villa 'Quinta dos Redes' — 'Farm of the Nets'. There were no hotels or guest houses in Luz. Then began the search for a suitable property for ourselves. We had done this before on each visit to Portugal, but without success. We walked for miles over the fields in our quest for Shangri-la, but it seemed to be further and further away. Our two chums comforted us by saying we must have patience and keep trying, as they had done, and we would surely succeed. They made a point of advising us not to leap at something unsuitable out of despair. There was a considerable amount of land for sale in Luz, but the wise Portuguese, prompted perhaps by our presence, and our friends at 'Quinta dos Redes', sensed there was something in the wind and prices rose quickly — indeed astronomically, if it was near the sea.

One day, I had been lying in the sun for about half an hour when Hubert and our friends from the 'Quinta' descended upon me excitedly, saying there was some land for sale at the top of the hill overlooking Luz, owned by Senhor Lopes, the chemist in Lagos. A meeting on the site was arranged and there he was, dressed in an immaculate grey suit, with an impressive tie, polished shoes and a grey fedora hat. He was a tall man with a pleasant honest face which broke into a smile as he greeted us with an imposing grace. We four, by contrast, were dressed most casually. After the formalities of introduction, conducted by Hubert in perfect Portuguese, Senhor Lopes walked up the land to mark out which part was for sale. We all followed in a line. We surmised there would be about a quarter of an acre on offer, but Senhor Lopes kept on walking and we looked back at each other in happy amazement, wondering when he would stop. The land for sale was 2½ acres of almond and fig trees with a breathtaking view of the bay of Luz and the miles of lush countryside to left and right. The property sloped gently down to the main road, from which there was access via a long drive, and the whole was bounded by a substantial white wall. Finally Senhor Lopes stopped and, turning to us, his shoes by now covered in dust, asked if we wished to buy the property. The price he quoted was extremely low, quite refreshing after the inflated prices of the other properties we had seen.

Hubert, who was never shaken by unexpected situations, good or bad, kept his calm. 'Yeees,' he said, doubtfully, 'but what about the olive trees?' These bordered the end of the land overlooking the sea views and there were plenty of them. Senhor Lopes gave a resounding 'No' to this and explained that he would not part with the olive trees, which I knew were extremely valuable. Hubert coolly insisted that the olive trees be included. Suddenly Senhor Lopes, who had been gradually approaching an explosion, threw down his hat fiercely and walked away — but not far. The four of us waited. He returned looking tired. Hubert suggested that we should go away and think things over and then meet again. Lopes agreed reluctantly; we shook hands and left after agreeing the date and time of the next meeting. Hubert remained calm and quiet, the rest of us numbed, myself fearful that we should lose the property.

On the appointed day we four dressed in our best, I in a dress, and Hubert and the boys in suits with collars and ties, to match the anticipated sartorial splendour of Senhor Lopes. He was already at the meeting place, but this time it was he that was in casual clothes as we had been when we first met. We all laughed at our failure to agree a standard dress code for the occasion, Senhor Lopes gleefully enjoying the incongruity of the situation. It was obvious from the start that this was going to be a good meeting and so it was, Senhor Lopes gracefully conceding his precious olive trees — he really was a dear man and honest to boot. We all returned to the village and had a celebratory bottle of wine at the Quinta, agreeing that we would all consult about our dress for the next meeting. Then everything leapt ahead. Harold Tyrrel, a friend from Ferragudo, found us a builder who worked only for the *camera* — the town council. He had never built a private house before, just schools and town halls, which we went to see. We were impressed with the quality of the workmanship and design and hoped that he would agree to build a house for us — it would certainly be built to last. His name was Senhor Cebola, which in English means 'Mr Onion'. We were not surprised as we had already met a beach guard named Senhor Coelho — 'Mr

Rabbit' — and the vet, Senhor Cabrita — 'Mr Goat'! Also there was an elderly man in Espiche, the next village, called Senhor Pois Bem, which we were informed meant 'Mr Well Allright'! These names conjured up all the charm of early Disney as, indeed, did the Algarve in those early days.

Then began the most exciting experience: our house was about to become a reality through the combined talents of Hubert as the architect, not yet able to speak much Portuguese; and Senhor Cebola, as builder, who spoke not a word of English and had never built a house before, only town halls and schools. We were helped enormously by Senhor Helio Cruz, who was born in Luz but lived for a time in Gibraltar and spoke perfect English. Cebola was a real discovery — decisive, optimistic and professional. We did have a small setback when Hubert drew the plans in metres rather than feet, and the first design resembled Buckingham Palace! The labourers were a revelation with their painstaking work. When we inspected progress, which Cebola advised, they would say how much they appreciated a show of interest; the look of pride and joy on their faces was greatly touching.

The foundations had been laid on 14 May 1962 — our wedding anniversary — and by 29 January the next year the house was ready for our furniture from England. Hubert, however, was committed to return to London to re-direct *The Mousetrap* for Peter Saunders and to direct a musical version of *Three Men in a Boat* that he had written for the BBC. A further complication was that I had a serious car accident: I was the passenger in a car which was driven into the back of an unlit lorry and I sustained serious injuries which necessitated hospitalization and a long period of convalescence. During this time the Portuguese specialist gave me to understand that I would probably never be able to sing again and, perhaps, not even speak. I could not believe this and continued to write long letters to Hubert, keeping quiet about the accident but informing him about how the house was progressing.

The house we named *Lar do Cerro* — 'Home on the Hill' — emphasizing the prominent position it occupied, overlooking Praia da Luz and the bay to the south and with splendid views to the north of the village of Espiche and the hills beyond. There were no other houses nearby in either direction. It was the first 'foreign' house to be built in the Lagos area, and it was built to last. All the materials we used were of top quality, mostly coming from Lisbon; sadly, few of them are available today.

There was one amusing incident which occurred shortly before we moved in. The electrician who wired up the house had lived in Lisbon where his principal experience had been installing traffic lights. One evening when Hubert and I were approaching the house and still some distance away, we saw lights in the house for the first time. And what a splendid sight it was! Every light inside and outside was on, the whole edifice illuminated as if by floodlighting. When we entered the electrician greeted us, jumping up and down with excitement, shouting 'Luz, Luz.' We were completely dazzled, for he had fitted 200-watt bulbs in every holder.

Shortly after we moved in and were more settled, I decided to tell Hubert of my voice disaster. As was usual with Hubert he took it on the chin quietly, no doubt wondering how I was ever going to be able to work again. Then one evening when he was playing the piano upstairs and I was listening below whilst cooking supper, I heard a song I had sung many times before. I wondered if I could try my voice and see what, if anything, was left of it. To my utter amazement it came out clear and strong and I fled upstairs to Hubert, who appeared stunned but so happy. He put his arms round me and we laughed and cried. It was a miracle, we both believed, and we thanked the Lord together. What the specialist had prophesied was true: my high notes, the top register, were not there, but my middle and lower registers were stronger even than before the accident.

After some weeks the press arrived — the *Daily Mail* and the *Daily Express* — complete with interviewers and cameras. I was dismayed. How on earth did they know where we were? But Hubert had that sly grin on his face when he knew that he had done something that would not be popular with me — the understatement of the century. I was furious with him. One of the reasons that I had come to Portugal was to get away from all the fuss and palaver of the press and the whole business of being in the public eye. I had thought how wonderful it would be to live in a place where no one knew who I was from a hole in the ground, to be accepted as an ordinary person, which is how I have always regarded myself, and live a normal happy life as Mrs Gregg. In the resulting publicity we were allotted half a page in the *Daily Mail*, with a large photograph of us and the house and an interview given by Hubert. A similar spread appeared in the *Daily Express* with another large photograph of us standing on the rocks above the sea. Hubert thought this was all splendid publicity, but I hated it and hoped that it would soon be forgotten: it was not to be, however. Within two years there was a broad trail of Britons emigrating to Luz, and some Germans too, all building their own houses.

We were most fortunate to employ a young girl of eighteen who became like a daughter to us. This was her first domestic job, but she could cook like a dream, loved Lar do Cerro and the house shone with the care she gave to it. Maria Francesca was lovely to look at and possessed a tremendous sense of humour. Whenever we had to return to England to work she would say to me, 'When the Senhora is not here I like to imagine that this house is mine.' There was much laughter and love in Lar do Cerro and we were so very happy. Maria would stay all day at the house, arriving at nine in the morning and not leaving until eight in the evening. When I suggested that she might like to leave earlier she was most indignant and thought we did not want her to stay, so I never suggested it again.

In our early days at Lar do Cerro we gave a house-warming party for the twenty-eight British residents we knew. One of them later wrote, 'You and Hubert are what we need here — leaders.' We were flattered but wary, as the last thing we wanted was to be seen as 'social leaders' so we went easy on further invitations. When we arrived back from working in London we were too exhausted to be 'social' anything and just wished to rest for a week or so. Once encouraged, however, the residents would not give up, so we devised a method of stemming the tide by informing them all that until we put a large white handkerchief on the upper balcony we were in purdah. It worked.

Tio (Uncle) Raimunde, the gardener, was a genius. A wizened little man, about five foot two inches and brown as a chestnut, it was impossible to tell his age, for his vitality and acrobatic skills as he shinned up the almond and olive trees belied his deeply wrinkled face. He made the vegetable garden a work of art. We had everything in it — serried ranks of carrots, cauliflowers, cabbages — like a well-drilled army. Alas, Tio bought himself a motorcycle and in 1974 whilst I was in Newcastle in *Aladdin* I received a message that he had had an accident and had died during the five-hour journey to hospital in Lisbon. Hubert and I were shocked and we grieved to lose both a friend and a unique character, the like of whom we should not meet again.

Mother, who had been staying with us in Portugal for the last six months, returned to

London to arrange for the release of her flat and for the transfer of some of her furniture to Portugal, where we had a large bedroom *en suite* and a sitting-room built just for her. We were expecting her to return, but Aunt Freda telephoned to say that she had suddenly decided to go to California to see my brother Brian. We did not hear from her and were very worried and quite unable to communicate as I had no idea where Brian was — he was always a loner, changing addresses frequently. We waited anxiously for several weeks and then received a further call from Freda. She had received a cable from Brian saying that he had put Mother on a plane and asking for her to be met at Heathrow, adding that she was 'very ill'. Aunt Pop and Uncle Joe met her at Heathrow; she was in a terrible state, crying dreadfully and saying that 'Pat has died in Portugal; I read it in the paper.' The staff on the plane talked to Uncle Joe, telling him that Mother had been walking up and down the aisle, crying and upsetting the passengers and it had been necessary to restrain her. She was now back in her flat, and thanks to the care shown by her nearest neighbours from the flat opposite, she was now calm, said Uncle Joe. I was appalled and desperate. 'I must go,' I said to Hubert, 'right away.' Hubert said I should first ring my own doctor and ask him to go and see Mother then ring us with his opinion. This I did, and my dear doctor, who had always been there in times of trouble since I was eighteen, rang me the next day. What he said amazed me. 'There is no need at all for you to come back;

your Mother is perfectly all right; you must not come.' He was stern, but I remembered how reserved he had always been towards Mother and how he had called her 'a cannibal mother'.

Then a call came from Uncle Joe, a stalwart, sensible man. He had taken Mother to the Battersea hospital and arranged for her to have her own room. She was quite lucid and normal but was under surveillance by the doctors. That did it. We would have to leave. After only eight months in our new home we had to decide what to do. I rang the doctor at Battersea. He told me that Mother would not recover — in fact might worsen. So we packed up. It was August and there were no planes available, but we managed to get a berth on a cruise ship on the way to London. Hubert packed up all his precious books. We had a lot of luggage, as we did not know when we would be coming back. A woman from an estate agent's, the first one in the Algarve ever, asked whether we wanted to let the villa or sell it. We were silent, not wanting to do either. Hubert looked at me. 'I suppose we had better let it,' I managed to say. When the woman departed I saw Hubert's unhappy face. 'Never mind, darling, they can't take away the bricks and mortar,' I said.

19

Mother's Illness

As soon as we arrived back in England we dumped our belongings in Mother's flat and rushed to the hospital. The doctor did not mince words. Mother had Alzheimer's disease, which, he said, was incurable and would get worse, with temporary remissions at times. When I saw her I was shocked: she looked like an old lady of ninety, her eyes quite expressionless; she did not immediately recognize me and, when she did, showed no reaction at all. It was tragic. I was greatly distressed, as was Hubert, who had always been a wonderful son-in-law. I later learned that two years before, Aunt Pop had taken her to see a specialist who had also diagnosed Alzheimer's. I was amazed at this latest intelligence and more than a little annoyed with my Aunt for not having told me, as we would not have gone to Portugal so soon and would have prevented the mix-up over Mother's financial affairs which came to light later.

I could not speak; I was shattered. 'Is Alzheimer's hereditary?' I asked.

The answer was a firm No.

'Is there a chance I might have it one day?' was my next worry.

The doctor laughed loudly saying, 'You will never have it.'

'How do you know?'

'I know,' he replied sternly.

Mother's room was quiet and within easy reach of the rest of the ward. I stayed quite a while trying to make her speak and show some sign of herself, but it was hopeless and I left with a heavy heart.

We moved into a house in Purley belonging to one of Hubert's friends, who was planning a visit to China. I went to visit Mother several times before we moved, but there was still no reaction from her — on the last visit she did not even recognize me, which was too painful to bear. Hubert and I had to go to work — and quickly. I played cabaret at the Society Restaurant and Hubert invented a radio programme for himself called *Square Deal* — a most apt title as our generation were being labelled 'squares' in those days, reflecting the perception that we were 'behind the times'. Though it was laughable, we were not laughing. The programme was an immediate success, despite going through two name changes — first *Thanks for the Memory* and then simply *Hubert Gregg*. He was given half a page in the *Daily Telegraph* which reported, 'this is the most unique and interesting programme on the air.' The programme continued for over thirty years and became a national classic of radio.

As the cabaret did not finish at the Society until the early hours of the morning it was not possible to return to Purley each night, so I went to stay with Colin Beck and his friend in central London for a month. One evening at the Society

I spied Herbert Wilcox sitting alone at the back of the restaurant. I had met him once at the Caprice, and when I was introduced to him he said, 'Ah, we should have met years ago.'

Not knowing how to respond to this politely I replied, somewhat coolly, 'If you say so.' This particular evening, after I had finished my act and had changed ready to leave the restaurant, a waiter came to me to say that Herbert Wilcox wished to see me and was waiting in the foyer. What was all this about? When we met he was most complimentary about my performance, adding emphatically, 'You are the most exciting woman in the world!' a phrase I remembered that Orson Welles delivered to Eartha Kitt some years previously. He suggested that he should drive me home, but I already had a car and driver which Hubert had arranged to meet me every night after the show. I declined with thanks, but he would not accept this and said that he would cancel the car and pay the driver and that we could take a taxi. I did not like to refuse, as I thought perhaps he had an idea for some film work for me and so we drove off. Colin Beck's flat was quite near and in any case I had no qualms about Herbert Wilcox. After all, he was married to Anna Neagle and had a most respectable reputation, I thought. We had been driving for only a few minutes when I found myself fighting off his attentions, which were not only surprising but wholly unwelcome. He was very strong for his age, but I was younger and fought well despite my shock! In the middle of this wrestling match I managed to gasp, 'What about Anna?'

'Oh, Anna's all right,' was his reply. A few minutes later we arrived at Colin's flat and I wrenched the door open and fled. It was my first and, thankfully, my last experience of 'taxi fighting' — and from a most unexpected source. I was furious, and then depressed that he should perpetrate such degrading behaviour on me, happily married as I was. Hubert, once I'd recounted this revolting experience to him, was incandescent with rage, needless to say. It was all so tacky and chimed with my experience of playing in cabaret in restaurants. So much for an English knight.

The next unwelcome event was that Battersea Hospital said they could no longer keep Mother and that she must leave in six weeks. Six weeks! To find a place for us all to live and with all our possessions in Portugal — we did not even have a teaspoon. So we began trawling through the *Evening Standard, Country Life* and so on, searching for somewhere suitable. We came across one in Benenden, Kent, which we leapt at, as it was where Aunt Freda was matron of the Benenden Chest Hospital. We drove down there and found a lovely old house, overlooking fields, the last house before France, whose lights one could see on a clear night. The address consisted of just three words — 'Ramsden', Benenden, Kent — so it would be easy for us to remember where we were living.

Hubert and I had both been booked to do a tour of *Villa Sleep Four*, a play written by Hubert inspired by an earlier visit to Portugal.

We had performed in it together before but now that Mother was living with us I had, regretfully, to opt out in order to look after her. So the separation threat was back again, as the tour was to last for three months. Hubert planned to come home at the weekends, though this was not entirely practicable as many of the theatres were in the provinces and I was 1½ miles from the nearest village. The separation posed other difficulties for me as I did not drive and had to use the bus to get to the village or to Cranbrook, the nearest town. We did however have the good fortune to secure the services of Mrs Butler as a daily help, a woman imbued with the same sterling qualities as Millie Joyce — a happy nature, a sense of humour and a strong country accent. She cycled to work from the village in all weathers and was once stopped at night by the local policeman. 'Where are your lights?' he hollered.

'Next to me liver,' she retorted and pedalled away like mad.

One day, when the doctor came to see Mother, I opened the door, saying she was in the sitting-room. 'I don't want to see your mother,' he answered quietly. 'I came to see you. Let us sit down in the kitchen.' He closed the door and said, 'You cannot nurse your mother any more. If you do you are going to be very ill. You are going to have to find her a home.' I burst into tears aware that I was exhausted but reluctant to do such a dreadful thing. The doctor continued, 'Telephone your Aunt; she will know of somewhere suitable. I will speak to her today.' I could hardly bear to look at Mother, so quiet and distant, so far away from me. How could I let her go?

After a sleepless night Mrs Butler arrived like a fresh breeze. She could see something was wrong, so I told her what the doctor had said. She was so sweet and comforting, saying in her quiet country voice that it would be good for mother to be with other people round her who could look after her if she got worse — she might even get better if surrounded by others of her own age. I knew that this was kind of Mrs Butler, but I also knew that Mother would never get better from this hateful Alzheimer's disease, only worse. The only thing I could do for her was to find the best place for her, as near as possible. I telephoned Aunt Freda and within a few hours she rang back to say that she had the name of a home which sounded ideal. Hubert and I went to see it and it was.

The day we drove Mother to the home I shall never forget. We had explained to her that she was going on holiday to a nice house with people whom she would like. This seemed to please her. She met the owner with her customary dignity towards strangers. Hubert and I showed her into the lounge where some of the residents were sitting. She walked in with her usual panache, paused, then said, 'Isn't it a lovely day?' From the hall, where we had retreated, we could hear no reply, but I thought that as the residents had never seen Mother before and as her appearance was imposing they might have become a little timorous. Then something dreadful happened.

Mother looked at the residents and turned to face us, with tears streaming down her face. I made a move towards her, but Hubert put both his arms round me and steered me firmly to the front door, saying, 'You cannot do anything more now.'

Hubert suggested we should go to Lar do Cerro for two weeks, as it was not the letting season. It was heaven to be back and our friends were considerate enough not to bother us with invitations — we needed a break and simply wanted peace and quiet. Francesca was overjoyed to see us and spoilt us disgracefully. Hubert wrote a play called *The Rumpus*, a comedy poking fun at the fashionable suburban wife-swapping scene. It was hilarious, almost farcical, with its foolish young couples abandoning their conventional lifestyles and attempting to find alternative partners, with unsuccessful and riotous results. It was one of Hubert's best — and there were parts for both of us, which was wonderful.

We then heard the unbelievable news that Hugh Williams had written a play with an identical theme called *Never Say Die*. How on earth this happened is a mystery, as Hugh and Hubert had not been in touch for years. Some time later when we returned to England we went on tour with it just the same, although we avoided the theatres where Hugh was playing. *The Rumpus* was a notable success and we were playing together again.

Hubert had almost finished writing his musical *Nell* when we received a telephone call from a senior executive at 20th-Century Fox. The studio was interested in the script and could he and a colleague visit us at Benenden to discuss the matter. This was exciting news and we awaited the visit hopefully. We had no idea how he had heard about the musical. The visit was a success; Hubert played some of the songs and recounted the story and our visitors appeared as enthusiastic as they could allow themselves to be. We were told that the chief of the booking department, Mr Skouras, and an equally influential Hollywood bigwig, Mr Brown, would be informed. We were in a high state of excitement after this visit, as we were told that the two top representatives they had named would be coming to England to meet us and hear the music and read the script.

One morning I received a telephone call from the matron of the nursing home, telling me that Mother had died peacefully in her sleep during the night. 'No, no,' I cried, but this woman was wonderful. Straight away she told me what I had to do — inform the coroner, ring the undertaker and so on — so that I could avert the pain, at least temporarily. Mrs Butler was with me and was a great comfort, holding me tightly. Before the funeral Mother 'lay in state' at the Croydon Chapel and I engaged a make-up woman to make her look her best. When we went to see her for the last time she looked beautiful, calm and seemed to be smiling slightly. We were silent, simply standing looking at her and remembering how remarkable she had been. Hubert finally remarked gently, 'I would like to take her home with us.' This touched me so much that finally the tears fell. Mother had died on 3 July 1965 at the age of sixty-eight.

The cremation was held at a small chapel at Golders Green, as Mother had wished, for that was where Daddy had been laid. There was a stage platform and the mourners sat below, exactly like a theatre, and when the coffin moved slowly from stage left a spot-light played upon it until it disappeared stage right. A thought came to me as it reached stage centre: Dear Mother is a star at last!

20

Straight Theatre

We decided we must return to live in London, as Benenden was too far away and as Mother was now gone it was also too large. It had not been a happy house. We had experienced a fire, a flood and a plague of rats and mice that took over the house one night when I was alone. That was a real life 'Hitchock' experience. The house was close to a farm, too close for comfort, it seemed. So we sold 'Ramsden' and auctioned off the furniture and so on in the garden. It had served its purpose for Mother. As we drove away we met Albert in the village — he who had told me that he had found rats' skeletons in the music-room: 'Had enough, have you?' he grinned. We answered in the affirmative and bid farewell to Benenden.

We had a stroke of luck: Hubert took me to see a flat he had found in Piccadilly which faced on to the Devonshire gates of Green Park. As it was a penthouse, the view was fabulous, with Buckingham Palace across the park on our right, Big Ben and the Ritz Hotel on the left and an avenue of trees in Green Park leading to the Mall. The entrance was in Mount Street and came with a porter and a staircase of deep blue carpet. Piccadilly could not be seen as the flat was so high; we could not even hear the traffic below. The strangest discovery came to light on the consul table in the hall, where the mail was set. There we saw a letter addressed to the Duke of St Albans, the descendant of King Charles II and Mistress Gwynne — a good omen, we thought, for Hubert's *Nell*. The porter told us that the duke and duchess had a flat in the same block and that it had been chambers at one time when Harold Macmillan had a flat there. Our correct address was 10 Green Park House, Piccadilly W1, or '91 Piccadilly' for lazy letter writers! When Hubert had taken me to see it and meet the then owner, I thought it was heaven.

We had only been in our new home two days when my agent rang. This was a surprise, as he hardly ever used the telephone himself but sat and waited for everyone to ring him. The news was that the Twentieth-Century Fox contingent had arrived in London and wished to see us the next day about *Nell*. Our flat was already bringing us luck. So the next day was a busy one. We were due at Grosvenor Square, where the Americans were staying, and an appointment was made for five o'clock in the afternoon to 'set out our stall'. When we arrived at the ground-floor flat, we gasped to see that the large window facing the square had been removed and a grand piano was being hauled through the gap by workmen. O, the power of Hollywood, unimaginable to ordinary mortals! Spyros Skouras was a genial, quiet-spoken man with invincible eyes. Mr Brown was a slightly nervous but smiling chap, also rather quiet. The grand piano was soon in place and so was a table laden with a magnificent buffet and champagne. Hubert and I were straining at the bit, however, ready to go into battle and fight for *Nell*. A buffet and champagne were the last things we required. I noticed that our agent was sitting there too — a rarity indeed. We began with Hubert speaking the narrative and playing the piano, I singing the Nell Gwynne songs and both of us singing the duets of Charles and Nell. We were inspired and worked fast, with all stops out. Mr Skouros and Mr Brown were transfixed, almost hypnotized, and our agent was beaming with anticipation of all those 10 per cents. Finally we finished. The Hollywood contingent leapt to their feet, applauding. 'Gee, that was great — what a show.' Their enthusiasm was tremendous. Hubert and I were on top of the world. Now we were ready for some of the buffet and a glass of champagne. We had been working for two hours solid and with all the strength we had.

Mr Skouros and Mr Brown and their representative in the UK, who was also present, were flying back to Hollywood the next day to report to Darryl Zanuck, the great white chief of Twentieth-Century Fox. We would be hearing from them immediately after. Our agent came with us when we left, declaring, 'I have never seen anyone sell a show like you two did tonight.'

The next day I received from Mr Skouros an enormous bouquet and a card saying, 'Thank you for your virtuoso performance.' Within a few days, there arrived from the studio a thick contract for *Nell*, including rights to any

355

merchandising spin-offs.

Hubert and I left for Portugal to cool off and to rejoice in our Lar do Cerro; my cousin Michael accompanied us. Just before we left we visited our agent to go through the enormous contract. We all left this office together and our agent, who was normally taciturn, linked arms with us, exclaiming, as we almost danced down Piccadilly, 'We are all going to be rich. We are all going to be rich!'

A week later Hubert, Michael and I were sitting on the terrace at Lar having some tea, when the postman came with a cable three pages long. Hubert read it. His face went white. 'The worst possible news,' he said quietly; 'the worst possible news.' I was shaken and took the cable from him. It was from our agent and said there had been a coup at Twentieth-Century Fox led by Darryl Zanuck's son; he had taken over completely and discarded all the productions planned by his father, including *Nell*. We were silent. Then Michael said, 'That must be quite a blow.' I took Hubert's arm and we went inside. He was quite calm — too calm, I feared — but he took this bad news on the chin, just as he always did and never once complained or mentioned it.

When we returned to London Hubert met his old friend Kenneth More, who wanted to know what was happening. He asked Hubert to lend him the script as he was interested in playing King Charles. Great news, as Kenny's name alone would guarantee the success of any play. He read the script and approved it, subject to the condition that Charles should be the dominant part — not Nell as planned. Hubert went to work again on the script and practically rewrote it. I prayed that he would not again be disappointed after all the prodigious energy he had spent on it. With the rewrite completed Hubert and Kenny decided to approach Bernard Delfont, who declared interest and said he would like to hear the music and songs. Off we went to sing and play the score of *Nell* again. Bernard Delfont was enthusiastic as the Fox people had been and we left his office in a mood of hope, though perhaps rather more subdued. A few days after that a column appeared in the *Evening Standard*, quoting Bernard as saying that 'This show, *Nell*, is going to be bigger than *Oklahoma*.' Kenneth More was named as the star. Everything seemed set fair. We waited. And waited.

In the meantime we were invited to the Savoy Hotel for a luncheon promoting health food and vitamins that was presided over by Barbara Cartland. From our first meeting with her we became great admirers — I especially so, as she impressed me as being not only a good businesswoman, but a true innocent, without malice or female wiles. In other words, to quote Mae West, 'I don't like females, I like dames' — women who are honest, independent and do not rely on their gender to gain what they desire. The three of us got on splendidly and Barbara Cartland invited us to lunch at her house the following Sunday. 'Don't dress up, darlings,' she cooed. 'There will only be a few old friends, a quiet simple lunch.' We arrived at Camfield Place, Hatfield, Hubert in a tweed jacket with grey slacks and I in a simple summer dress. We were shown into the drawing-room to meet the Duke and Duchess of Bedford, the Duke and Duchess of St Albans, the Countess of Suffolk and a large lady who was introduced to us as a 'famous Russian poetess', all standing in a row as we entered. However, they were beaming and welcoming, so we soon settled down. During the luncheon, which was fabulous, Barbara turned the conversation to *Nell* and the Duke of St Albans was most interested to hear about it in detail — possibly because his ancestor was the natural child of Charles and Nell. I realized at once that this was the reason for the luncheon party, as dear Barbara had shown much sympathy for and interest in our account of the ups and downs of the show when we met her at the Savoy. St Albans seemed to be serious about knowing all the problems we had experienced and everything we could tell him about the story, the music and who to play Charles and Nell and so on. The whole table joined in and it became an exciting *Nell* lunch, with questions coming fast and furious, as though it was the most important show ever. None of the guests was flippant or bored. All were on our side, and it was heartening. Barbara looked delighted and satisfied, smiling and nodding at Hubert from time to time.

A meeting was arranged with St Albans for lunch at our flat. As he entered I could see that he was carrying an enormous, heavy book which

358

looked extremely old. He handed it to me and asked me to open it. I saw the signatures of King Charles II and Nell Gwynne, with fascinating lists of domestic things — comestibles and other mysterious kitchen items — written in the old English of the day — one, 'a dozen of quail', I recall. As the Duke had handed the book to me I had assumed it was our guest's gift and I thanked him profusely, 'O! Your Grace, what a lovely present!' The duke paled; Hubert collapsed in laughter, explaining to me that the book was an invaluable historical treasure, not a present. The Duke was relaxed and natural, and during lunch we discussed the mechanics of getting *Nell* into the theatre. He stayed quite a long time and we enjoyed his company, but, as we had still not heard from Bernie Delfont, *Nell* appeared to have come to another full stop. Hubert had decided not to ring or write to him, saying 'If there is any news, Bernie will be in contact.'

We then had an offer from a new producer whose name was unknown to us, but we went to meet him at the Café Anglais in Leicester Square. The offer delighted us — a musical version of *Beaux Stratagem* — with us playing the leading parts. In a few days the artists he had already contacted began to turn up at our flat, obviously delighted at having signed contracts. I learned the first act, including the songs. Hubert had a strict law that 'lines' should come last and that studying the play was more important, but I was always anxious until I had the lines burned into my brain. Then the blow fell. In spite of the fact that contracts had been signed, the producer rang to say the backers had withdrawn. It was unbelievable but true.

Hubert, never down for long, had the idea of me playing the title role in the Somerset Maugham play *The Constant Wife*, which was about to go on tour for a new management. When I read it I was shattered. The part seemed like a female Hamlet; it went on forever. 'I can't do it,' I moaned.

'Yes, you can,' said my optimistic spouse. 'I shall direct it.' I pinned myself once more to learning the words, working night and day on the mass of material but fright was my constant companion — partnering *The Constant Wife* closely.

We opened at the Pavilion Theatre, Bournemouth. I was word perfect and that was all; my performance was out of a deep freeze and so was I. Hubert came round backstage, beaming, 'Well, darling,' he announced, 'now you can say you have played one of the classics.' I said nothing but I thought, Yes, but how did I play it? I did not read the reviews, as I had already written my own in my head. Hubert had been so sure that I could do it that he did not bother to give me any direction at all. Instead he concentrated on an actor, in an important part, who could not act at all and never would. The night before we opened he did give me some help, but why had he not given it me before, I asked. 'Well, I thought you would just do your own thing,' he explained.

The tour began and I was most unhappy

knowing that I had failed to conquer this difficult part. The rest of the cast were polite but distant, as they wondered what I thought I was doing in a straight play, a Maugham at that. They were not 'Kirkwood friendly'. The weeks dragged by, but to my amazement I found I was progressing and learning the character of Constance; my confidence was slowly returning. Also the cast were less cool and I found a friend in Valerie Taylor, no longer young but a consummate actress of formidable power.

Maugham writes so concisely that it is almost impossible to ad lib if a line is forgotten. If one slips on a 'but' or an 'and' one is sunk at once, but, happily, this did not happen to me. There is a legendary story of a great and revered American actress who was playing the part of Constance in New York. She was known to be partial to a glass of wine or two, and one fateful night she came to a full stop in the middle of one of the endless speeches. The set had a fireplace and chimney-piece which was placed centre stage. The prompt corner was to the left of the fireplace. So this bemused actress made for the prompt corner, as she thought, but arrived at the fireplace instead, put her head up the chimney and in her powerful theatre voice asked, 'What do I say now?'

Suddenly, fortune shone on us once more. Prince Littler, who had given me my first break when I was at the Prince's Theatre — now the Shaftesbury — and who was now the owner of many West End theatres, rang us to say he would like to hear the score of *Nell* and also read the script. This was good news, as we had thought that *Nell* was defunct forever. So, Hubert, my pianist and I, wended our way to the Theatre Royal, Drury Lane, and into his magnificent office. His Man Friday and producer, Toby Rowlands, was also there. Once again we presented our *Nell*, as we had done so many times before. When we had finished there was a silence. We held our breath. 'You can have the Theatre Royal, Drury Lane, in March,' he said. We stared at him stupidly. He smiled. I wanted to cry, but instead smiled too.

We floated home in a happy delirium, rang Kenny More, who was delighted, and embraced each other joyfully. A week or two later a friend rang to ask us if *Nell* had opened yet. She then informed us that Tony Hatch, the composer, and his wife Jackie Trent, a singer, had opened on tour in a show called *Nell* with Lonnie Donegan as Charles II and Jackie Trent as Nell Gwynne. There was a newspaper article that quoted Jackie Trent as saying, 'I am Nell Gwynne — a busty red-head!' The show was to be a spoof on the history of Charles and Nell. There was nothing we could do, even though they were using our title and benefiting from the publicity that Bernie Delfont had given our *Nell*, saying it would be 'the greatest musical since *Oklahoma*.' Then Prince Littler rang to say that all his backers had withdrawn because of this disgraceful *coup*. The spoof pop version played a few weeks on tour and was a disaster, gaining terrible reviews — no help to us in our shock and misery. Hubert's wonderful music has never been heard . . .

I then had a telephone call from an independent manager called Henry Sherwood, who offered me the title role in Somerset Maugham's play *Lady Frederick*, which was to tour for three months. I realized that *The Constant Wife*, probably seen in Brighton, had sparked this off and I rejoiced that I had finally cracked the elusive Constance by that time! Lady Frederick was a wonderful part, but it meant another long separation from Hubert and the thought chilled me.

Rehearsals took place in Croydon, where we were to open in two weeks' time. The director, Malcolm Farquhar, was an enormous help to me. He worked me hard — three complete run-throughs the day before we opened; but he knew what he was doing and I could have gone through the play in my sleep — which I nearly did. I would have done five run-throughs had he wanted it, for he was such a fine director. He gave me confidence and I trusted him completely.

Hubert came with me to Croydon and we stayed at the Selsdon Park Hotel, where I had lived for a while in the forties. He would see me open and then go home to Brighton. I was glad to have his presence and support and I dreaded the long separation that lay ahead. I thought back to the tour of *The Constant Wife* when he had come to see the play at Birmingham. We had argued a lot; I resented his not giving me the direction I needed whilst I was struggling to find my feet. He had seemed detached, preoccupied and unsympathetic. It was mean of me to think of this, for he had been tired and dispirited after the *Nell* débâcle, though he never spoke of it. I would have been very lonely, had it not been for Valerie Taylor. This was all behind us, though, as we had a new house to attend to and which I could look forward to enjoying.

Lady Frederick opened to a full house at Croydon; the reviews were good but mixed for me. This did not worry me greatly, as I knew that when I had played the role for longer I would make the part my own — it was so ideal for me. It was rather like wearing a new costume for the first time; it needed to settle and become a second skin. The next date I proved this. We opened at Norwich and I gained the best review I have ever had. On the opening night the play triumphed and Henry Sherwood and Malcolm Farquhar were full of joy. They accompanied me to my hotel, where Henry, having already presented me with a bouquet, now proposed a bottle of champagne. I declined and drank some milk instead, much to their amusement; but my mind was on the play and the need to keep my performance up to standard, if not improve on it for the rest of the tour. I had again experienced hostility from some of the cast who had been in the play in London when Margaret Lockwood had taken the lead. They were rather resentful of a new Lady Frederick and a 'musical' one at that. After Norwich they warmed a bit and all was well; it became a happy company. I had never played a part that some other artist had played in the West End before.

I recall that when I first went to my hotel in Norwich — The Maid's Head — the reception desk was manned by a lone porter. I gave my name and asked for some help with my luggage. The porter, who was of late middle age in a good light, gave me a shocked look. 'You're not Pat Kirkwood?' he blurted out.

I replied with an equally firm 'Yes, I am.'

He smiled mockingly. 'No, no, I mean the original Pat Kirkwood.'

'That's me — I am,' was my reply through gritted teeth.

'But I saw Pat Kirkwood at the Empire Theatre, Liverpool, in the forties,' was his triumphant answer. By this time I was heartily sick of trying to establish my identity. 'That was me — I am the one and only Pat Kirkwood. Now what is my room number? I need help with my luggage, please.' This settled the matter and gained me the services of an awed porter for the rest of the week.

The tour continued with great success as I had by now made Lady Frederick the important 'second skin' and the part was a joy to play. Before I left, Hubert gave me a small transistor radio with a cord which fitted over my wrist, and I used to walk home after the show with it dangling comfortingly beside me. As the part was so demanding, I could not join the company for a drink after the show but went straight back to my hotel to supper and bed. This was a routine I habitually followed to enable me to conserve my energy and keep me fit. To me, being quite small — five feet four inches — and not carrying much weight, this has from the very start of my career been an important ritual. It often meant living a lonely life on tour, and I missed Hubert, especially as we were not working together. We spoke on the telephone every day but this is a poor substitute for togetherness, especially as I am phone-shy, unable to communicate easily all that I feel. I would always forget to say what I had intended, usually remembering the moment I put the receiver down! However, I was happy in my work, even when the curtain came down and there was an empty space. When we came to the last week of the three-month tour, at the Theatre Royal, Bath, I packed happily for home. Shortly after, Hubert returned home and was glad to see me but preoccupied with his writing and broadcasting. He was always working on two or three things at the same time — no sluggard he!

We then had an offer to play Mr and Mrs Squeezem in *Lock up your Daughters* at the Everyman Theatre, Cheltenham. This was a most happy experience, as the parts were perfect for both of us — three cheers for casting — and the company were marvellously talented and also great fun. The show was an enormous success and Hubert and I had found each other again — the laughter and closeness. Then we both appeared at the newly opened University Theatre, Newcastle, in Noël Coward's *Hay Fever*. I played Judith Bliss, or tried to, as I could not understand the character at all and thought she was a silly and irritating woman. Hubert played Mr Bliss. It was not a happy experience. The company were very young and seemingly hostile towards us, especially after we refused to support a proposal for a strike over something so trivial I have forgotten what it was about.

My next part was Robin Hood in the pantomime *Babes in the Wood* at His Majesty's Theatre, Aberdeen. Hubert was deeply immersed in his writing but managed to come up for two days at Christmas. Two or three weeks later, Henry Sherwood asked me to play a 'two hander' with Irene Handl in a play called *A Chorus of Murder*. I was ready to accept as I had been an admirer of Irene for some time, but had never done a play with only one other character in it. Could I do it? There was only one way to find out, so I did it and Irene, being such a consummate professional, was a joy to work with; it was hard work, exciting, challenging, and we ended up having a successful three-month tour. *A Chorus of Murder* came to an end and I remember saying to Hubert that I never wanted to work for any management other than Henry Sherwood.

After *A Chorus of Murder* I did another pantomime for Henry Sherwood — *Dick Whittington* at His Majesty's Theatre, Aberdeen. Hubert came up for Christmas and stayed over for the New Year, and on New Year's Eve we were invited to the owner manager's house for supper with his family. The small children were brought in to meet 'Dick Whittington', as they had seen the pantomime the previous day. They all tripped in shyly and were introduced to me, when suddenly the youngest gave me a long stare then burst into tears. 'She's a grown-up' the little one cried, 'she's an adult', and had to be led away to bed. Although I was sorry for the upset I had caused it seemed to me to be quite a compliment that in the role of Dick I had managed to transform myself into a young lad.

It was about this time that I heard that Noël Coward was ill in Switzerland, his adopted home, so I thought I would write an amusing letter to him to cheer him up. I wrote about the pantomime and some things that I knew would make him laugh. I wrote about the rehearsals, the hilarious temperament of the Fairy Queen, of all people, who threw her tiara at no one in particular and was seen standing beside a green sidelight meant for the Demon King, which transformed her golden locks into dishevelled seaweed. If the audience had seen this performance they would have been very confused! After I had written a few more letters I received word from dear Coley (Lesley), who wrote that Noël had laughed his head off; they were filing away my letters as they had all been enormously entertained by them. He ended his letter by saying, 'You can write — you must write.' I was both delighted and surprised.

I had been on tour on my own for over a year, including four pantomimes. Hubert and I were drifting further and further apart; we seemed to have lost the ability to communicate with each other, which was strange as we had always had plenty to talk about. It seemed impossible that such a wonderful companionship should wither.

We had always been so close, but I knew, as I had seen it happen so many times before, that the months away from one another had begun to take their toll. I had never thought it could happen to us. We began to fight a lot; we were lost, tired, tired of trying, tired of disappointments. There seemed to be nothing in our lives, now that we could not find each other.

We had an offer to play *Move Over, Mrs Markham* on tour after its successful West End run, so at last we would be working together again. Everything fell into place except that Hubert was not happy with his part, an eccentric butler, although he gave a delightfully comic performance. When it ended I was glad to go home to our sunny Georgian cottage in Brighton, which we had transformed by painting the outside chocolate brown with a pale lemon door and shutters; it sounds bizarre but it looked marvellous and we named it the 'Brown House'. We had put some boxes outside the first floor windows and filled them with red geraniums; the whole operation worked delightfully. After a few weeks at home I did not want to do anything else but stay put, but an offer came from Howard and Wyndhams, the leading management for straight theatre, to play *Aladdin* at the Theatre Royal, Newcastle, for a Christmas run, so I was off again. The show was a success for the whole run. Dave Willis, the Scottish comedian, played the Dame and gave a gloriously robust performance. Hubert came up for Christmas Day. It was nice of him to make the long journey when he was so busy, but he never missed being with me at Christmas no matter where I was performing.

When the show finished I went home. Things were not right between us and we both knew it. Silence too often ruled the day, although we sometimes had a return to the old camaraderie. Life was beginning to be rough and difficult in Brighton. Our house in The Lanes, although normally quiet, now began to suffer when the pubs closed. Many houses had their windows smashed regularly, and one morning, when I opened the door, I found a drug addict asleep on the step. I did not disturb him, just stepping over his prone body! Then our window looking on to the Lanes was smashed in during the daytime, when I had left the house for half an hour. The police came round but confessed they could do nothing; that they were understaffed. The window was mended and then during the night we began to hear the intimate conversations of couples outside the house, not to mention animal noises in abundance. The front door was splashed with red paint. This was all mildly irritating, but one night something happened to make us decide to move: a petrol bomb was thrown through our neighbour's window and exploded in the centre of the dining table as the family were at supper. We had had enough. One week later it was sold to a couple who declared it was the house of their dreams, even though we had warned them of the situation.

We found a Victorian terraced house at

Westgate-on-Sea, four miles from Margate; it was situated on a quiet road only yards away from a large beautiful bay and the sea. Hubert, after working in London, came home at the weekends. We were so far apart it was obvious that we could not go on as we were. Our marriage was sinking slowly and inevitably into the icy waters of divorce. We had put up a good fight — almost twenty years — against implacable odds. It was all so sad and grim that when 'Boo' Laye rang to ask me if I would like to play the part of The Honourable Mrs Gaylustre in the Pinero farce *The Cabinet Minister*, I accepted at once, glad to get away from the unhappy situation. The play was a challenge for me as I had never performed in a classic farce before, and Pinero was a sophisticated play-wright. But the part was fun to play, as it turned out, even though I was playing a 'baddie' for the first time. Michael Denison and Dulcie Gray were the principal characters, and 'Boo' played a beautiful and witty lady, which was no trouble for her at all.

We opened at the Theatre Royal, Windsor, for three weeks, with the understanding that we would be moving to the West End at the end of the tour. We were packed out, breaking the theatre record, so we were all well pleased with ourselves. The experience was a happy one for me, taking my mind off the situation at home for a while. Vanessa Lee and her husband Peter Graves thoughtfully came to see the show on the first night. They were sincerely complimentary about my performance, which cheered me considerably. In Birmingham, 'Boo' and I stayed at the same hotel and used to walk home together after the show with our alarm 'torches'. It was a busy city, but both of us were too scared to use them as they made such an ear-piercing noise.

'Boo' was aware of the trouble between Hubert and me. One matinée day when I was feeling low and tearful she grabbed me by the arms and shook me, saying, 'Let go, let go, it will all pass.' I noticed that she was about to cry as well; her blue eyes filled up but she swallowed hard, exerting the strong discipline that had brought her through the traumas and tragedies of her own life. No wonder she was so loved by all who knew her and the thousands who did not. 'Evelyn Layes' did not grow on trees — which is a pity as they would vastly improve our parks and gardens.

The play was set to come to London, as we expected, but closed at Richmond nearby — not in the West End, after all. On returning to Westgate-on-Sea, Hubert and I discussed our divorce and engaged solicitors. I had never appointed a solicitor before and did not know of one, but my cousin Michael, son of my Aunt Pop, was a high-flying businessman who knew everyone. He gave me the name of a highly reputable lawyer — Michael Cook — who later became a judge. We continued living together despite the fact we were 'separated' for a trial period of two years as the law then required, though Hubert was only at home at weekends. I cooked, as always, so we had our meals together and even had a few laughs. We sold the house; Hubert returned to his flat in London; I migrated to Lar do Cerro. Dealing with all the bureaucracy kept me fully occupied, which was a good thing.

21

Lar do Cerro

I was tired after the long tour of *The Cabinet Minister* and numbed by the divorce, but it was good to be back again in beautiful Luz. It was soon the letting season, however, and I had to stay with friends for a while until I solved the problem of where to live from April to October. At the back of the house, there was a gardener's cottage, where Tio Raimunde used to crack the almonds and spread the figs to dry on wooden slats outside in the sun. With the advice of Senhor Cebola, who had built the main house and had a nostalgic feeling for Lar do Cerro, I converted the cottage into a nice little 'snug' for myself, adding a kitchen and sitting room.

I then had an idea to ask 'Boo' Laye if she would like to come and stay with me for a while before the letting season began. She accepted and I was overjoyed to see her dear face again. She had a marvellous time, bewitching all in sight. One morning, when we were walking to the village, she even popped her head into the fisherman's bar which was out-of-bounds to all, no matter who. They were the sardine fishermen, a rough, tough, jolly crew, but not to be taken lightly. When 'Boo' put her head through the door, which was open to the cobbled street, the place went quiet. No wonder, for she was wearing a flowered straw hat, underneath which her large blue eyes gazed, whilst her eyelashes fluttered coquettishly.

The men looked as if they had seen an angel, forgetting their drinks and gazing open-mouthed at this vision. She was delighted by the stir she was creating. I got worried and whispered to her that we must go as we were not supposed to be there. She replied 'pooh' but floated out of the bar with a regal wave of the hand. A cheer rang out from the fishermen along with various complimentary remarks like linde ('beautiful') and senhora buenita ('pretty lady'), which was unheard-of from these strong, grim and hard-working men of the sea. I am sure none of them ever forgot the day a blonde angel paid them a visit!

We had a great time together. One evening when we were sitting on the terrace in the evening sun, 'Boo' decided to give me a lecture about my work in the theatre. 'Do not go towards the audience so strongly. Wait for them to come to you,' she said, wagging her fore-finger at me. This was, strangely, just the gesture Noël Coward always made when he was trying to impress a recalcitrant actor. What 'Boo' was saying to me was, in effect, the same as Charles B Cochran's telegram after a first night: 'Do not give so much — hold something in reserve.' I thanked 'Boo' for her advice, but explained how difficult it would be for me to change the way I worked. I always felt so happy to be onstage that I showed it and wanted the audience to know too. This was not thought out or rehearsed, it was just my natural self. I could not, however hard I tried, disguise my delight at seeing the audience. Something I learned in my early days in the theatre was to be myself and never to let anyone try to mould me into something I was not. This was a strong instinct, and since then I have heard many wiser and more knowledgeable theatre lovers than myself give the same advice. Even in a play, in a straight part, it is necessary to retain one's own self, to make the part fit you and not the other way round.

After three weeks 'Boo' had to return to London. I missed her, but soon after, the cottage was finished, just in time for the start of the letting season. Then I had a telephone call from Hubert to say that Oxford Playhouse were putting on the musical *Pal Joey*, by Rodgers and Hart, and would be ringing to offer me the lead part of Vera Simpson, the part played by Rita Hayworth in the film. It had been a great success in the New York theatre in 1940, when Gene Kelly played the title role, and Vivienne Segal played Vera. Van Johnson was in the chorus. Hubert argued it was a marvellous part with wonderful songs by Rodgers and Hart, such as 'Bewitched, Bothered and Bewildered' and many more. Also the show was to be a part of the Edinburgh Festival and would open at the Lyceum Theatre, which fact alone was worth my going to Scotland. He was right of course and generously offered his flat in London whilst he stayed at the house in Westgate to which the buyers had not yet moved. Of course I was delighted to think of singing the Rodgers and

Hart numbers, but doubtful that I was suited to the part of Vera Simpson, a highly sophisticated lady who was tough as old boots and expert at getting what or whom she wanted, no matter what. Hubert said 'not to be silly' and that I should take the part at once. So off I went, leaving a most reliable and loyal married couple, Eulalia and Manuel, to look after the house and garden, Eulalia taking responsibility for the clients without a qualm.

I arrived in London to begin rehearsals. Philip Hedley was the producer and also the artistic director at the Theatre Royal, Stratford East, where I did a one-woman show later in 1983. I told Philip on the first day of rehearsals that I was wrong for the part. He, wisely, just laughed. We had had our ups and downs at rehearsals, mostly because the sets and scenery were complicated and included a 'revolve', which was temperamental and often not flush with the stage. Thus on the day before dress rehearsal, when I leapt into Robert Sherman's arms during our dance — he was playing Joey — my foot crashed into the space on the revolve and I was in agony and unable to walk. I was rushed off to hospital. This was the first of many disasters, for one of the leading players became ill and Joyce Blair stepped into the part at short notice and gave a wonderful performance, word perfect and full of vitality. Vanessa Redgrave gave a quotable quote for once when she said, 'Anyone who steps onstage is brave.'

We opened at the Royal Lyceum Theatre, Edinburgh, and were an instant success — a great relief for me. I am grateful for an excellent interview conducted by John Barber, whom I had thought of as being 'Kirkwood unfriendly'. In the end he gave me a splendid half page in the *Daily Telegraph* under the headline 'Glimpsing a star out of West End sight':

'If anything,' said one of the critics, 'she looked even more stunning than she did 25 years ago. A star we had forgotten turned up at the Edinburgh Festival and became the talk of the town. [I had been touring for a year] The perdurability of Pat Kirkwood's charm amazed people even more than the height of Dietrich Fischer-Dieskau or the attendance at highbrow concerts of Burt Lancaster. Some said it was her delicious smile; some her exuberant personality; some her ability not so much to sell a song as to inhabit it and make it her own. All agreed we had not seen for a generation a woman with that easy, glorious command of the stage. And, since the music halls where she learned it have gone, we may never see it again.'

After Edinburgh we went on tour for four weeks, starting in Stevenage. On the first night I knew I was developing a dreadful cold and to cap it all, a piece of scenery collapsed on me — the first time I had experienced a slap on the back from that quarter! The next day I had laryngitis and the cold had settled in. I rang Philip and he suggested I come to the theatre and give it a try, but when I did nothing but a croak came out. I was off the show for two days but came back on the Friday, and strangely my old friend 'voice' returned loud and clear. In my whole career I had rarely been offstage with illness and only if my voice was affected. It caused such trauma to the company, especially the understudies, and one felt dreadfully guilty for putting them through the experience. There was a saying in the theatre: 'Singers are always off'. While untrue in general, the voice is a delicate and sensitive part of the physical make-up, vulnerable to climate and state of health, so singers have to be fitter than actors or instrumentalists. The very act of singing live, on a stage, requires physical fitness and this in turn demands a healthy lifestyle, almost that of an athlete.

The most treasured memory I have of *Pal Joey* was meeting Patricia Hodge. At rehearsals we eyed one another but did not speak. She is remarkably talented and I could sense this was no ordinary person, but in the hassle of rehearsals we did not have much time to give thought to anything but the show. It was not until we travelled from London to Edinburgh and were booked into a sleeper together that I found that we were perfectly at ease with each other, as if we had been friends for years. This was a new experience for me as I had always suffered from shyness except when on stage and did not make friends easily. I was also wary of giving my trust, especially to other women, as a result of unfortunate experiences that I did not forget. I discovered that we both went through the same routine upon retiring, even in a train — removing make-up, brushing our hair, putting on nighties — all the while talking and laughing. We had the same sense of humour. Then Patricia climbed into the top bunk, insisting that I took the lower one. I was grateful. We continued our sleepy conversation for a while then went to sleep. My last thought was, I've found a sister.

This discovery brightened the show, especially when we were on tour. Patricia's — or 'Trish' as she preferred to be called — outstanding qualities were her serenity and poise, two rare gifts that did not appear to repress her sense of fun nor her 'gurgly' schoolgirl laugh. Our relationship blossomed; we bought each other little presents and talked a lot. She was a great comfort to me when I had laryngitis at Stevenage. After *Pal Joey* finished I had a visit from Trish at Westgate-on-Sea, where I was staying for the time being, and she insisted on seeing my books of press cuttings extending back over many years. I had wanted to talk. Anyway, time went so quickly that I remember we had to run like hell to catch her train back to London. Later I visited her and her handsome husband Peter at Barnes, where she cooked me a gorgeous meal. Later our ways diverged and I saw little of her. Now she has two lovely boys and her life has become as busy as is possible. She is now recognized as one of the few fine actresses we have and will go on to even greater achievements. The last time I met her was some years later, in 1994, when she appeared on my *This Is Your Life* programme. She gave me a touching tribute in her usual quiet, impressive and inimitable style. She is one of the four women I have met in my life completely devoid of envy, malice or wiles. I shall never forget her. One unhappy fact about the theatre is that it is well nigh impossible to keep a friendship going as artists are rarely — or never — in the same show or town, so one has to learn to be thankful for the short time in which to enjoy a close and rewarding relationship and to treasure the memories.

After *Pal Joey* I went to Rancho Santa Fé, California, to stay with an American friend named Frances F. Beachy, but known to her intimates as 'Billie Stiff'. She had attended a small party Hubert and I had given in Luz some years before and had been late in arriving. As she came into the house she announced, 'I want a dry martini and a footstool', a reference to one we had brought over from England, which she considered very British and eccentric. We became friends from that moment and when she left I called after her, 'I love Billie Stiff — I don't care what they say about her!' This time I stayed with her for three months and met many of her friends. Among these was a man called Al Redmond whom she recommended I marry, saying he was a millionaire. I liked him very much but had no desire to marry him. I always believed in marrying for love rather than for money — marriage is difficult enough, but without love it must be hell. When the time came for me to leave there were tears. We have from first acquaintance to last been good friends and will ever remain so, even if Billie is in California and I am in England. When I got home to Lar do Cerro and entered my cottage a letter awaited me on the table. The decree absolute of my divorce stared me in the face. I went to bed.

I settled down once more as a resident of Portugal, having dealt with a mass of bureaucratic detail before securing a resident's permit and identity card. There were the clients to deal with. Eulalia had managed splendidly in my absence but now she introduced me to some of their idiosyncrasies. The most recent couple never left the premises. The husband used to walk around the house stark naked and his wife complained to Eulalia (who was furious) that he was having kidney trouble because the lavatory bowl was not kept clean. We later discovered a great pile of empty Portuguese champagne bottles stacked in the garage. They left with two splendid sun tans, thanked me for an enjoyable stay and departed in an aura of charm.

One Sunday, when we had an Indian family staying, Manuel, who had come to clean the swimming pool, hurried towards the cottage appearing pale and shaky. 'Senhora, minha senhora' he cried anxiously. I went out to see what the trouble was. 'What is the matter, Manuel? Tell me calmly,' I said to him in Portuguese. He swallowed hard. 'Tudo nu, tudo nu,' he cried — 'All nude, all nude!' And so they were, Mr and Mrs India and their two beautiful daughters, seated round the pool. When Manuel finally cleaned the pool they gathered round him and patted him on the back and said what a good job he had done. Manuel, his composure restored, came into the kitchen, saying, 'Boa pessoas' — 'Good people.'

A time came when there were no bookings for the house and it was now July. So I went to see Barry Sadler, the joint owner of the Luz Bay Club, explained the position and said I was going to have to find a job. He was most reassuring and helpful, as was his wont, as I discovered later from his many kindnesses to me and others. 'Go home now,' he said, 'and I'll think of something.' And he did. Two days later two executives of a new travel agency offered me a contract on very generous terms. So I had more clients and more problems, but not the one I had feared the most.

Then the season was over and I was packing up ready to move from the cottage back into the house. About three o'clock in the afternoon I heard a knock on the door and there appeared Al Redmond, Billie Stiff's friend from California. He was on his way to see Barry Sadler on some business or other, on behalf of Billie who owned some property in the Algarve. He wanted me to go with him as he did not know where Barry lived. I sent him off for a bathe in the swimming pool whilst I had my customary siesta. I tried to persuade him to wait until the next day, as it was evening and Barry might have some guests, but Al would not agree. He had come down from the Ritz Hotel, Lisbon, with a liveried chauffeur and was insistent on seeing Barry without delay. We found the house with some difficulty, and sure enough when we arrived some cars were parked in the driveway and a dinner party was evidently underway. I apologized profusely to Barry's wife Michelle about our intrusion.

She asked me to sit down and have a drink. Suddenly I heard a male voice behind me: 'Never apologize, never explain.' I turned round to see a smiling face and two blue sparkling eyes.

I was not amused. 'I was brought up with some good manners,' I announced pompously, but as there was nowhere to sit except next to this impertinent person my 'dignity' was wasted. So I sat next to him. Out of my right eye I noted that this over-confident male had a female sitting next to him, who glowered at me as I sat down. I assumed they were an 'item', which turned out to be far from the truth, but even so, this chap and I began to talk quite easily together. After a few minutes' conversation he declared, 'You are the most charming woman I have met in the Algarve,' which he could have improved upon, I thought. Michelle had introduced us, but because names were not my strong suit, all I could remember was that he came from Bingley, Yorkshire.

The next morning, I walked as usual to the supermarket. Coming to the check-out, I almost bumped into the tall — as I could see now — blue-eyed chap who had instructed me on what not to do. I could not remember his name but I recalled where he came from so I asked him, 'Isn't it Mr Bingley?' His face lit up with a warm, attractive smile and his blue eyes danced with amusement as he again corrected me. Revealing his proper name as James Peter Knight

— Peter — he asked if I would care to go to Lagos the next day and have a coffee with him. I accepted. As I went home to Lar I felt a warm glow, a kind of peace, and all day I looked forward to the next morning.

Thus began a tremulous and romantic courtship, which seemed to belong to another, more gracious age. It was not without its difficulties as I was in the process of selling Lar do Cerro, which I decided was far too big for just me, especially after the fright of getting no bookings over the summer. I arranged to move into a smaller house closer to the sea and the shops. Eulalia and Manuel would, of course, stay with the house and the new owners. Peter was also in the process of selling his holiday house in Luz as he had lost his wife some time before. Although he had had a holiday house in Luz for ten years I had never seen nor heard of him. So there we were, passing each other in the skies. I was flying to London to deal with the prospective buyers of Lar de Cerro and back to Luz; Peter was off to Luz to sell his villa and back to Yorkshire, so we only had a few rushed meetings between flights, but he wrote every day and phoned twice a day. I wrote every day too. It was quite ridiculous behaviour between two 'middle-agers', but it proved that people are as young as they feel and never mind the passports.

A few months later Peter was talking of marriage, but this scared me out of my romantic haze and gave me a nasty shock as I could not imagine the thought of marrying again. I had been living alone for four years quite happily. On an impulse I wrote to him to say that I thought it would be better if we did not see or contact each other again. It was sheer panic on my part — I was afraid of marriage — and after I had posted the letter I returned home to the silence of the telephone that had buzzed so cheerfully; to the absence of the daily letters; and to the disapproving quiet of the whole house, which seemed to have withdrawn itself from me in disgust.

This situation lasted one week before I had a letter from Aunt Pop, who lived at Lymington, where Peter had a boat at Buckler's Hard nearby. He had planned to visit her at Lymington. He set off the fateful day he received my letter, and as he later told me, he was so upset that he found himself in Oxford High Street instead of miles away on the by-pass. Aunt Pop later faced a pitiful, wet figure — it was pouring with rain — clutching a bunch of flowers and staring mournfully through woebegone blue eyes. Aunt Pop exuded her usual warmth and cheerful charm and her husband, Harry, having sized up the situation, poured a sizeable whisky which he handed to Peter with a grin and a wink. So Aunt Pop drew the whole sad story from Peter who, she said in her letter, was in a most unhappy state. She added bluntly that she was appalled that I could so ill-treat such a nice man and that she had told him to ignore my letter completely and carry on as if it had never been written. All in all I had a proper dressing-down from Aunt Pop — always an unforgettable event — and I was glad that this one was only by letter and not face to face.

She did not seem to realize that I too had been going through a miserable time. I had lost seven pounds in weight in one week, pacing up and down in Lar trying to come to a decision and quite unable to sleep. My closest friend, Phyllis Bonsey, who was in her eighties but as bright as a button, declared, 'You're under siege! The man's a wolf!' Eulalia thought I should marry whom she called 'Senhor Pão — 'Mr Bread' — from Peter's habit of bringing bread to Lar whenever he visited.

Manuel was dead against it. 'The Senhora should not marry — we can look after the Senhora,' he said.

But Eulalia was all for it: 'The Senhora should not be alone' — it was the fourth year of my spinster state — 'she should marry Senhor Pão — he is a good man!' How I missed them both, after I sold the house; they had been my loyal and caring friends.

Of course, I now wished I had never written my 'don't write, don't ring' letter, but how could I undo what had been done? Then Peter, encouraged by Aunt Pop, telephoned and everything was soon as it had been before. We resumed our courtship, and he came out to Portugal and asked me once more to marry him, extracting a promise that I would let him know by an agreed date. Peter went on a course at Perkins of Peterborough, learning about diesel engines for his boat. I telephoned him at his hotel, said I had made my decision, and announced shakily, 'I could not *not* marry you!' We had known each other for eight months.

We arranged to meet at the Hotel Principé Real, in Lisbon. When I got to the airport at Farö to catch my plane Air Portugal was on strike, so I told my taxi driver to drive me to Lisbon. My first thought was that this was an omen and I should drive back to Luz at once. But I went nevertheless. Peter arrived at the hotel shortly after me and immediately whisked me away in another taxi. I asked where we were going and he told me to wait and see. The taxi deposited us outside the city on the banks of the Tagus, where, at the time when the Salazar bridge had been built across the river, the Portuguese had erected a large and impressive monument to celebrate the occasion. It was an exuberant expression of the nation's statehood, quite magnificent, somewhere that must be seen by all who visit that delightful city. Peter told the taxi driver to wait and we walked towards the great stone monument. Here, in the best formal tradition, he fell on his knees and asked me to marry him. Upon my affirmation, he slipped an engagement ring on my finger. As we embraced, we became aware of a small throng of Portuguese spectators, who thoroughly enjoyed this romantic drama and gave us a round of applause and large smiles as we walked towards the taxi for the journey back to the hotel.

Then the complications began to develop. I was resident in Portugal, Peter in England, and there was no way we could be married in

Portugal without a long delay. We went to see an Embassy official in Lisbon with Peter's idea that we should be married by a ship's captain at the port. This was greeted with some polite mirth by the various people we saw, but the top man did not turn a hair or crack a smile. 'I am sorry to have to inform you, Mr Knight, that we have not done anything like that since *Casablanca*.' We were finally married in a register office in Gibraltar by a dear little man called Mr Luka, who looked like Charlie Chaplin. Strangely, when we were taking our vows, he cried like a baby, with tears running down his cheeks. I thought this very odd, for he must have married many couples. Was he crying for them all or, perish the thought, did he think we were too late?

The excitement of the occasion and the prospect of a new life had hidden the grief that I experienced when we returned to Luz to complete the sale of Lar and had to say goodbye to the house and garden; to all the happy memories and laughter which had filled it; to my faithful friends Eulalia and Manuel, to Phyllis Bonsey and her husband Bruce, and to Anne and Darry Durant, all of whom had supported my spirit and given me strength. Peter gripped my hands in his and comforted me. He reminded me that I still had the little house by the sea — Number 91 Luz Bay Club — which I had intended to be my future home; that we could come out and stay in it whenever we had a mind to do so; that we should see Eulalia and Manuel again and my little Jack Russell, Bertie, now at home with them where he had been born.

Peter returned to England. He still had many responsibilities, for, although retired as senior partner from his practice as a solicitor in Bradford, he was president of the Bradford & Bingley Building Society. I was to follow shortly. I had a lovely letter from Peter's daughter, which helped to settle my nerves at the thought of meeting Peter's large family. When she met me at Heathrow it was a great relief to discover that she had a strong sense of humour, and we had a most enjoyable supper at the airport hotel before being carried off to Yorkshire.

22

Finale

I now began to rehearse for the entirely new role I was shortly to play, one I had never played before — stepmother to Peter's daughter Carolyn and to his son Nicholas, each with their own children. I also had to meet, for the first time, a host of his relations and friends. It was all rather daunting. Peter's two children were naturally wary at first about meeting their stepmother, particularly one who was an actress. It took them some time to realize that I was just as nervous as they. But as we got to know one another we all finally 'clicked' and that was a happy day that has improved over the years — seventeen of them as I write today. For a short while after our return we lived in Bingley, later moving to Suffolk to live in a sixteenth-century thatched house at Hitcham, a grade-2 listed building. During this period I was asked by Philip Hedley to appear at the Theatre Royal, Stratford East, in *An Evening with Pat Kirkwood* — a one-woman show. It was particularly pleasurable for me as Peter had never seen me on the stage before. Also in the audience was my old friend of many years, June Davis, the widow of snooker champion Joe Davis and, as June Marlowe, a beautiful and much admired singer.

When Peter retired as director from the Bradford & Bingley Building Society in 1984, we returned to Praia da Luz once again for nigh-on two years. There we found a new house and made great improvements so that it became a beautiful home much as Lar had been, only nearer to the sea. Alas, Peter was diagnosed as having a serious heart condition. During this worrying period, when I had been privately advised by a heart specialist who practised in Praia da Rocha that the illness would be fatal unless he lived the life of a semi-invalid, I was approached by Cameron Mackintosh with an offer to appear in the first London production of Stephen Sondheim's Broadway musical *Follies*. I was to play a former American singer and sing a nostalgic song, 'I'm Still Here'. I told Cameron that I did not think I was suited to the part and that it was more suited to an American actress. Though this was true he brushed the objection aside and sent me the tape, to which I listened. Taking into account Peter's condition, and the need to get him home as soon as I could, it was quite out of the question. I could not tell Cameron the real story why I had to turn down his offer, because the specialist had warned me that on no account was Peter to be given any idea of his condition, as it might cause a crisis. Soon after this we returned to England for Peter's check-up, only to be told there was absolutely nothing whatsoever wrong with him — he had merely been suffering from homesickness and the diagnosis had been completely false. I am afraid Cameron was a bit cross with me, but he did not know the situation, so I hope he will read this.

We were without a home in England for a while until we found a house in West Burton, Wensleydale — a North Yorkshire village with a population of 200 people and 200,000 sheep. It was here that we were discovered by the press, who importuned us with an unscheduled visit and a persistent cameraman who had to be cautioned by the local constable. Then there were again, as there had been many times before, lurid headlines linking my name with that of Prince Philip. This was particularly distressing to me, living as a newcomer in a small village with a strong Methodist tradition. I wrote to the prince and asked him if anything could be done, but his kind reply was that it was 'part of the mythology of the press, which the Royal Family has also suffered and nothing can be done'. What the villagers felt about all this went unspoken, to me at least, but I was conscious of it. Indeed it was not until comparatively recently, ten years later, that I was solemnly told by a lady who helps me in the house that I had been accepted.

In 1989, I was pleased to be asked to appear in a tribute to Noël Coward at the Barbican, especially as 'Boo' Laye was also to appear. It was called *A Talent to Amuse*. Also starring were Jonathon Morris, Kelly Hunter and Paul Jones. Peter was quite enthusiastic about my doing it and entered into the spirit of the occasion to the extent of attending the rehearsals — he simply walked into the rehearsal room, sat down and started chatting to the director. I told him he really shouldn't be there, but he did not seem impressed with this statement and wandered round the theatre advising all the artists to 'break a leg' in the best theatrical tradition. He has that fortunate gift of being perfectly at home wherever he is and liked by whomever he meets.

In 1992 I was asked to take part in a tribute to 'Boo' Laye. Would I not! Appearing again at the London Palladium where I had played so many happy times — and paying tribute to my dear 'Boo'. I was already there! When the taxi deposited Peter and me at the theatre I was besieged by autograph hunters, many with old photographs of me. We were so thronged about during my signing session that Peter was forced to walk a few paces away. Later he told me that a fan had come up to him and said, 'Excuse me, are you important?' to which he replied. 'Yes.' When asked who he was he said, 'I'm David Mellor's grandfather.'

I could think of only one song to sing that was perfect for the occasion — the evergreen 'There's No Business Like Show Business' by Irving Berlin. Our friend, the author Michael Thornton, who had written amongst other books *Royal Feud* and a most compassionate biography of Jessie Matthews, and whose knowledge of the theatre is encyclopaedic, evidently had the same idea. He rang me to suggest some new words for the lyric, which he had put together praising 'Boo' and her artistry. I sat down then and wrote my version, melding the best of both together. It was no easy thing to remember the words of the old and the new versions mixed together, but I rehearsed it until I was blue in the face and could have sung it in my sleep. To the evident delight of a theatre packed with Boo's fans, I sang Berlin's anthem to the words: 'There's no lady like *that* lady, like no lady I know . . . ' Standing alone once more on the vast Palladium stage, my mind went back more than half a century to my first appearance there in *Top of the World*, when I sang to audiences while the bombs were falling on London, never knowing if we would survive to the end of the performance, let alone live to see that 'lovely day tomorrow' I used to sing about. I am still thankful to have lived through that 'finest hour' for Britain. There was a feeling for life that none of us will ever forget. We all sensed it, and perhaps were more alive then than at any times in our lives.

Boo's Palladium tribute was a wonderful success and was produced by Christopher Wren with a cast of more than a hundred stars, including Sir John Mills, his daughters Hayley and Juliet, Ronnie Corbett and many others. At the finale, all the ladies walked down to the strains of Stephen Sondheim's 'Beautiful Girls', while Boo sat enthroned and resplendent, greeting every star. She was 92, but had still stopped the show singing 'In the Pink'.

The following year, 1993, I was asked to do a one-woman show, *Glamorous Nights of Music*, at the Wimbledon Theatre, supported by Sheila Mathews and Clifton Todd and again with Christopher Wren producing. I was pleased to work with him once more — he was greatly talented and knew exactly what he was doing, always cheerful and optimistic — rare gifts in a producer in my long experience. I worked hard getting my songs organized and rehearsed in readiness for 27 and 28 April, a matinée and two evening performances. The show was helped greatly by the support and enthusiasm of my good friends in the audience, June Whitfield, Judy Campbell, Irving Davies, Gerry Phillips and many more — it is impossible to name them all. It was thrilling, yet touching to see so many of my former colleagues of years ago sitting in front. I had a cable from Zoë Gail and Julie Andrews in America and from Helen Parnell in the South of France, whose return address was damaged in the post and, sadly, I was not able to write and thank her. On the two nights before the show there had been a struggle to get into my dressing-room through the crowds at the stage door and in the street — the stage doorman said he had never seen anything like it at Wimbledon. What a scene there was in my dressing-room after the show, with all those well-remembered faces around me.

Something extremely pleasant happened on 20 January 1994, although the beginning was rather mysterious. In December 1993, Barry Burnett, my new agent, rang to say he had been asked to arrange an interview with me for Thames Television at the Prince of Wales Theatre. They were holding an anniversary celebration for the theatre's birthday and all the principal artists who had played there had been invited to give an interview on their stage experiences. I was delighted to accept, as I had done two shows there — one of them *Chrysanthemum*. Then strange things began to happen at home. Peter was, as usual, talking a lot on the telephone, but now would close the door for prolonged periods. When I entered the room for some papers he would mutter down the phone, 'Sorry, can't talk any more now,' and put it down. I thought this was a bit odd, and when I asked him who he was talking to he said it was the vicar, but without much conviction. Then one evening when he had gone to bed I went upstairs and heard the murmur of a voice, rather muffled, and opening the bedroom door I gazed on a large lump of bedclothes under which Peter was whispering into his mobile telephone. He immediately surfaced, giving me a sickly smile. What was going on? Had Peter a secret companion? I was mystified but did not ask him anything. Shortly after, he announced that he had to go to. W.H. Smith's in Darlington, about thirty miles away. I still kept quiet.

On the day before the interview on 20 January, we set off for the Cavendish Club, near Marble Arch, and the following morning presented ourselves at the Prince of Wales Theatre in readiness for my interview. The television cameras were set up in the downstairs bar, the cameramen and the interviewer — whom I had not met before — were already there, but there was no sign of any other artists. Either they were late or I was early. We began the interview, but shortly after we had started the interviewer began to move away from behind the camera and

I had to bend in my chair towards him, still talking and wondering what was going on. In the middle of my sentence I sensed someone standing next to me and turned. Close to me was Michael Aspel with an enormous red book in his hands. I completely lost my cool and gave what I can only describe as a loud, inelegant yelp, reminiscent of Eliza in *Pygmalion*. 'It's the man with the book,' I cried tremulously, although I knew it was Michael as I had seen him on television many times; now, however, his name deserted me. 'This is your life,' said Michael, but I felt it was just the opposite. What a shock! Michael laughed his handsome head off, as did the cameraman, the interviewer and, lurking in a corner, my scheming husband!

I was whisked off to the Teddington studios, shown into a dressing-room and provided with champagne and delicious sandwiches, neither of which I could touch at the time. Also I noticed a familiar-looking suitcase, which, the make-up woman explained, had been packed by my husband with some dresses for me to choose from. Later I learned that he had organized the whole operation and kept it all secret so that I would not know. He was aided and abetted by our good friend, Michael Thornton. The television staff were marvellous and helped me back to earth and to relax. I was then shepherded to the set, where I waited for Michael Aspel to call my name. When he did and I came onstage the reception I received was heart-warming. The audience had not known who was appearing and, thankfully, welcomed me most generously. Sitting on seats on either side were a host of old colleagues and friends — it was like a happy dream.

Then a galaxy of talented artists with whom I had worked over the years began to appear: Roma Beaumont and her husband Alfred, the son of George Black; Michael Denison and Dulcie Gray; Wendy Toye; Shani Wallis, on video from America; Van Johnson, flown over from the United States; Lord Delfont and his wife Carole Lynne, together on the video screen with a warm message; Lewis Gilbert, my film director in *Once a Sinner*, likewise; Evelyn Laye, too — seated at her piano in her home — raised her glass to me; Robert Nesbitt, now alas deceased, my director in many shows; June Whitfield; Hubert Gregg with his wife Carmel and their two children Kathy and Robert; Gerry Phillips, stage director, and not least, Patricia Hodge.

The surprise of the evening, its culmination, was the entrance of my brother Brian, whom I had not seen for nine years. He had been flown over from his home in Palm Springs, California. He made a splendid entrance and contribution, as confident as ever and exciting the television crew to comment upon his professionalism. After hanging on, amidst all these nostalgic memories, hoping I would not give way to the tears I was on the point of shedding, this last emotive meeting was very nearly more than I could bear. It was one of the happiest and most touching nights of 'my life', thanks to my colleagues and friends, who had made the effort to support the programme, and to the meticulous organization of the director and the team responsible for it. Later I was to receive the 'Red Book' in remembrance of the occasion. I shall always treasure it.

Almost immediately after the programme we went for a winter break in Luz. Whilst there I received an unexpected telephone call with an offer to appear as special guest star in a musical show at the Festival Theatre, Chichester, for twelve weeks starting in July 1994. The show was called *Noël/Cole — Let's Do It* — a musical symposium of Noël Coward's and Cole Porter's songs compiled by David Kernan and written by Robin Ray and Dick Vosburgh. There was a talented and hard-working cast — David Kernan, Robin Ray, Liz Robertson and Louise Gold — and Peter Greenwell, who played the piano and sang Noël's songs so brilliantly.

I sang three numbers: Noël's 'Chase Me, Charlie', written for me in *Ace of Clubs*, and Cole Porter's 'You're the Top' and 'Begin the Beguine'. Everything was so well produced and happy at the theatre, and my own performance was received better each night than ever I could have wished — 'stopping the show' on several occasions. *Let's Do It* turned out to be a 'smash-hit', with full houses every performance, although one young girl, with skirts up to her unmentionables and a jewel planted to one side of her nose, complained to me: 'I thought it was going to be a dirty play.' That was down to the title, I suppose, but she stayed for the rest of the performance, so perhaps a whole new world was opened to her.

During our last week I asked one of the theatre executives how the show had compared with the other presentations with which we were alternating, this being a repertory season as usual. He grinned: '*Let's Do It* has been the success of the season and made us very happy, particularly financially!'

'The success of the season,' I repeated happily.

'Definitely,' he answered. 'And not only of this season but many.'

Well, what a lovely surprise indeed. And what a wonderful way to end my career.

Reprise

I left Chichester resolved never to appear in the theatre again. I felt I had done enough and wanted a normal life. It was a difficult decision to make but one I was happy to live with. It was October 1994 and I felt a great deal of relief after making my decision and a certain happiness to know that my last appearance had been a successful one. I have never missed the life, strangely enough, except for the audience, who were my friends, and the love they gave to me — the feeling that I was at home onstage. Yes, I have missed them, but I am thankful for being fortunate enough to have done the work I loved for so long — nearly sixty years. I have also been blessed with three happy marriages which, finally, took away the emotional scars of my disastrous first one, during which I lived in limbo for nine years before regaining my freedom. I was fortunate to discover how happy marriage could be with husbands who were tolerant and sympathetic to my work, which many lesser men would not have been.

Whatever my achievements, I am grateful for having been able to take what came, to keep my feet on the ground and be myself without any false ideas or illusions. Life was a roller coaster, sometimes wonderful, often not, but always interesting and worthwhile. I am also grateful for the many friends I met in the theatre, many of whose names I have recalled in the chapters of this book. I ask forgiveness for the ones I have omitted to mention.

I would advise any young person who wants to go on the stage to have some training, if possible, and not to be too ambitious. The main thing is to enjoy it and to work hard, making it the main purpose in life. One must not be side-tracked by too much praise or too much criticism; then you will be in full possession of your faculties and most of your wits, always remembering to make a close friend of 'Lady Luck', who plays a prominent role in the theatre — almost, perhaps, as necessary as talent.

Will I ever be tempted to change my mind about working again? You never can tell what lurks around the next corner. It might be the role of a lifetime, which nobody could refuse. Or it may be just a peaceful and contented walk with Peter and our West Highland terrier, Jamie McGregor. Whichever it is, I will settle, gratefully and happily, for the wonderful life God has given me.

We do hope that you have enjoyed reading this large print book.

Did you know that all of our titles are available for purchase?

We publish a wide range of high quality large print books including:
Romances, Mysteries, Classics
General Fiction
Non Fiction and Westerns

Special interest titles available in large print are:
The Little Oxford Dictionary
Music Book
Song Book
Hymn Book
Service Book

Also available from us courtesy of Oxford University Press:
Young Readers' Dictionary
(large print edition)
Young Readers' Thesaurus
(large print edition)

For further information or a free brochure, please contact us at:
Ulverscroft Large Print Books Ltd.,
The Green, Bradgate Road, Anstey,
Leicester, LE7 7FU, England.
Tel: (00 44) 0116 236 4325
Fax: (00 44) 0116 234 0205

LOVE ME OR LEAVE ME

Josephine Cox

Beautiful Eva Bereton has only three friends in the world: Patsy, who she looks upon as a sister; Bill, her adopted cousin, and her mother, to whom she is devoted. With Eva's father increasingly angry about life as a cripple, she and her mother support each other, keeping their spirits high despite the abuse. So when a tragic accident robs Eva of both parents, Patsy, a loveable Irish rogue, is the only one left to support her. Tragedy strikes yet again when Eva's uncle comes to reclaim the farm that Eva had always believed belonged to her parents. Together with Patsy, Eva has no choice but to start a new life far away . . .